Circumcision on the Couch

PSYCHOANALYTIC HORIZONS

Psychoanalysis is unique in being at once a theory and a therapy, a method of critical thinking and a form of clinical practice. Now in its second century, this fusion of science and humanism derived from Freud has outlived all predictions of its demise. **Psychoanalytic Horizons** evokes the idea of a convergence between realms as well as the outer limits of a vision. Books in the series tests disciplinary boundaries and will appeal to scholars and therapists who are passionate not only about the theory of literature, culture, media, and philosophy but also, above all, about the real life of ideas in the world.

Series Editors
Esther Rashkin, Mari Ruti, and Peter L. Rudnytsky

Advisory Board
Salman Akhtar, Doris Brothers, Aleksandar Dimitrijevic, Lewis Kirshner, Humphrey Morris, Hilary Neroni, Dany Nobus, Lois Oppenheim, Donna Orange, Peter Redman, Laura Salisbury, Alenka Zupančič

Volumes in the Series:

Circumcision on the Couch

The Cultural, Psychological, and Gendered Dimensions of the World's Oldest Surgery

Jordan Osserman

BLOOMSBURY ACADEMIC

NEW YORK • LONDON • OXFORD • NEW DELHI • SYDNEY

BLOOMSBURY ACADEMIC
Bloomsbury Publishing Inc
1385 Broadway, New York, NY 10018, USA
50 Bedford Square, London, WC1B 3DP, UK
29 Earlsfort Terrace, Dublin 2, Ireland

BLOOMSBURY, BLOOMSBURY ACADEMIC and the Diana logo are trademarks
of Bloomsbury Publishing Plc

First published in the United States of America 2022

For legal purposes the Acknowledgments on p. 219 constitute an extension of
this copyright page.

Cover design by Daniel Benneworth-Gray
Cover image: Sigmund Freud by Max Halberstadt, 1921

A catalog record for this book is available from the Library of Congress.

ISBN: HB: 978-1-5013-6816-5
ePDF: 978-1-5013-6818-9
eBook: 978-1-5013-6817-2

Series: Psychoanalytic Horizons

Typeset by Deanta Global Publishing Services, Chennai, India

To find out more about our authors and books visit www.bloomsbury.com and
sign up for our newsletters.

Contents

Figures

Allison Bechdel, Are You My Mother? (London: Jonathan Cape, 2012), p. 168

Introduction

The Snipped Subject

Male circumcision first caught my attention as a subject of inquiry when I was a high school student attending an Amnesty International conference. At this event, I noticed something peculiar: a group of men, angry and determined, who appeared only at the session where members were called upon to vote on the organization's priorities, and otherwise did not seem involved in the conference or human rights activism more generally. They had come to convince Amnesty to recognize male circumcision—which they dubbed "MGM," male genital mutilation—as a human rights abuse no different in nature from "FGM" (an issue the organization actively campaigns against). They were armed with literature that detailed the alleged physical and psychological harms caused by circumcision and "debunked" commonly accepted beliefs about the procedure, such as its prophylactic benefits. I would later learn that these activists represented members of the so-called "intactivist" movement, which aims to end the practice of routine male circumcision.

As a Jew growing up in America, I knew that circumcision was both considered the province of my religion and that it was ubiquitous in American society, a routine procedure performed after birth on boys of all backgrounds in the name of hygiene. This was the first time I had really thought about circumcision as a *choice*, made by an authority, about an intimate part of my body—and potentially a bad choice. I was equally struck by the single-minded fervor these men seemed to display. They appeared filled with hate and righteous anger at those who advocated circumcision and eager to malign Amnesty and its members as hypocritical and potentially "misandrist" (i.e., "anti-man," as opposed to "misogynist") for failing to take on their cause, or see matters the same way. I was mistrustful but nevertheless intrigued.

Several years later, I was about to embark on a graduate program in psychoanalytic studies, and the idea to write one of my papers about circumcision came to me initially as a kind of joke. What if I tried to "psychoanalyze" the odd intensity of anti-circumcision sentiment? I tweeted this idea, intending to be ironic. I received a reply from an intactivist organization, which didn't hear the irony. They offered to share with me testimonials of men who felt traumatized by circumcision.

I realized there might be something to this idea. The term "intactivist," after all, invites psychoanalytic criticism, as it references that wish for "intactness" that psychoanalysis tends to consider a major defensive fantasy against the subject's foundational fracture—the wish to "restore" a prelapsarian unity and wholeness that never, in fact, existed.

But, besides my fascination with the fantasies undergirding intactivism, I discovered a wealth of additional questions, emerging from my attempt to think through intactivist claims in terms of my own life history, yet with much larger research implications. How could a procedure which has become commonplace in American society nevertheless stand for something which marks one as a Jew or Muslim, a minority? How would one evaluate intactivist arguments regarding the deleterious effects of circumcision on sexuality when the procedure usually occurs before one has reached sexual maturity, indeed before one typically has any memories at all? What, in other words, might be the relation between something that has happened to someone—outside one's control and memory—and who one is as a subject, with a "sexuality" and an "identity"?

Eliza Slavet points out that the Jew's "discovery" of his circumcision may be compared to the moment Frantz Fanon famously recounts, in *Black Skin, White Masks*, when he is suddenly jolted into being conscious of his blackness.[1] Fanon describes sitting on a train and overhearing a child say to her mother, "Look, a Negro!"[2] While in the moments before, he was simply going about his business, not paying any attention to the racial or other features distinguishing him from others, suddenly he became marked, interpellated, "responsible at the same time for my body, for my race, for my ancestors."[3] Fanon's reflections on the encounter, as Slavet observes, evoke the image of a violent or botched circumcision: "What else could it be for me but an amputation, an excision, a hemorrhage that spattered my whole body with black blood?"[4] In the contemporary Jewish American context, one almost never experiences such an abjecting interpellative encounter in relation to circumcision. Yet, in my run-in with the intactivists, perhaps something related took place; for, until this moment, I knew "about" circumcision before I understood myself *as* circumcised in any meaningful sense—as belonging to a group for whom circumcision represents a mark of difference. (And indeed, a group which anti-circumcision activists sometimes hold responsible for the loss of their "intactness.")

[1]   Slavet, *Racial Fever*, 115–16.
[2]   Fanon, *Black Skin*, 84.
[3]   Fanon.
[4]   Fanon, 85.

I had taken the ordinariness of male circumcision for granted. Only with the medicalization of the rite in the late-nineteenth-century, I learned, did circumcision become a facet of mainstream American life. Overall, the practice has occupied a deeply ambiguous place in the Western imagination. While its status as the founding covenant of Jewish monotheism places circumcision at the center of the so-called Judeo-Christian tradition, it has largely functioned as this tradition's haunting "internal Other," a sort of organizing trope or "dispositive," as Jay Geller calls it,[5] for the whole range of anti-Semitic beliefs throughout the centuries.

Today, countless people have encountered anti-circumcision activism or at least heard arguments against the practice. Several films and documentaries have been produced on circumcision, including the intactivist-aligned *American Circumcision* on Netflix, which features many of the intactivists I discuss in the following and final chapters. Highly publicized attempts to ban nonmedical male circumcision via courts and legislatures have occurred in Germany, Iceland, Norway, and elsewhere in Europe, although none have succeeded—yet. In the United States, disputes between parents over whether to circumcise have been heard in multiple courts, and a local intactivist-led ordinance to ban circumcision nearly appeared on a San Francisco ballot before a judge intervened to have it withdrawn.[6] The presidential hopeful Andrew Yang, whose 2020 Democratic primaries campaign attracted a motley crew of internet startup fans and believers in Universal Basic Income, declared publicly, "I'm highly aligned with the intactivists," bringing the term from the fringes into mainstream national discourse.[7] "Holy shit. A candidate actually redpilled on circumcision?" responded a user of the web forum 4chan, referencing the anti-feminist terminology of the "manosphere."[8] Meanwhile, former British Labour Party leader Jeremy Corbyn, besieged by accusations of anti-Semitism, proudly proclaimed his support for the right to practice ritual circumcision as part of a wider effort to reassure Jewish voters.[9] Most recently, one of the protesters who took part in the 2021 Trump rally that led to the storming of the US Capitol held intactivist placards that read, "Make America's penis great again, with a foreskin! No foreskin, no peace!"; others treated the Covid-19 pandemic as an opportunity to demand hospitals stop performing circumcisions.[10] Those who have fallen afoul

[5] Geller, *Freud's Jewish Body.*
[6] See Wikipedia, "Circumcision and Law."
[7] Yang subsequently ran for mayor of New York, and backtracked on the issue, calling it a matter of "religious freedom" and a "personal decision," possibly due to its electoral unpopularity in the city. See Levine, "Andrew Yang's Anti-Circumcision Stance."
[8] Quoted in Sommer, "Andrew Yang."
[9] Dysch, "Jeremy Corbyn."
[10] Bromley, "Thank You"; Riminton, "America"; Circumcision Choice, "Intactivists."

of the movement have at times faced serious consequences; psychologist Jennifer Bossio received death threats "for years" after she published research contesting the claim that circumcision leads to reduced penile sensitivity.[11] Online discussions of my own work on the subject have included comments such as "No, asshole, don't you dare decide for me what I need" and "Why is it necessary for psychoanalysis and all kinds of nonsense when, using logical thought, you can see that you do not cut healthy tissues of children?"[12] (I can only hope it doesn't become darker.)

Derrida writes that circumcision is a "memory without memory of a mark [that] returns everywhere."[13] The more I delved into this topic, the more I discovered that, indeed, circumcision "returns everywhere," leaving its enigmatic mark on some of the most fundamental problems involved in psychosocial life: from the constitution of raced and sexed identity, to the question of universalism, to the discovery—and repudiation—of infantile sexuality. Male circumcision, it turns out, is a powerful site through which questions of gender, race, sexuality, and psyche have been negotiated throughout human history. As James Boon puts it, "Foreskins are facts—cultural facts—whether removed or retained . . . (non)circumcision involves signs separating an 'us' from a 'them' entangled in various discourses of identity and distancing."[14]

While most contemporary work on the subject has preoccupied itself with whether circumcision is "right" or "wrong," "safe" or "harmful," in this book, we will proceed from the premise that, whatever its medical consequences, the significance of male circumcision exceeds anatomical and juridical considerations. Throughout history and context, circumcision serves as a potent receptacle for fantasy. The field of psychoanalysis, I will argue, helps us shed light on the nature and function of these fantasies. Moreover, the repository of conflicting and paradoxical meanings attributed to circumcision—alternately portrayed as a "phallicizing" procedure that initiates a boy into manhood and a form of penile "feminization"—provides a unique lens through which we can reexamine crucial and contested aspects of psychoanalytic theory, including castration, sexual difference, and the relationship between discourse and embodiment.

Jay Geller offers a compelling explanation of a psychoanalytic approach to reading:

> We look for clues, traces of the concerns (not always conscious or intentional) on the margins of his text; we keep our eyes open for the

[11] Schofield, "Anti-Circumcision Movement."
[12] Anonymous, "r/MensRights—Conference."
[13] Derrida, *Archive Fever*, 42.
[14] Boon, "Verging on Extra-Vagance," 43.

various *Entstellungen*—wrenching distortions of both form and content. We also attempt to discern what is avoided, omitted, de-emphasized. We ask ourselves: what doesn't seem to fit? what sticks out as strange?[15]

However, as the "foreskin question" makes clear, "wrenching distortions of form" are in the eye of the beholder. Thus we will ask not only what appears out of place in discourse on circumcision but also in what ways circumcision has been marked *as* out of place.

In each case we will examine, stances and controversies surrounding circumcision reveal a preoccupation with the question of mastery in the face of lack, played out—not incidentally—on the site of the penis. Circumcision figures either as an attempt to consolidate "phallic mastery" that winds up revealing the inherent impossibility of such an enterprise, or alternatively, it foregrounds an experience of castration, thus provoking defensive responses. If these psychoanalytic concepts are not yet familiar to the reader, I hope their meaning will become clearer in the next chapter, where I will set out my understanding of the relevant theory that forms the backbone of this book, alongside a critical reading of the extant psychoanalytic literature on the meaning of circumcision and the "cut." If you're more familiar with the psychoanalytic jargon, then I hope my exploration of circumcision throughout this book will occasion its reassessment. In short, circumcision has something to say about the "split," or "snipped," subject of psychoanalysis—and psychoanalysis offers exceptional tools through which to hear it.

I will offer now a brief survey of the history of circumcision, highlighting the moments that I develop as case studies for this book.

A Short History and Chapter Overview

As the title of the book states, circumcision is considered, along with trepanning, the world's oldest known surgical procedure.[16] Civilizations and tribal societies around the world, including parts of Africa, Asia, the Middle East, Australia, and the Americas, are known to have practiced circumcision from ancient times onwards, often as integral parts of complex initiation

---

[15] Geller, *Freud's Jewish Body*, 13.
[16] Cox and Morris, "Why Circumcision"; Alanis and Lucidi, "Neonatal Circumcision." Some argue the term is misleading, as "surgery" implies a curative medical intervention, whereas ancient circumcision was ritualistic in nature. As we'll see in Chapter 3, nineteenth-century medical circumcisions were infused with symbolism in ways that undermine the neatness of the distinction.

ceremonies. Cave paintings and sculptures from the Paleolithic period depict what appear to be circumcised, if not foreskin-retracted penises.[17] The oldest known visual representation of a surgical operation taking place appears on an ancient Egyptian bas-relief, dated approximately 2400 BC. It depicts a young nobleman undergoing circumcision, possibly as a marker of elite status.[18] An assistant grasps the hands of the boy while a priest circumcises him with a stone knife. The inscription reads, "Hold him fast. Do not allow him to faint!" In the Western world, by the time of the Roman Empire onwards, circumcision becomes strongly associated with Judaism, with the *bris* or *brit milah* (ritual circumcision) performed by a *mohel* (ritual circumciser) on the eighth day of a Jewish boy's birth, rather than during childhood or later.

The meaning of this central rite within Judaism varies widely across Jewish texts, time periods, and interpreters. It makes its most prominent appearance in Genesis, as a foundational covenant between God and Abraham:

> Every male among you shall be circumcised. You shall circumcise the flesh of your foreskins, and it shall be a sign of the covenant between me and you. . . . Any uncircumcised male who is not circumcised in the flesh of his foreskin shall be cut off from his people; he has broken my covenant.[19]

The rite regularly reappears throughout the Torah. Often, it is associated with the unique national character and identity of the Jews, and is a requirement to participate in various aspects of Temple life. In Deuteronomy, and throughout Prophets, circumcision receives a metaphorical character; for example, Jeremiah declares that the house of Israel is "uncircumcised in heart."[20] Additionally, in Exodus, Moses, expressing doubt in his oratorical skills, describes himself as "of uncircumcised lips."[21] This biblical significance is supplemented and transformed by centuries of subsequent rabbinical commentary, which constructed the physical rite as necessary to "complete" the male Jew, with a strong emphasis on blood imagery.[22] Prominent Jewish thinkers Philo of Alexandria (*c.* 20 BCE–*c.* 50 CE) and Maimonides (*c.* 1135 CE–1204) both offered ascetic perspectives on circumcision, associating

[17] Angulo and García-Díez, "Male Genital Representation."
[18] Badawy, *Tomb*, 19.
[19] Gen. 17:9-14. I use the New Revised Standard Version of the Bible unless otherwise noted.
[20] Jer. 9:25.
[21] Exod. 6:12. See English Standard Version (and other translations); NRSV replaces "uncircumcised lips" with the less literal phrase "poor speaker."
[22] Jonathan et al., "Circumcision," 732.

it with the weakening of sexual pleasure and potency, thereby enabling greater focus on spiritual pursuits.[23] By contrast, Kabbalistic texts have treated the rite as enacting a kind of divine intercourse between man and god, as well as having apotropaic effects such as the warding off of demons.[24]

Outside of its immediate religious significance, circumcision has served as the symbol upon which countless battles have been waged within the history of Jewish struggle in hostile environments. The ancient Greeks opposed circumcision both morally and aesthetically, considering it immodest for the head of a man's penis to be visible when he participated in athletics (which were usually done in the nude) or visited the public baths.[25] Emperor Hadrian outlawed circumcision across the Roman Empire under penalty of death.[26] Some Jewish men therefore disguised their circumcision, including attempting to "undo" the procedure by stretching the remaining foreskin, a procedure called *epispasmos* in Greek.[27] (In a sense, this practice persists today: some intactivists attempt "foreskin restoration" using various skin-tugging devices designed for the purpose.[28]) Possibly as a response to this, by about the middle of the second century CE, rabbis made the traditional circumcision procedure more radical, requiring a second cut that barred the glans completely and was much more difficult to undo.[29] *Periah* is the Hebrew name for this "second step." It remains an integral part of the *bris*, invested with theological justifications that obscure its likely political origins.[30]

Circumcision becomes fundamental in the process through which Christianity differentiates itself from or "supersedes" Judaism. In defense of uncircumcised Gentiles, St. Paul declared that the significance of circumcision was "spiritual" rather than "literal," and therefore the physical rite was not necessary for salvation.[31] This set the stage for Christians to substitute the figurative and bloodless rite of baptism for the more carnal cut, and to understand the latter as anachronistic, sign of the Jews' stubborn refusal of Christ (even though some Christians, such as the Copts, have continued the practice). Kathleen Biddick writes, "In his new theology of

[23] Jonathan et al.; see also Glick, *Marked in Your Flesh*, 32–3 and 64–6.
[24] Jonathan et al., 733; see also Wolfson, "Circumcision."
[25] Hall, "Epispasm."
[26] Hodges, "The Ideal Prepuce."
[27] Hall, "Epispasm"; 1 Mac. 1:15.
[28] Kennedy, "Masculinity and Embodiment."
[29] Jonathan et al., "Circumcision," 731.
[30] See, for example, Krohn, *Bris Milah*, 30, where *periah* is explained as symbolizing the divine intervention necessary for a circumcision to be complete.
[31] Rom. 2:29.

circumcision, the circumcision of the heart, Paul severed a Christian 'now' from a Jewish 'then.'"[32]

This particular Judeo-Christian controversy is the backdrop of my first case study, where I consider the relevance of circumcision to political-philosophical interpretations of St. Paul. How does Paul's stance on Jewish circumcision influence the way theorists embrace or oppose "Pauline" universalism? I explore this question by juxtaposing two influential books on Paul published in the same year, Alain Badiou's *Paul: The Foundation of Universalism* and Daniel Boyarin's *A Radical Jew: Paul and the Politics of Identity*. The two books, with their opposed conclusions on the meaning and value of Paul's universalism, provide the coordinates of a larger opposition between "universalists" and "particularists." I argue that a close study of Lacan's "formulas of sexuation" allows us to reconcile Badiou's admiration of Paul with Boyarin's skepticism by demonstrating how both authors share a commitment to a Lacanian "feminine" approach to collectivity, made visible in their different readings of the significance of Jewish circumcision.

After Christianity's general abandonment of the rite, circumcision made a monotheistic return with Islam. Although not mentioned in the Quran, male circumcision (*khitan* in Arabic) appears in several *Hadith* and is practiced throughout the Muslim world.[33] While it is not central to Islamic theology or legal scholarship, it tends to be highly valued within Muslim communities, generally understood as *fitra*, acts considered "refined" or "ideal" if not legally mandated.[34] (Female circumcision, although popular in some Muslim communities, is less widespread.[35]) Unlike in Judaism, where the basic elements of the rite are fairly uniform, there is little standardization of the timing and the traditions surrounding Islamic circumcision, with significant variation between different Muslim communities.[36] In many cases, pre-Islamic indigenous circumcision rituals have been absorbed into local Muslim practice.[37]

European anti-Semitism and Islamophobia, throughout the centuries, has often taken the form of an obsession with, and "pervasive dread"[38] of, circumcision, understood as disfiguring and perverse. "Central to the definition of the Jew," writes Sander Gilman, has been "the image of the male Jew's circumcised penis as impaired, damaged, or incomplete, and

[32] Biddick, *Typological Imaginary*, 11.
[33] Wensinck, "Khitan."
[34] Wensinck.
[35] Bearman et al., "Khafd."
[36] Wensinck, "Khitan."
[37] Wensinck.
[38] Silverman, *Abraham to America*, 145.

therefore threatening to the wholeness and health of the male Aryan."[39] In the notorious "blood libels" of the Middle Ages, Jews were accused of abducting and circumcising Christian children or using Christian blood to heal the wounds from their own circumcisions.[40] Many mohels were also kosher slaughterers, confirming, in anti-Semitic fantasy, an association between Jews, knives, and blood.[41] This libidinal fascination with the Jewish rite also had its inverse form of expression. In medieval times, numerable churches proudly claimed to possess the relic of Christ's severed foreskin. "A common test for foreskinned authenticity," explains Eric Silverman, "was taste. A physician, supervised by a priest, sampled the skin for the flavor of genuine holiness. The taster was called a *croque-prépuce,* or 'foreskin cruncher.'"[42] Yet, while the circumcised Jew both titillated and threatened the body politic from within, the Muslim circumciser terrorized from without: "To most Englishman," writes Robert Darby, "circumcision was a threat from which they had been saved by the defeat of Islamic armies."[43] As Julia Reinhard Lupton explains, for Christians, whereas "modern Judaism" was "a residual phenomenon, a stubborn carryover from an earlier moment," Islam "came to represent . . . a redoubling of Jewish intransigence to the Christian revelation . . . a double scandal."[44] In modern times, both Jews and Muslims have been forcibly undressed by perpetrators of genocide and ethnic cleansing who used circumcision status as a means of detection, including during the Holocaust and recent anti-Muslim riots in India.[45]

Despite—or possibly because of—the long history of anti-Semitic attitudes toward circumcision, attempts to eliminate the rite within Jewish modernizing movements have largely failed. In nineteenth-century Germany, an emergent Jewish Reform movement sought to assimilate Jews into wider German society and secular Enlightenment ideals, rejecting claims of ethnic difference as well as large portions of rabbinical law. Yet, despite overturning crucial aspects of Jewish observance, those few rabbis who circulated proposals to end the practice of circumcision were met with vehement condemnation, not only from Orthodox Jews outside the movement but also from their allies within. Leopold Zunz, a pioneer of the movement, summed up popular sentiment on the rejection of circumcision with the declaration,

[39] Gilman, *Freud*, 61.
[40] Gross, "Blood Libel."
[41] Judd, *Contested Rituals.*
[42] Silverman, *Abraham to America*, 156.
[43] Darby, *Surgical Temptation*, 32.
[44] Lupton, "Ethnos and Circumcision," 204–5.
[45] Ellis-Peterson, "Inside Delhi."

"Suicide is not reform."[46] A small number of Jews, associated with intactivism and Humanistic Judaism, began in the 1970s to practice and attempt to popularize a ceremonial alternative to circumcision named "brit shalom"; although gaining some traction, it remains a fringe practice.[47]

Negative attitudes toward circumcision experienced an unusual modification in the late-nineteenth-century when a number of British and American doctors began promoting the procedure. The libidinal dynamics surrounding this Anglo-American medicalization of circumcision form the basis of my second case study. The first "medical circumcisions"—those justified in the discourse of modern medicine rather than cultural practice or religious ritual—were performed on young boys as supposed cures for poorly defined disorders labeled "reflex irritations" or "reflex neuroses." The symptoms of these disorders were wide-ranging, from seizures and paralysis to bedwetting and constipation. Doctors blamed these disorders on masturbation, due to its supposedly disturbing effects on the nervous system, and argued that circumcision would relieve the "irritating" foreskin that, they argued, induced them to masturbate. The point of this case study is threefold: First, to offer a close reading of nineteenth-century medical texts on circumcision, highlighting the anxieties around sex, sexuality, and race that pervaded medical discourse. Second, to compare the theoretical paradigm surrounding nervous illness that justified the medicalization of circumcision with the ideas Freud developed around the same time. Finally, through this process, to gain an appreciation for the symptomatic nature of the "circumcision doctors'" approach. Like a fetish, medical circumcision functioned both to reencounter and to repudiate the "enigmatic seduction" constitutive of human sexuality. I offer here an extended analysis of sexuality in psychoanalysis by way of Jean Laplanche's theory of generalized enigmatic seduction, to demonstrate the crucial difference between the "talking cure" and the "circumcision cure."

Although, as medicine evolved, these initial justifications for circumcision mostly disappeared, the procedure long remained associated with health and sexual-moral hygiene in the United States and the United Kingdom, sometimes under the banner of philo-Semitism.[48] It became standard hospital procedure for newborn boys in America and was fairly popular in the UK, particularly among the upper classes, and for "future servants of empire"

---

[46] Quoted in Glick, *Marked in Your Flesh*, 121, further detail on 115–47; see also Silverman, *Abraham to America*, 183–7.

[47] See Wald and Moss, *Celebrating Brit Shalom*.

[48] Glick, *Marked in Your Flesh*, 179–214.

whose "sensitive foreskins" might not adapt well to "hot, humid climates."[49] The practice was reinforced during the world wars due to concerns about the urogenital hygiene of uncircumcised soldiers.[50] However, the founding of UK's nationalized healthcare system in 1948 occasioned cost-benefit analyses of procedures like circumcision. This centralization of healthcare, combined with growing professional skepticism around the value of practice, led to its precipitous decline among the British.[51] American medical organizations remain at odds with their European counterparts in continuing to take pro-circumcision stances.[52]

Today, approximately 80 percent of American males are circumcised.[53] The numbers of neonatal circumcisions performed in US hospitals are declining, influenced by demographic shifts (circumcision is less popular among Latino people), but also possibly in response to intactivist-informed skepticism.[54] Nevertheless, routine infant circumcision performed within a medical (rather than religious) context is uniquely popular in the US compared to the rest of the world, leading Jonathan Allan to suggest it "has become a part of the American civic religion."[55] By contrast, approximately 16 percent of UK males are circumcised, and the numbers hover between 0 and 20 percent throughout the rest of Europe.[56] (Contrary to an intriguing urban legend, the British royal family does not traditionally circumcise its members.[57]) The World Health Organization estimates that one in three males worldwide are circumcised, due largely to the influence of Islam (68 percent of circumcised men are Muslim).[58] Islamic scholars holding a 1987 conference "for the Scientific Aspects of Qur'an and Sunnah" in Pakistan

---

[49] Hyam, *Empire*, 77.
[50] Dunsmuir and Gordon, "History of Circumcision."
[51] Gairdner, "Fate of the Foreskin."
[52] For example, the latest American Academy of Pediatrics "Circumcision Policy Statement" concluded that "the health benefits of newborn male circumcision outweigh the risks." Their stance on the practice has undergone numerous revisions over the decades, from initially arguing there were "no valid medical indications for circumcision" in 1971 (Circumcision Reference Library, "Circumcision Statements"). European doctors expressed opposition to the AAP's latest position in Frisch et al., "Cultural Bias"; cf. AAP "Cultural Bias and Circumcision." Under the US private healthcare system, doctors receive reimbursements for covered procedures, providing a potential financial incentive for circumcision's continued popularity. See Carpenter, "On Remedicalisation."
[53] Introcaso et al., "Prevalence of Circumcision."
[54] Owings, Uddin, and Williams, "Trends in Circumcision"; Morris, Bailis, and Wiswell, "Circumcision Rates."
[55] Allan, "Is the Foreskin a Grave?" 11; see also Dekkers, "Routine (Non-Religious) Neonatal Circumcision."
[56] Dave et al., "Male Circumcision in Britain."
[57] Darby and Cozijn, "British Royal Family's Circumcision Tradition."
[58] WHO, "Neonatal Male Circumcision," 7.

reviewed American medical journals on circumcision and concluded that the practice "is medically beneficial . . . and reflects the wisdom of Islamic statements," illuminating the porosity of religious and scientific discourses on circumcision.[59] Circumcision also remains popular for nonobservant/ secular Jews and Muslims throughout the world—suggesting deep psychic ties to the practice that invite psychoanalytic consideration.

The practice is uncommon in East Asia, with the notable exception of South Korea, where circumcision rates have historically been as high as 95.2 percent, due to the influence of the American military during the Korean War; and, although still rare, circumcision has become an aesthetic trend in Japan.[60] Recently, circumcision has received new support in the global public health arena as an HIV/AIDS prophylactic; studies claim that it reduces the risk of HIV transmission by 50 to 60 percent in heterosexual males.[61] World Health Organization-backed public health campaigns have been launched in East and Southern Africa to promote circumcision for this purpose.[62]

My final case study looks at this current context, highlighting recent political and human rights controversies surrounding circumcision. I offer close readings of intactivist discourse, recent attempts to ban circumcision in Germany, multicultural defenders of male circumcision, popular opposition to FGM, and public health disputes over the dangers of *metzizah b'peh* (an aspect of the Jewish circumcision rite, performed mostly by the ultra-Orthodox community, involving oral-penile suction). I demonstrate how contemporary perspectives on circumcision, whether for or against, are just as legibly permeated with libidinal excess as those espoused by nineteenth-century circumcision doctors. Seemingly opposed stances on circumcision often evince the same wish to secure mastery in the face of the subversiveness of sexuality, and in the process, they wind up reproducing the very sexual excesses they wish to eliminate.

Making a Cut

As this brief history should suggest, there are innumerable issues, moments in time, and geographical locations that a book on circumcision might focus

[59] Quoted in Gollaher, *Circumcision*, 47.
[60] Kim et al., "Decline in Male Circumcision"; Castro-Vázquez, *Circumcision in Japan*. See also Allan, "The Foreskin Aesthetic."
[61] WHO, "Neonatal Male Circumcision." On homophobic anxieties underlying public health discourse on circumcision, see Allan, "Is The Foreskin A Grave?"
[62] See WHO's "Clearing House on Male Circumcision." Challenges to this approach include Lyons, "Male Infant Circumcision"; Bonner, "Male Circumcision."

on, whether it be an anthropological interpretation of the practice in tribal societies, an ethical analysis of circumcision and bodily autonomy, a study of how circumcision is symbolically registered within processes of racialization, or anything else besides. Indeed, as we will see in the next chapter, there exists a fair amount of scholarship on these questions, although most contemporary books on circumcision take a more polemical, rather than critical or theoretical, approach. To address the subject, a cut—or several—need to be made across themes, ideas, histories, and spaces. My solution is to identify a series of case studies where the question of castration or "the cut" within psychoanalytic theory can be brought to bear on a discrete period in the history of circumcision: ancient Christianity, discussed in Chapter 2; nineteenth-century medicine, discussed in Chapters 3 and 4; and contemporary politics, discussed in Chapter 5. Considered together, these case studies provide fruitful terrain on which to examine and distill key psychological, gendered, and cultural dimensions of the world's oldest surgery. Additionally, the sweep of disciplines and time periods that the case studies cover situate circumcision and the controversies surrounding it at the very heart of struggles over the constitution and definition of so-called Western civilization.

That being said, it is important to address some particular exclusions and editorial decisions I have made.

"Female Genital Mutilation" and the Question of Moral Neutrality

Most white Westerners believe male circumcision is "completely different" from so-called "FGM." The latter is often understood as a dangerous and "barbaric" practice concerned with reducing or eliminating a woman's capacity for sexual pleasure, whereas male circumcision, it is often argued, is a relatively minor operation that does not negatively impact male sexuality and may also confer hygienic benefits.[63] Intactivists have responded that the two practices share much in common and that mainstream opposition to FGM belies a double standard.[64] Male circumcision, they argue, does actually pose various dangers: the procedure involves a significant amount of pain, it can be botched or lead to infection (especially when performed by people without medical training or access to adequate sanitation), and, intactivists

[63] See, for example, Burke, "Female Circumcision," 440; and Hochhauser, "Don't Compare."
[64] See Earp, "Female Genital Mutilation"; Bodenner, "How Similar is FGM to Male Circumcision?"

claim, it also reduces male sexual pleasure. Moreover, some inactivists argue that the impetus for the routine medical circumcision of boys in the West arose from the same "anti-sensualist" ethos that justifies FGM.[65]

Although I reject the anti-feminist undertow of some intactivists' perspectives (believing men are the "true victims" because the "plight" of male circumcision goes unrecognized), I am equally opposed to the "civilized/savage" distinction that underlies the more commonplace division between "male circumcision" and "female genital mutilation."[66] However much male circumcision may carry the stamp of civilized respectability, a close examination of the practice (that we will undertake) reveals a relation to those same "primitive" elements of violence and aggression—inherent to all human cultures, whether they practice genital cutting or not—that are often commented on in opposition to FGM. This problematic binary is reinforced by the apparent neutrality of the term "circumcision," versus the use of the word "mutilation." For this reason, I will use the more value-neutral term "female genital cutting," or FGC. The actual interventions that constitute FGC vary widely across communities, from more extreme procedures such as the partial removal of the clitoris or the sewing together of the vaginal opening, to relatively minor acts such as a small genital nick.[67] Therefore, I also prefer the term FGC over "female circumcision," as the former designates that there exist various forms of genital cutting. I find the term "circumcision" more applicable in the male case because, while there exist different techniques and different degrees of foreskin removal, the overall surgical intent—removal of the foreskin—is consistent across cultures.[68]

Like male circumcision, the meanings or ritual significations of FGC are complex, polyvalent, and variable across communities.[69] (However, in nearly every society where FGC is customary, male circumcision is also customary and ritually interlinked.[70]) Many African and postcolonial

---

[65] Darby, *Surgical Temptation*.

[66] See Androus, "Critiquing Circumcision"; Lévi-Strauss, "Social Problems."

[67] See Public Policy Advisory Network on Female Genital Surgeries in Africa, "Seven Things." WHO classifies FGM according to four "types" (see "Female Genital Mutilation"). For a critical discussion of this classification, see Earp, "Moral Relativism," 108–11.

[68] Readers may question whether the term "male circumcision" reinforces gender normativity, as it assumes the gender identity of the person subjected to it. This is an interesting problem, as circumcision is typically part of a gendering process that, by its very nature, does not take the individual's preferences into account. I hope my use of the term is not taken to endorse an essentialist or transphobic view with regard to genital anatomy and gender.

[69] See, for example, Shweder, "Female Genital Mutilation"; Shell-Duncan and Hernlund, *Female "Circumcision" in Africa*; Wade, "Learning from 'Female Genital Mutilation.'"

[70] Public Policy Advisory Network on Female Genital Surgeries in Africa, "Seven Things."

feminists oppose what they view as the white liberal presumption that all women who have undergone some form of FGC are victims of patriarchy who require foreign saviors. Some have argued, not without controversy, that FGC rites might even be understood as empowering and generative of female solidarity.[71] Additionally, FGC is not the exclusive province of the non-Western "Other." There exists a history of female genital surgeries practiced in the West as treatments for a range of female "disorders," usually with the intent of managing or suppressing female sexuality.[72] Many vaginal operations practiced under the name of "cosmetic surgery" in the West today are anatomically identical to those labeled "FGM."[73]

The issues of FGC and intactivism open up a larger question about whether I ought to make a judgment on the morality of genital cutting. To the likely consternation of some readers, this book critically examines both pro- and anti-circumcision arguments without coming down in favor at all. I believe that by sidestepping the question of "for" or "against," we can better evaluate what is really at stake in the often-impassioned stances that surround the procedure. Like in the clinical practice of psychoanalysis, this suspension of judgment sustains a generative tension, enabling us to grapple with contradiction and uncertainty. By avoiding the temptation to choose a side, we are able to see how contradictory positions on the removal of the foreskin often present a "unity of opposites," sharing the same underlying anxieties around phallic potency and mastery.

Thinking about genitals and what can be done to them—your own, or someone else's—can feel threatening. It requires an encounter in the mind between an intimate part of the self and a potentially violent "Other," which can occasion a desire for reassuring certainty about what is safe and harmful, right and wrong. Some of the more graphic images I've encountered while researching—I've spared the reader the discomfort of viewing these—have made me feel dizzy. (It's not called castration anxiety for nothing.) In his ethnographic study of the practice of "bareback" sex amongst gay men who put themselves at risk of HIV infection, the psychoanalytic critic Tim Dean makes a similar point: "Far too often our desire to identify the politics of a phenomenon such as barebacking serves as a cover for deciding very quickly whether we approve or disapprove of it, thereby locating ourselves securely in relation to what may seem difficult or disturbing." Dean stresses both the

---

[71] See, for example, Shell-Duncan and Hernlund, *Female "Circumcision" in Africa*; Ahmadu, "Ain't I a Woman Too?"; and Gunning, "Arrogant Perception."

[72] See Darby, *Surgical Temptation*, 142–66; and Moscucci, "Clitoridectomy."

[73] Earp, "Between Moral Relativism," 121.

difficulty and ethical imperative of suspending judgment in order to free up the capacity to think.

This is not to suggest that readers shouldn't make decisions about where they stand in relation to genital cutting or the broader questions of consent and the body that it opens up (some of which we will explore in the final chapter). It is, rather, to suggest that, as with the experience of undergoing an analysis, we might obtain a better, and potentially more ethical, perspective by permitting ourselves to think freely about what we would rather avoid— including our own motivations for taking a side. Relatedly, I do not wish to discredit those who articulate experiences of harm or trauma from undergoing FGC or male circumcision. I suggest that we can both recognize, as genuine, one's testimony of pain or suffering in relation to an event such as circumcision, *and* retain an ability to question or remain curious about the conclusions such testimonies may offer about the procedure. Rather than advocating a position of distrust, I see this as in keeping with the psychoanalytic notion that the ideas one has about oneself and one's history are deeply felt and real, yet also partly unconscious, contradictory, and bound up in relational and discursive networks that may require unpacking and translation.[74]

A Jewish Emphasis

Another noticeable limitation of this work concerns an emphasis on controversies involving circumcision and Judaism, rather than Muslim or pagan circumcision practices. Partly this stems from my personal history and the contingencies of what I have chosen to study. However, there is also some justification for this focus within the larger context of this book. Looking closely at Jewish, male circumcision brings to light its uniquely "uncanny" position within Western identity (with all that term's Freudian/ German resonance—*unheimlich*/ "unhomely": something both integral to

---

[74] This point has particular resonance given the rise of #MeToo, and the concern that attention to the unconscious risks dismissing testimonies of sexual violence as "hysterical fantasies." I examine the status Freud accords to fantasy in Chapter 4. Suffice to say, I agree with Rose's evaluation that "The psychoanalytic attention to fantasy does not . . . discredit the utterance of the patient . . . [and] . . . was never assigned by Freud to the category of wilful untruth. In fact Freud's move was the reverse—toward a dimension of reality all the more important for the subject because it goes way beyond anything that can, or needs to be, attested as fact" (*Sexuality*, 13). See also Angel, *Tomorrow Sex Will Be Good Again*; and Osserman and Dousos, "Psychoanalysis and 'Post-Truth.'"

and disturbing of one's sense of "home").[75] In so doing, I hope not to shore up a West versus non-West dichotomy, but, rather, to interrogate the intimate yet inassimilable relation to Otherness that is constitutive of identity as such. Stephen Frosh helpfully illuminates this paradoxical centrality of Jewishness in the Western psyche:

> Through its historically derived cultural pervasiveness [the figure of the Jew] is perpetuated as the representation of that which is needed yet despised, that which holds in place the otherwise potentially intolerable destructiveness of a social system founded on inequality and alienation. . . . The Jew, and more generally the figure of the "other," is a constitutive feature of Western consciousness, an element out of which subjectivity is made.[76]

I would add that it is particularly through the image of circumcision that this process takes place.

To put it generally, circumcision has haunted and titillated the Western imagination since its foundation. This book explores some of the ways that this has occurred and sharpens our understanding of the impasses that it reveals.

---

[75] Freud, "The 'Uncanny'"; see also Dolar, "I Shall Be with You on Your Wedding-Night," which situates the uncanny at the heart of psychoanalysis.
[76] Frosh, *Hate and the "Jewish Science,"* 196.

1

Freud's Foreskin

Psychoanalytic Interpretations of Circumcision

Perhaps the most astonishing fact about circumcision is simply that it has arisen in different places across the world, and in societies that, in some cases, did not have contact with one another. Why would different groups of people independently think that the surgical removal of the foreskin— often in contexts where the risks of complications greatly outweighed any possible medical benefits—was a good idea? As the psychoanalyst Bruno Bettelheim pointed out, even when circumcision rites *can* be traced to cross-cultural contact, one still wonders what makes *this* cultural practice compelling enough to adopt?[1] Some have offered, unconvincingly in my view, explanations grounded in evolutionary theory, suggesting that pubertal circumcision historically conferred selective advantages as it delayed the age of reproduction.[2] Others have highlighted important anthropological themes related to circumcision rites: birth, fertility, social initiation and affiliation, the locus of authority, the differing bodily functions of men and women, and so on. Often, such interpreters attempt to synthesize these themes to pronounce on circumcision's overarching meaning, either for a particular society or more generally.

In this chapter, we will examine some psychoanalytic explanations of the impetus and psychic effects of circumcision, as well as the symbolic import of circumcision in Freud's own life and work. As we wind our way through the relevant literature and consider its occasional contradictions, I will develop the following arguments: (i) circumcision is one of the ways that the biological penis is imaginarily rendered the symbolic phallus, with all of the ambiguities involved therein; (ii) acts of circumcision are fundamentally ambivalent, representing simultaneously a masculinization and feminization of the participants; and (iii) stances toward circumcision involve a preoccupation with the question of phallic mastery in the face of lack.

---

[1] See Bettelheim, *Symbolic Wounds.*
[2] Cox and Morris, "Why Circumcision."

However, before we dive into this, I wish to introduce my theoretical framework. Inspired by Lacan's emphasis on the way the unconscious *undoes* meaning, I suggest that we begin with the *cut* that is at the center of every act of circumcision. Before it provides anything "positive"—an identity, a medical effect, a type of knowledge—circumcision opens something up and takes something away. It does so not just anywhere on the body, but on the male organ of generation. Thus at a basic level, we can say that circumcision draws a relation between the penis and negativity. It brings the sexual organ into a system of human representation by removing something from it. It therefore takes us into the heart of the question of sexual difference and the phallus, as theorized in psychoanalysis.

Charles Shepherdson, drawing on the imagery of circumcision and other initiation rites, explains the significance of such cuts through a distinction between the organism as a purely biological phenomenon and the subjective experience of the body as acquired through representation:

> In contrast to the organism, the body is constitutively denaturalized, "organ-ized" . . . by the image and the word. . . . Born as an organism, the human animal nevertheless has to acquire a body, come into the possession of its body (to be "born again," as suggested by many rituals involving tattooing, circumcision, baptism, and so on), through the image and the signifier.[3]

Of course, for psychoanalysis, you do not need to be circumcised to be subjected to "the cut"—you merely need to speak. Language already tears something vital away from us. This is a fundamental trauma which, psychoanalysis maintains, demands representation. Here, I am referring to the reformulation of "castration" and "sexual difference" inaugurated by Lacan's linguistic "return to Freud." Lacanian psychoanalysis brings to the fore the question of how a subject comes into being in relation to others via the system of meaning-making we call language. This process involves a fundamental break from "nature" that is experienced, retroactively, as an inassimilable trauma. For Lacan, this is the ontological substrate, the ultimate "real," of Freudian castration, and the entry into what Lacanians call "sexed" (or "divided") subjectivity.

Circumcision, I would argue, draws our attention to embodied aspects of this phenomenon, the ways signification leaves its mark on the reproductive body. We speak, and therefore, we are governed by a logic irreducible to

---

[3] Shepherdson, *Vital Signs*, 99–100.

biology. Yet, we remain biological beings, wedded to our corporeality, dependent on the products and processes of our anatomically differentiated bodies for the continuation of life. How can we give form to the intersection of these two aspects of subjectivity, the representational and the vital? As Judith Butler writes, "Sexual difference is the site where a question concerning the relation of the biological to the cultural is posed and reposed, where it must and can be posed, but where it cannot, strictly speaking, be answered."[4]

What Is Sexual Difference?

Although the term "sexual difference" often refers to Freudian and Lacanian theory, neither Freud nor Lacan used this particular phrase. It was produced in the Anglophone feminist appropriation of Lacan, out of the attempt to formalize psychoanalytic theory on castration, sexuality, the phallus, and the psychic "positions" of masculinity and femininity.[5] The term is usefully polyvalent: "sexual difference" suggests both "difference between the sexes," and the interrelation of sexuality and difference—the encounter with "difference," or something "other" to oneself, that psychoanalysis holds to be constitutive of the (sexual) self.

For psychoanalysis, sexual identity is never straightforwardly secured. Freud theorized that the child is innately "bisexual" and "polymorphously perverse."[6] The acquisition of a masculine or feminine identity, and a set of sexual aims and objects, occurs through a tumultuous process of repressions and identifications, in which one's encounter and struggle with "law" or prohibition is central. As Freud writes apropos of femininity, "psycho-analysis does not try to describe what a woman is—that would be a task it could scarcely perform—but sets about enquiring how she comes into being, how a woman develops out of a child with a bisexual disposition."[7] Lacan downplayed Freud's more maturational and developmental accounts of human sexuality—those which suggested a teleology toward heterosexual "genitality"—and foregrounded, instead, Freud's observations regarding the sexual drive's essential perversity, its stubborn refusal to submit to any normative schema of reproductive sexuality.[8]

---

[4] Butler, *Undoing Gender*, 186.
[5] Mitchell, "Sexual Difference in the New Millennium."
[6] Freud, *Three Essays*, 191–3 and 141–4.
[7] Freud, *New Introductory Lectures*, 116.
[8] See, for example, Lacan, "Function and Field," 217–18.

Yet, against those strands of queer theory that posit a Manichean battle between the innate subversiveness of human sexuality and the oppressiveness of external social norms, psychoanalysis theorizes a subject generated *through* the "symbolic order," Lacan's name for the social world of language, intersubjective relations, and law. The unconscious subverts the societal norms and strictures placed upon sexuality only insofar as the ego has at least partially identified with these in its bid to achieve lawful belonging within the symbolic. For Lacan, this tension stems from the human need to secure meaning, to participate in a regulated symbolic system. As Jacqueline Rose writes:

> Lacan's statements on language need to be taken in two directions—towards the fixing of meaning itself (that which is enjoined on the subject), and away from that very fixing to the point of its constant slippage, the risk or vanishing-point which it always contains (the unconscious). Sexuality is placed on both these dimensions at once. The difficulty is to hold these two emphases together—sexuality in the symbolic (an ordering), sexuality as that which constantly fails.[9]

Humans are both enjoined to line themselves up in a symbolic male/female opposition and exist in permanent rebellion against this fiction. This need to secure meaning—our constitutive reliance on the symbolic order—occurs, according to Lacan, as a result of the human animal's "premature birth." We are born with preciously few survival instincts, in a state of total and prolonged reliance on our caregivers, yet with an unusually high capacity for imaginative thinking, leading to a "narcissistic alienation in the other's body image."[10] An "artificial" system is needed for us to escape this narcissistic/incestuous enclosure and acquire the means to survive and reproduce the species. "Without a symbolic 'superimposition' on the realm of animal sexual instincts," explains Lorenzo Chiesa, "the human Imaginary and the . . . libido would inevitably reduce us to aggressive self-destruction. . . . The Symbolic constitutes the structural condition of possibility for any sort of (reproductive) human sexual relationship to occur."[11]

Although this emphasis on sexual reproduction may sound suspiciously naturalistic, especially in light of Lacan's emphasis on the nonexistence of the sexual relationship, what we are actually presented with here is an account of *both* the persistence of heteronormative ideology *and* its ultimately

[9]   Rose, *Sexuality*, 66–7.
[10] Chiesa, *Subjectivity and Otherness*, 83.
[11] Chiesa, 83.

artificial character. As Chiesa writes, "the Symbolic may, broadly speaking, be understood as a successful 'reaction' against the disadaptation of man as animal."[12] The symbolic generates the "reactionary" myths about men and women that provide the impetus for exogamous sexual relationships, yet it is not a "natural" inheritance but, rather, an artificial and constitutively malfunctioning system, into which the subject must find his own way to insert himself, and at a cost that will manifest in his psychic life. "Language is always-already there for the [child], but the symbolic relations that structurally accompany it remain utterly enigmatic," explains Chiesa. "As a consequence, the child has to 'learn' how to actively enter the Other *qua* Symbolic, and to enter it as an individual."[13] We each attempt, in our own way, to participate in the myth of a harmonious sexual relationship —and thereby encounter its inherent impasses and failures.

Moreover, this imaginary fantasy of sexual complementarity is propped up by the symbolic to disguise the latter's fundamentally abstract and even "mathematical" character. Because it is ultimately based on linguistic principles of difference and exchange, the symbolic relies on our belief in deeper sexualized meaning to sustain itself, which it was to Lacan's credit to debunk. As Rose writes, for Lacan, "there is no longer imaginary 'unity' and then symbolic difference or exchange, but rather an indictment of the symbolic for the imaginary unity which its most persistent myths continue to promote."[14] Coming back to circumcision, we might therefore view its initiatory dimensions as illuminating a contradiction between human sexual anatomy and the symbolic. The cut represents both our reliance on the symbolic in order to make (re)productive use of our "natural," sexed bodies, and the way in which the entry into symbolization cuts us away from nature in the process.

The Phallus and the Penis

What is the relationship between sexual difference in psychoanalysis and the anatomical distinction of the sexes? This question is of vital importance in relation to circumcision's mark on the penis. For psychoanalysis, what matters is not the anatomical body as such but, rather, the fantasmatic interpretations of what the body *means* and the symbolic places to which

---

[12] Chiesa, 61.
[13] Chiesa, 61.
[14] Rose, *Sexuality*, 71.

different types of bodies are assigned. In the Lacanian conceptualization of sexual difference, the subject is enjoined to identify with the meanings assigned to its anatomical sex, yet at the same time must confront meaning's precariousness. This is linked to the entry into symbolization, and a single signifier is charged with carrying out this process for both sexes: the phallus.

The concept of the phallus is essentially concerned with why a speaking being consents to taking up a desiring position in the symbolic order. Lacan described it as "the privileged signifier . . . in which the role of Logos is wedded to the advent of desire."[15] It appears as a solution for an initial, imaginary encounter with lack that serves ultimately to reproduce this lack at a higher and more complex (symbolic) level. As the Lacanian analyst Patricia Gherovici puts it, "The phallus is the object that appears to veil a symbolic lack to create it."[16]

The problem begins at the mirror stage. The ideal unity of the child's body in the mirror image does not correspond to its own intuitive sense of its body as inchoate and fragmented; the child alienates itself in the images and signifiers coming from the Other in an attempt to achieve a longed-for coherence. By "Other," I mean both the mirror image and the child's primary caregiver—the "(m)Other"—insofar as both hold the promise of rectifying the child's organic insufficiency. This Other frustrates the child, for in this process of alienation in the Other it encounters the Other's own lack; the Other cannot provide the completion that the child desperately seeks. This can be thought of in terms of the mother's unpredictable comings and goings, which suggest to the child that the (m)Other is wanting, as well as the gap encountered in relation to the mirror image itself, the point where the specular image fails to entirely account for and incorporate the "real" of the body. This induces the child into an attempt to fill in the lack in the Other by becoming that which it presumes the Other lacks.[17]

The phallus comes into operation at this juncture as the name for the child's hypothesis of what would complete the Other. At the imaginary level, this involves the notion that there is a concrete "thing" that is lacking or threatened, which, if secured, will allow for unity and wholeness.[18] As language intervenes, this lack in the Other becomes differentiated and diffuse. It is no longer an imagined "thing" but, rather, a complex *desire* of the Other's. The child then endeavors to decipher the Other's desire, whether

---

[15] Lacan, "Signification of the Phallus," 581.

[16] Gherovici, *Please Select Your Gender*, 20.

[17] See Lacan, "Mirror Stage" and "Subversion of the Subject"; and Van Haute, *Against Adaptation*.

[18] See Chiesa, *Subjectivity and Otherness*, 60–96.

through its attention to the Other's overt expressions of dissatisfaction, or more fundamentally, the unsaid or "beyond" consubstantial with signification. It is here that the *symbolic* phallus emerges as the signifier that stands for the desire of the Other. This signifier functions as a veil, covering over the traumatic emptiness that the child has encountered with a positive signification. As Paul Verhaeghe writes, the "phallic instance is . . . already an interpretation of [a more] radical lack."[19]

Replacing the pursuit of imaginary completion with a relation to the symbolic phallus is a difficult and never fully accomplished task, involving an encounter with law. The child must find a way to accept that the Other's desire is not for itself as an imaginary phallus, but for something beyond, belonging to the order of language, culture, and society. The inherent impossibility of completing the Other is supplemented by an (Oedipal) prohibition against it. In the more traditional Freudian narrative, this is represented by the figure of the father, presumed bearer of the phallus, who puts a limit on the child's incestuous bond with the mother and compels the child to pursue other socially acceptable alternatives. However, what matters for Lacan is not the physical father but the imposition of a third term, a structural place beyond the (m)Other–child dyad. The symbolic phallus thus becomes the means through which the child appreciates the larger network of socially viable positions it can inhabit. The child cannot "be" the phallus for the Other, but it can take on various phallic signifiers: interests, accomplishments, and ways of being in society that it deems desirable. These desires are never wholly independent of what one thinks the Other—which is no longer solely the mother—wants/lacks. Rather, they are the subject's symbolic interpretations of the desire of the Other, once it has confronted the prohibition against/ impossibility of the incestuous completion of the mother.[20]

Drawing on Freud's theory of the universality of the phallic phase for boys and girls, Lacan holds that it is only through the phallus that the entry into sexual difference takes place. The symbolic "positions" of masculinity and femininity do not have complementary signifiers attached to them but, rather, involve different relations to a unitary phallic signifier.[21] This presents us with the following problems: Given the obvious "penile" referent, what is the relationship between the phallus and the anatomical organ? Second, why is this penile signifier held to carry out the work of sexual difference for both sexes?

Within the Lacanian literature, there are three related explanations for why the image of the penis serves as an initial representative of the phallus.

---

[19] Verhaeghe, "Lacan on the Body," 122.
[20] See Hook, "Lacan."
[21] Lacan, "Signification of the Phallus," 583.

The first two relate to the organ's anatomical peculiarity and the way its image lends itself to an initial entry into symbolization. In *Subversion of the Subject*, Lacan emphasizes the apparent detachability of the penis in relation to its "negativization" in the specular image.[22] The argument is essentially Freudian. While typically, parents positively reinforce the child's narcissistic identification with its body image (we can think of games like "this little piggy went to the market," where the toes are identified, delimited, and tickled), Lacan suggests that the penis is "negativized," invested if not with shame then at least with the sense that its relation to the Other is uniquely problematic.[23] In combination with this, the little boy discovers that the penis's "position as a 'pointy extremity' in the form predisposes it to the fantasy of it falling off."[24] The penis is thus held to be the first imaginary representative of the phallus because it presents itself as uniquely precarious, prone to detachment and the traumatic loss of autoerotic pleasure. The morphology of the penis—the simple fact that it protrudes from the body—coincides with its psychical inscription ("negativization") as something exceptional in relation to the other body parts, to produce the fantasy that this unique and excessive presence may all too easily become an absence. This somewhat comic description essentially suggests that, at the level of fantasy, the image of the penis is an ideal object to represent an initial absence or lack in the imaginary, a concrete "thing" that may be missing or an initial "interpretation" of "radical lack." Of course, this implies a different experience for boys and girls. For Lacan, writes Van Haute, "the phallus marks for both sexes a crack in the specular image," but it does so in different ways: "an organ that might have been there for girls, and for boys, one that might have not."[25] Both sexes experience a lack in relation to the image, but one is characterized more by the specter of loss (leading to the question, *what must I do to preserve this?*), the other by the sense of it already having gone (or not having emerged yet).

A second and related explanation concerns the way the organic functions of the penis provide a potential entry point into binary phallic logic. Lacan suggests this at various points in his teachings, for example:

> The signifier avails itself of a series of elements which are linked . . . to the body. . . . There are a certain number of elements, given to experience as accidents of the body, which are resumed in the signifier and which, as it were, give it its novitiate. We are dealing here with things that are

[22] Lacan, "Subversion of the Subject," 696–7.
[23] See Fink, *Lacan to the Letter*, 136.
[24] Lacan, "Subversion of the Subject," 696–7.
[25] Van Haute, *Against Adaptation*, 183.

both elusive and irreducible, amongst which there is the phallic term, plain erection.[26]

Here, Lacan appears to suggest that the penile binary flaccid/erect allows for an initial bodily representation of the dialectics of presence/absence necessary to enter into signification. Malcolm Bowie draws these connections more explicitly:

> The penis here provides a stepping-stone between sex and logic.... What of the everyday uncertainties that beset the male member? . . . The penis may be rigid or flaccid, and either condition may arise opportunistically or not. Its discharge may be premature or infinitely delayed. It may be short and wished longer, or long and wished shorter. It may be proudly displayed, or apologetically concealed. It may be the instrument of will or seem to possess a will of its own, an object of fear, disgust, admiration, envy. . . . This capacity for variation within pre-ordained limits seems to make it into a dialectician par excellence, a nexus of signifying opportunities, a fine example, in all its modes, of the Freudian fort/da.[27]

While Bowie helps us visualize the ways in which the anatomical behavior of the penis lends itself to an engagement with the differential structure of language, we can presume that Lacan's resistance to making the links too explicit emerges out of a wish to avoid a naturalistic trap that would render null the distinction between the penis and the phallus. The point is not that biology produces signification, but, rather, that we interpret the body *against the preexisting background of the symbolic* as a way of entering into language as corporeal subjects. Although she intends her comments as a critique of Lacan, Judith Butler seems to capture Lacanian logic on the phallus quite precisely when she writes, "One might be tempted to argue that in the course of being set into play by the narcissistic imaginary, the penis becomes the phallus."[28]

In Lacanian theory, the process of entering into signification begins from the subject's body and moves outwards. The child learns to differentiate the various parts and functions of its body in the imaginary and applies this rudimentary form of signification to its relations with the world. For example, a child sees a running tap and may think it is urinating. Gradually, the autonomy of the signifier will increase, such that a "running tap" acquires a unique signification of its own; its connection to the body will be repressed

[26] Quoted in Chiesa, *Subjectivity and Otherness*, 70.
[27] Bowie, *Lacan*, 125.
[28] Butler, *Bodies that Matter*, 77.

and manifested only unconsciously, such as when the sound of a running tap incites the need to urinate. Thus, the dynamics involved in the passage from the imaginary to the symbolic are a kind of psychic acquisition and negotiation of signifying operations. The phallus is held to be the initial instance of this operation: through a process of metaphorical substitution, the imaginary organ is transformed into a signifier, its connection to the body diminished but never totally extinguished. This signifier, the paradoxical signifier of lack, corresponds to the necessary gap in signification itself, the minimal difference required to set the chain of signifiers in motion.[29] As Theresa Brennan writes, "The visual recognition of sexual difference is a channel connecting the heterogenous experience of the feeling, sensing body to something that is alien to it: the differential structure of language."[30] A subject finds a place for itself in language, without being *reduced* to language, by aligning its bodily encounter with imaginary lack to the lack in signification.

In fact, in Lacan's Seminar Five, it is through reference to the signifying function of circumcision that Lacan designates the complicated relationship between the penis and the phallus. He notes that "the religious incarnations in which we recognize the castration complex, circumcision for example" underscore how what is at stake in castration is not "the genital organs in their totality" but "something that has a particular relationship with the organs, but a certain relationship whose signifying character is not in doubt."[31] Alenka Zupančič highlights how, far from assigning the penis a transcendental status, Lacan's work on the phallus actually functions as a critique of the organ's traditional importance:

> By spelling out the link between the traditional almighty phallus (which, by the way, functioned symbolically, and as a symbol of power, long before Lacan came along) to an anatomical particularity, he (and psychoanalysis) made a crucial contribution to the removal of the phallus from the mode of necessity to that of contingency.[32]

A final explanation for the penile underpinnings of the phallus relates to its place within the child's interpretation of the (m)Other's desire. In Seminars Three and Four, Lacan discusses the child's registration of imaginary phallic lack in relation to its appreciation of the mother's desire for the father's penis, and of the apparent superiority of the paternal sexual organ.[33] The child finds

[29] Van Haute, *Against Adaptation*, 174.
[30] Brennan, *Between Feminism and Psychoanalysis*, 4.
[31] Lacan, *V*, 289–90.
[32] Zupančič, *Odd One In*, 205.
[33] Lacan, *III*; *IV*. See also Chiesa, *Subjectivity and Otherness*, 60–96.

his or her genitals traumatically inadequate in comparison with the father's, ushering him or her into a sexually differentiated position of lack. The penis is significant here not because of any inherent anatomical function but because of the role it plays in the interpretation of the mother's desire. It is a process that we might imagine modified under alternate social structures (in which the penis is not valorized) and child-rearing scenarios.

Sexual Difference and the Phallus

The subject's encounter with the phallus is a way of structuring, along the lines of sexual difference, a primordial encounter with lack, desire, and law. As the hypothesis of the Other's desire, it presents the subject with a binary choice: can I have it, or not? Am I someone who may possess the phallus if I consent to submit to law (give up the mother in exchange for an eventual, "legitimate" substitute)? Or, have I been altogether denied the phallus (in which case I might pursue an alternative system of valuation, such as becoming the object of another's desire)? These are the questions and pursuits which, according to psychoanalysis, guide masculine and feminine identifications. Sexual difference thus concerns two possible responses to castration—two ways a subject copes with the impossibility of imaginary wholeness—made possible by a single signifier. In a sense, the phallus is a fetish for both sexes, a symptomatic solution that both disavows and sustains castration.[34] It enables reproductive heterosexuality via symbolic imposition, tearing one out of an incestuous bond, while at the same its artificial and fantasmatic character makes sexuality, and sexual identifications, go haywire—opening the door for nonnormative sexual and gender practices and identifications. As Rose puts it, "The phallus can only take up its place by indicating the precariousness of any identity assumed as its token."[35] Her account of the relation between anatomical and sexual difference as symbolically mediated by the phallus, and the psychic instability it produces, is worth quoting in full:

> Sexual difference is ... assigned according to whether individual subjects do or do not possess the phallus, which means not that anatomical difference *is* sexual difference (the one as strictly deducible from the other), but that anatomical difference comes to *figure* sexual difference, that is, it becomes the sole representative of what that difference is

[34] See Lacan, "Signification of the Phallus," 583.
[35] Rose, *Sexuality*, 64.

allowed to be. It thus covers over the complexity of the child's early sexual life with a crude opposition in which that very complexity is refused or repressed. The phallus thus indicates the reduction of difference to an instance of visible perception, a seeming value.

> Freud gave the moment when the boy and girl child saw that they were different the status of trauma in which the girl is seen to be lacking (the objections often start here). But something can only be seen to be missing according to a pre-existing hierarchy of values. . . . What counts is not the perception but its already assigned meaning—the moment therefore belongs in the symbolic. And if Lacan stated that the symbolic usage of the phallus stems from its visibility (something for which he was often criticised), it is only in so far as the order of the visible, the apparent, the seeming is the object of his attack.[36]

Once again, foregrounding the cut of circumcision helps to illuminate the contradictions involved in phallic symbolization as discussed by Rose. In circumcision, the penis is affirmed as the anatomical site fundamental to a boy's social and symbolic initiation, yet at the same time, the "givenness" of anatomy is challenged: the reification of the penis, and the value it accrues through circumcision, require that the penis be subjected to symbolization, incurring a loss of "intactness," a subtraction that is imaginarily represented through the act of the cut. If, as Butler writes, "the phallus appears as symbolic only to the extent that its construction through the transfigurative and specular mechanisms of the imaginary is denied," in the act of circumcision we can see these mechanisms made manifest.[37] Moreover, circumcision underscores the way in which language and symbolization are not simply "external" things we participate in but, rather, constitute phenomena for which we must *carve out a (corporeal) space*. Circumcision both presents the promise of a complementarity between culture and the sexual body, and shows this to be a discursive fiction.

"Femininity" in Psychoanalysis

Women have come to figure as a "problem" for psychoanalytic theory, evidenced by Freud's notorious question, "What does a woman want?"[38] In Oedipal terms, women not only have to give up the mother but, unlike men,

---

[36] Rose, 66.
[37] Butler, *Bodies That Matter*, 47.
[38] Quoted in Jones, *Freud, v. 2*, 421.

they are enjoined to fashion themselves into the passive object of a man's love, sacrificing both their initial object choice *and* their active sexual aims. Freud could not understand how women managed to make these demanding renunciations of universal infantile wishes, arguing that they only occurred incompletely, if at all.[39]

Lacan argued that there is no signifier for femininity in the unconscious. Femininity only appears in reference to, or as an effect of, the phallus. Whereas masculinity constructs itself around the pretense of phallic ownership, femininity is consigned to the problematics of the masquerade: "It is for what she is not that [woman] expects to be desired as well as loved," writes Lacan.[40] Because she cannot have the phallus, she must, instead, participate in games which mark her as castrated, lacking the phallus, in order to "be" it for a man (who wants to "have" it) and thereby secure a symbolic position as a woman. As Stephen Heath explains:

> The masquerade serves to show what she does not have, the penis, by showing—the adornment, the putting-on—something else, the phallus she becomes, as woman to man, sustaining his identity and an order of exchange of which she is the object—"the fantasy of The man in her finds its moment of truth": "Such is the woman behind her veil: it is the absence of the penis that makes her the phallus, object of desire." . . . Disguising herself as a castrated woman, the woman represents man's desire and finds her identity as, precisely, woman—genuine womanliness and the masquerade are the same thing.[41]

To put these claims in terms more compatible with feminist thinking, we might say that, while masculinity is structured around the claim of an essence —the essence of a man is that he (supposedly) possesses the phallus— femininity concerns the subjective consequences of the impossibility of phallic ownership, and the ultimate lack of an essence behind sexed identity. The phallus, we recall, is ultimately a veil, a way of disavowing the traumatic absence that constitutes desire by making it appear as a full presence. If one is denied possession of this mechanism, the question of how to secure a symbolic position for oneself becomes especially fraught. The means through which one attempts nevertheless to secure this position will consequently show up the precarious, discursive nature of the phallus. Women, Lacan

---

[39] See Freud, "Female Sexuality."

[40] Lacan, "Signification of the Phallus," 583; see also Riviere, "Womanliness as a Masquerade."

[41] Heath, "Joan Riviere," 52. (The nested quotes are Lacan's.)

suggests, are induced to place themselves as objects into a circuit of exchange because, by lubricating the gears of this masculine system of possession, they find a symbolic place for themselves, an identity as a woman. Yet, by subjecting themselves to this system, assuaging its relentless need for fortification, women highlight the fraudulence at its core. "To be a woman is to dissimulate a fundamental masculinity, femininity is that dissimulation," writes Heath.[42] The only essence of sexual identity, this reading of femininity suggests, is the very *lack* of essence that fuels the attempt to take up a symbolic position. Femininity becomes the Other of the symbolic order as such, and therefore its repressed truth —a blessing and a curse:

> Lacan's reference to woman as Other needs . . . to be seen as an attempt to hold apart two moments which are in constant danger of collapsing into each other—that which assigns woman to the negative place of its own (phallic) system, and that which asks the question as to whether women might, as a very effect of that assignation, break against and beyond that system itself.[43]

Femininity is thus closely aligned with the unconscious, as that which escapes mastery, meaning, and possession *as the precise effect of submission to a phallic order that attempts to secure these things.* "We could say that the unconscious is feminine, that it is the negation, the un, the other, of phallic consciousness," writes the Lacanian analyst Bice Benvenuto.[44] In this formulation, the problems and paradoxes symbolically assigned to the female sex represent something fundamental about subjectivity as such, for both men and women.

Women's ambiguous positioning within the symbolic order (a positioning that calls that very order into question) leads to the production of fantasies about the "Other sex." For a masculine subject, symbolic castration is often defensively (and misogynistically) linked to notions of the "Woman," as alternately the uncastrated exception and the very abyss of castration. Both are masculine fantasies that attempt to make sense of something radically, threateningly "Other." In one, the woman possesses something man has been denied (such as superior sexual enjoyment and the capacity for childbirth). In the other, woman represents a black hole. In both, woman comes to stand for that which prevents man's phallic completion. It is Otherness as such that men struggle against here; only in a second instance is it fantasmatically purported to relate to the difference of the opposite sex.

[42] Heath, 49.
[43] Rose, *Sexuality*, 76.
[44] Benvenuto, *Concerning the Rites*, 75.

Sexual Difference and Gender

Is sexual difference the same thing as "gender"? Although the definitions of both terms are extremely slippery and vary widely, I do not believe they should be used interchangeably. Gender, as I understand it, concerns positive representations, performances, or social systems of sexed subjectivity. It involves a set of attributes or behaviors that cohere into identities socially designated as masculine or feminine, as well as the social organization of reproduction and divisions of labor. (More recent gender signifiers, such as "nonbinary," have expanded the range of socially identifiable genders; however, such identities are not simply additional genders but are also intended to transgress the ideology and power dynamics involved in gendering as such.) Butler's work has famously granted the term "gender" a high degree of theoretical sophistication; she defines gender as "a stylized repetition of acts . . . which are internally discontinuous . . . [so that] the appearance of substance is precisely that, a constructed identity, a performative accomplishment which the mundane social audience, including the actors themselves, come to believe and to perform in the mode of belief."[45] For Butler the very process of "performing" gender, in fact, creates it. As far as we, as discursive subjects, are concerned, there is no sex before gender (gender creates the fraudulent "appearance of substance" we call sex), yet at the same time, there is no subject independent of the "matrix of gender relations" in which "speaking subjects come into being."[46]

Sexual difference concerns something different: not the positive gendered attributes we perform, but the question of what form of subjective impasse gives rise to our use of gendered signifiers in the first place. As historian Joan Scott writes, in a psychoanalytic reformulation of her earlier work:

Gender is no longer simply a social construction, a way of organizing social, economic, and political divisions of labor along sexually differentiated lines. It is instead a historically and culturally specific attempt to resolve the dilemma of sexual difference, to assign fixed meaning to that which ultimately cannot be fixed.[47]

For Lacanian psychoanalysis, "that which ultimately cannot be fixed" is castration, the basic condition for subjectivity as such. Sexual difference involves the way a subject encounters, is subjectivized by, and negotiates the impossibility of phallic wholeness.

45 Butler, *Gender Trouble*, 179.
46 Butler, *Bodies That Matter*, xvi.
47 Scott, *Fantasy of Feminist History*, 5.

As we have seen, psychoanalysis theorizes a relationship between genital anatomy and sexual difference insofar as the former is mediated through the symbolic. Nevertheless, I do not think a psychoanalytic theory of sexual difference requires accepting anatomical determinism with regard to gender. There are many ways that subjects engage with the impasses of sexual difference, some of which may subvert how anatomy is traditionally symbolized (for example, the penis may not always be the exclusive site through which the phallus is symbolized).[48] While trans identity clearly engages with the problematics of sexual difference, there is no "one size fits all" approach through which trans identities might be "subsumed" into a psychoanalytic masculine/feminine opposition.[49] Oren Gozlan argues that "trans" functions as a "placeholder for the incommensurability between gender and sexual difference," insofar as trans people may highlight how *all* gender presentations attempt, and fail, to symbolize the impasse at the heart of sexual difference.[50]

Nevertheless, a psychoanalytic theory of sexual difference helps us understand, at an unconscious level, *how* the heteronormative gender binary comes to be established and maintain its hold on us, in addition to illuminating its structural weaknesses (qua the problematics of femininity). As Juliet Mitchell put it, "psychoanalysis is not a recommendation *for* a patriarchal society, but an analysis *of* one."[51] Psychoanalytic conceptualizations of "masculinity" and "femininity" offer a useful way to think through the desires undergirding gendered identifications and performances, as well as the symbolic and social organization that induces us into these identifications.[52]

Psychoanalysts on Circumcision

Psychoanalytic work on circumcision tends to focus on the relation between the practice and issues surrounding castration, sexual difference, and the

---

[48] See Carlson, "Transgender Subjectivity."
[49] A recent proliferation of Lacanian work challenges the pathologization of trans people and offers new ways to think about sexual difference in relation to trans. See, for example, Cavanagh, "Transpsychoanalytics"; Gherovici, *Transgender Psychoanalysis*; and Gozlan, *Current Critical Debates*. This literature opposes the once popular thesis put forward in Millot, *Horsexe*, that to undergo genital reassignment surgery is a psychotic endeavor to escape sexual difference altogether.
[50] Gozlan, *Transsexuality*, 7.
[51] Mitchell, *Psychoanalysis*, xiii (emphasis original).
[52] In *Siblings*, Juliet Mitchell argues that gender identifications emerge from the "lateral" axis of sibling and peer relations, whereas sexual difference emerges from the "vertical" axis of law and castration. See also Laplanche, "Gender": "The sexual is the unconscious residue of the repression/symbolization of gender by sex" (202).

phallus. However, authors differ in their views of how this relation ought to be defined and understood. By focusing on the cut of circumcision discussed earlier and considering the rite's ambivalence in relation to phallic mastery, I will suggest in the following sections that apparently contradictory interpretations of the practice might be reconciled.

Freud's own arguments on circumcision are developed most fully in *Moses and Monotheism*. Here, he proposes that the vitality and longevity of the Jewish people, and their transformative impact on the world, are premised on a repressed secret: the Hebrew people's murder of Moses and the consequent revolution in subjectivity that emerges out of their obsessive efforts to alleviate their guilt. The book is also an attempt to explain the unconscious roots of anti-Semitism, which Freud understood as a form of scapegoating occasioned by resistance to the renunciations required of modern monotheistic subjectivity. Freud examines circumcision within both these contexts: as a symbol of the Jews' attempt to repress their foundational crime and symbolically affirm their (belated) submission to Mosaic law, and also as a source of their persecution.

Moses, Freud proposes, was an elite Egyptian who, in his attempt to cultivate and lead a great nation, chose to liberate the Hebrew people from slavery and force upon them the quasi-monotheistic Aten cult. This cult represented a spiritual "advance" over other forms of paganism as it required the renunciation of sensuality and the elevation of abstract and intellectual principles. Moses had the Hebrews adopt the practice of circumcision as a sign of the elite status he wished to grant them. The Hebrews rebelled against Moses's burdensome demands, murdered their liberator and spiritual father, and returned to pagan worship. Yet, after a period of "latency" and driven by superegoic guilt, they renewed their submission to Mosaic law and attempted to efface the traces of their murder. Jewish circumcision functions for Freud as a "key-fossil"[53] in helping him reconstruct this secret history, for the attachment to it as a marker of Jewish identity presents a suggestive paradox: Why would the ancient Hebrews claim to differentiate themselves from the pagans using a rite which they knew very well was a popular Egyptian practice? The clumsy attempt to claim circumcision as their own, Freud argues, is a symptomatic distortion, a clue that points to the cover-up of the murder. Circumcision thus demonstrates both the Jews' willingness to submit to monotheistic renunciation and allows us to unravel the repressed crime which drove that very will to renounce.

---

[53]　Freud, *Moses and Monotheism*, 39.

Within this text Freud also pronounces on a deeper significance of circumcision, relating it to his arguments in *Totem and Taboo*:

> Circumcision is the symbolic substitute for the castration which the primal father once inflicted upon his sons in the plenitude of his absolute power, and whoever accepted that symbol was showing by it that he was prepared to submit to the father's will, even if it imposed the most painful sacrifice to him.[54]

The Moses story is, in fact, a variation or dialectical development of Freud's ur-myth of the primal horde. In *Totem*, Freud proposes that an original parricide lies at the origin of all civilization. An omnipotent father required absolute submission from his sons and punished their misdeeds with castration. The band of brothers conspired to murder their father to gain sexual access to the women he exclusively enjoyed. After the murder, the sons felt guilt for the father they both hated and loved; and they realized that none could achieve the full power and sexual license the father enjoyed, as that would render one susceptible to becoming a victim of the same crime. For Freud circumcision thus represents, from *Totem* to *Moses*, the sign of one's submission to a paternalistic law, driven by the guilt of repressed fantasies of patricide. We might, therefore, understand it as a "masculine" reading of circumcision; in Lacanian terms, the rite symbolizes man's entry into the symbolic via the Law of the Father and the phallic sacrifices it entails.

Further psychoanalytic literature on circumcision takes Freud's ideas in different directions. This literature can be organized into four major themes: (1) Circumcision and the imposition of paternal law, (2) Circumcision and bisexuality, (3) Circumcision and misogyny, and (4) Jewish versus pagan circumcision.

Circumcision and the Law

Theodore Reik's 1915 essay, "The Puberty Rites of Savages," develops a classically Freudian thesis on the significance of circumcision in relation to law. Reik reads the anthropological literature of his era on tribal circumcision practices alongside *Totem and Taboo*, arguing that circumcision rituals emanate from the desire of fathers to punish their sons for the latter's parricidal wishes. He focuses on the spectacular dramatized violence present in many tribal circumcision rites. A general set of rituals is shared across a variety of

---

[54] Freud, 122.

Australian tribes (with some elements also present in Native American and African contexts): First, sons of a similar age will be taken away and secluded for long periods from the women of the tribe. The women are told that the sons have been captured by a demon and likely will not return. Meanwhile, the sons will be exposed to various physical ordeals and tests of courage imposed by male elders. Often the men pretend to be demons themselves and threaten to eat or kill the sons. Finally, the sons will be circumcised and then permitted to return home. The women are told that they were killed by the demons and then resurrected, thanks to the intervention of their fathers or tribal elders. In many cases, the boys will experience amnesia upon returning home and may need to be "retaught" basic human functions.[55]

Reik interprets these rituals as a "primitive" demonstration of ambivalence through which fathers express hate and love, violently threatening their sons against parricide and subsequently expiating their own guilt. Drawing on Freud's story of the primal parricide and the installation of the incest taboo, Reik argues that the hostility and cruelty that fathers display toward their sons are the product of the fathers' *own* parricidal impulses. The sons reawaken in the fathers their childhood memories of their own wish to murder their fathers (the sons' paternal grandfathers) to commit incest with their mothers. In order to prevent being murdered themselves, the fathers must scare their sons into submission, circumcising them as a symbolic threat of castration. However, the process also reawakens the fathers' guilt for their murderous past. They therefore ritually "resurrect" their sons as an enactment of the wished-for resurrection of the primal father, and as an expression of the love they have for their own fathers, now redirected onto their sons. The rite thus involves a complex interplay of father-son identifications that serve to bring the sons into a fraternal bond ordered by the prohibition of incest. Reik places particular emphasis on the sexual license sometimes permitted to the sons after the circumcision is complete: in many tribes, the newly initiated/ circumcised youths are encouraged to take women as sexual partners (sometimes with unrestrained aggression), which Reik interprets as a way for the fathers to redirect their sons' libido away from the prohibited mother.[56] As Reik summarizes, "We recognize in all these rites the strong tendency to detach the youths from their mothers, to chain them more firmly to the community of men, and to seal more closely the union between father and son which has been loosened by the youth's unconscious striving towards incest."[57]

[55] Reik, *Ritual*, 91–9.
[56] Reik, 99–137.
[57] Reik, 145. Sandor Ferenczi makes a similar argument in the conclusion of his speculative work *Thalassa*.

In "Circumcision and Problems of Bisexuality," Herman Nunberg
extends and supplements Reik's thesis on the relation between circumcision
and the paternal prohibition, drawing on circumcision-related material
that emerged in his clinical work with patients. He discusses at length
the case of an orthodox Jewish patient who was reluctant to circumcise
his newborn son. The patient produced a dream near the date of his son's
anticipated circumcision, in which the patient struggled to drink wine
out of a ritual cup which he understood to be his father's. Nunberg took
this as an affirmation of Reik's theories on the links between circumcision,
castration, and parricide. The father's reluctance to circumcise his child
appeared to stem from the guilt surrounding his own parricidal impulses:
"He did not wish to repeat the primal sin, he did not wish to kill or castrate
his father in his son."[58]

Bruno Bettelheim, in his book *Symbolic Wounds*, departs from this
traditional Freudian reading of circumcision, arguing that the practice
should be understood not necessarily from the perspective of the authorities
who impose it, but from the initiates themselves, who, he suggests, desire to
undergo the ritual as part of their "efforts to find a solution" to the "sexual
antithesis."[59] He begins his analysis from an unexpected place: in the
Orthogenic School for Disturbed Children that he directed, he discovered
that a small group of preadolescent patients had formed a secret pact among
themselves involving an elaborate genital mutilation ceremony. Two girls,
who had reached menstruation, had convinced two boys that they should
mutilate, and draw blood from, their penises. The four believed that after
the rite, they would be able to have sex with whomever they wished in open
defiance of the authority of their caretakers in the hospital. Here, Bettelheim
claims, genital mutilation is not an imposition from paternal authority, but,
rather, an attempt among the "initiates" themselves to wrest control from
authority and claim sexual autonomy. Children, he argues, often experience
immense anxiety during puberty around the sex role they are due to inhabit.
Puberty confronts the child with unsymbolized mysteries: questions around
the significance of the passage from child to adult, and the meaning of the
difference between the sexes. Researchers should therefore approach puberty
rites such as circumcision from the perspective of the need for the maturing
ego to make sense of, and cope with the anxiety occasioned by, the social and
biological changes facing the child.[60] Bettelheim develops this hypothesis as an

---

[58] Nunberg, "Circumcision," 169.
[59] Bettelheim, *Symbolic Wounds*, 17–18.
[60] Bettelheim, 41.

alternative way to read the anthropological literature on tribal circumcision rites.[61]

Circumcision and Bisexuality

For both Bettelheim and Nunberg, attitudes toward circumcision reflect unconscious struggles over the inhabitation of sexed subjectivity. Bettelheim argues that circumcision rites function to symbolize and cope with "vagina envy," a masculine crisis which, he claims, occurs prior to, and is therefore more fundamental than, castration anxiety.[62] Femininity is a powerful, alluring, and threatening secret for men, he argues. The classical clinical literature includes abundant examples of males fantasizing about giving birth; yet somehow, he notes, psychoanalysts have failed to consider the dimension of envy in these fantasies, despite their readiness to identify signs of penis envy in girls.[63] Although Freudian theory typically places men on the side of "having" against feminine dispossession (the problematic of penis envy), for Bettelheim the most primary form of possession, from which men feel excluded, is the capacity for childbirth.

For men, argues Bettelheim, the female sex apparatus and its function are shrouded in secrecy; as an internal organ, its function cannot be directly observed. Yet equally, there are aspects of womanhood that involve the appearance of something "certain": female puberty is marked with the onset of menstruation, unlike the more diffuse and heterogenous signs of male sexual maturity, and maternity, unlike paternity, is rarely in doubt. These "facts of nature," argues Bettelheim, give rise to envy in men, a feeling of being left out of something mysterious and powerful. Circumcision rites, he argues, are one of the ways men attempt to symbolically acquire access to, or appropriate, these "secrets" of femininity. The blood shed from the penis during a circumcision, often granted a central place in ritual symbolism,

---

[61] In an unusual application of psychoanalytical social science, Michio Kitahara compared the sleeping arrangements of 111 different tribal societies to test the validity of the Freudian theory of circumcision as a symbolic substitute for castration ("Cross-Cultural Test"). Kitahara hypothesized that those societies in which mother and son shared a bed, and the father slept in a different hut, were more likely to practice circumcision, as the rite would assist the Oedipal prohibition compared to societies where greater physical separation existed between mother and son. His statistical analysis of the tribes matched his prediction. He therefore concluded that the Freudian, castrative account of circumcision was more empirically valid than Bettelheim's. The paper pays no heed to the symbolism involved in circumcision rites.

[62] Bettelheim, *Symbolic Wounds*, 20.

[63] Bettelheim, 20–6. A notable exception to this tendency occurs in Klein, "Early Stages," 171–2.

is a masculine attempt to experience menstruation, to "punctuate . . . a growth sequence that is inherently unpunctuated"; the "rebirth" of the sons by the fathers emphasized in many rites, an attempt to wrest control over parturition.[64] Tribal circumcision rituals are almost always kept secret from women, allowing men to ascribe to themselves the purported feminine mystery they envy. Through this exploration of "vagina envy" in circumcision rituals, Bettelheim casts further doubt on the Freudian emphasis on circumcision as the installation of paternal law. The libidinal appeal of circumcision, for both initiator and initiate, lies in its ability to gratify not the punitive superego but the id.[65]

Nunberg introduces bisexuality into his theory of circumcision while maintaining a Freudian/Reikian outlook: for him, the practice represents the threat of castration that both institutes sexual difference and evokes the fear of its dissolution, as demonstrated by his patients' neurotic conflicts over the practice. For example, the orthodox Jewish patient discussed earlier linked his dream image of the wine goblet to a menstruating vagina. Within this context, the patient recalled the memory of attending a ritual circumcision and fainting upon viewing the newly cut penis: "When I saw this gaping wound I thought the bleeding vagina must look like that . . . I wondered how it could ever heal."[66] Here, the circumcised penis is linked to the female genitals in their Freudian signification (i.e., the site of castration). The father feared imposing this punishment on his child.

This theme is complicated further in Nunberg's account of another adult patient who was circumcised at the age of five due to phimosis (tight foreskin). The patient recalled that, prior to his circumcision, he enviously admired the exposed head of his father's circumcised penis. His own circumcision initially gratified this homosexual identification with the father, according to Nunberg; the patient recalled being proud of his newly circumcised penis and displaying it to others. However, the loss of the foreskin brought with it the unexpected end to a pleasurable maternal cleaning ritual that soon led the boy to associate the event with the traumatic loss of his mother's love: before his circumcision, his mother used to gently clean the underside of his foreskin, but afterward she refused to continue the practice despite his desperate protestations. Over the course of his analysis it emerged that he unconsciously understood the circumcision as a prohibitive and masculinizing event that required the sacrifice of a "feminine" part of

---

[64] Bettelheim, *Symbolic Wounds*, 142.
[65] Bettelheim, 89.
[66] Nunberg, "Circumcision," 171.

himself; circumcision was an exit both from the incestuous bond with the mother and from a primary hermaphroditism.[67]

In his 1965 paper "Foreskin Fetishism and its Relation to Ego Pathology in a Male Homosexual," Masud Khan describes a circumcised patient for whom the foreskinned penis represented, as in Nunberg's account, "the ideal bisexual organ composed of the glans penis and foreskin-vagina united in inseparable (non-castrative) oneness."[68] The psychoanalyst Brian Bird offered a variation on Nunberg's views, describing the case of an uncircumcised boy who vocalized explicit castration fears, anxiously perceiving his foreskinned penis to resemble a vagina in contradistinction to his brother's circumcised penis.[69] "If the difference between a circumcised and an uncircumcised penis appears to a child greater than the difference between the uncircumcised penis and the female genital," Bird writes, "the latter two will tend to be classed together, i.e., the penis with a foreskin will be assumed to be feminine."[70]

How might we reconcile these different views on the relationship between circumcision, paternal law, and sexual difference? Drawing on our earlier exploration of the cut, we can juxtapose the ways these authors approach the dialectic of presence and loss as it concerns the penis and the foreskin in circumcision.

For Reik, a circumcised penis is a wounded penis, which has undergone an attack by hostile forces. However, a circumcised penis does not thereby resemble a vagina. Rather, it is a symbol of sexually mature, lawful, masculine belonging. We might say that for Reik, circumcision makes the penis into the phallus: the loss of the foreskin initiates the boy into a sexual order beyond the mother-child dyad, subjecting the physical organ to social/symbolic "organ"ization. For Nunberg (and those who echo his views), on the other hand, the loss of the foreskin symbolizes the loss of hermaphroditic wholeness. The cut removes a part of the penis that will subsequently come to be understood as its "feminine" part, initiating the man into the sexual divide and giving rise to the Aristophean fantasy of the missing other

---

[67] Nunberg, 150.
[68] Khan, "Foreskin Fetishism," 70.
[69] Bird, "Bisexual Meaning of the Foreskin."
[70] Bird, 304. Anthropological interpretations of circumcision often argue that the removal of the foreskin is intended to distinguish the male from the female and "rectify" a primary bisexuality/hermaphroditism. FGC is interpreted as male circumcision's complement, necessary to secure sexually differentiated womanhood. See, for example, Lévi-Strauss, "Social Problems." Such interpretations may obscure the more polyvalent psychodynamics of the rite that I discuss here.

half.[71] Finally, for Bettelheim, circumcision, in fact, makes the penis *more like* a vagina; it *adds* something to the penis (female reproductive capacity) rather than taking something away. What men feel they have been denied—menstruation and the parturitive powers associated with it—is granted to them via circumcision. If, for Nunberg, circumcision gives one a penis through *losing* the feminine part of the organ, for Bettelheim one *loses the lack*—the incomplete penis is transformed into Nunberg's hermaphroditic whole. For all these authors, then, there is an interplay of phallic ownership and loss—mastery and lack—that takes place on the male genital. Either a preexisting lack is filled through the act of the cut (Bettelheim), or the cut creates a lack which nevertheless provides something new, a place within a symbolic universe.

Circumcision and Misogyny

These psychoanalysts do not bring explicitly feminist questions to their analyses, yet it is clear in each of their readings that circumcision should give feminists cause for concern. Reik describes tribes where the sexual permissiveness granted the newly circumcised initiates includes the license to rape and abuse women. He interprets this as powered by an unconscious scapegoating of women for inciting the sexual desires that motivated the primal parricide of *Totem and Taboo*. United as fraternal equals under the law via the rite of circumcision, men redirect their hostility to women, whom they treat as the cause of the initial breakdown of the father-son relationship and the unrelenting guilt they have suffered. The "rebirth" characteristic of so many circumcision rites, Reik argues, enables fathers to place themselves at the origin of the boys' lives in repudiation of maternal parturitive primacy. Circumcision thus enables a male homosocial order that unleashes fury at its excluded "Other," femininity.[72]

Bettelheim proposes a similar idea when he interprets Freud's story of the primal father as an unconscious defensive formation screening the "much more feared, omnipotent mother who stands at the beginning of all our lives."[73] His discussion of "vagina envy" suggests that the rite compensates

---

[71] In Plato's *Sympoisum*, Aristophanes proposes that there once existed "round" creatures—male, female, and hermaphrodite—each of whom Zeus cut into half, eliminating the hermaphrodite class through the sexually differentiating split and creating homosexuals and heterosexuals in search of their missing complement (189–92). Nunberg notes, "The manner in which the wound is treated in the *Symposium* reminds us of circumcision" ("Circumcision," 150). Lacan offers a counterintuitive interpretation of this myth in *VIII*, 77–94.

[72] Reik, *Ritual*, 153–6.

[73] Bettelheim, *Symbolic Wounds*, 140.

for masculine fears of inferiority.[74] Nunberg also suggests that circumcision is bound up in a primal fear of womanhood. His patient fainted after viewing the bloodied genitals of a newly circumcised infant because, Nunberg argues, it called forth unconscious associations between castration and the female genitals. Although, in Nunberg's argument, circumcision initiates one into masculinity by representing the loss of hermaphroditic wholeness, this loss occurs unequally across the sexes: while men gain a penis via the loss of the "feminine" foreskin, women subsequently come to be understood as lacking any genitals whatsoever. The uncircumcised penis is pregenital and "whole"; the circumcised penis, through loss, becomes a masculine "half"; the vagina is not the other half, but the abyss of nothingness.

Jewish studies scholar Daniel Boyarin has put forward an alternate, "redemptive" interpretation of circumcision. He argues that the rite is symbolically coded as feminizing within Jewish practice, as not simply an externally imposed, anti-Semitic fantasy, "but also an internal one that represent[s] a genuine Jewish cultural difference."[75] For Boyarin, these feminine aspects of the rite are not misogynist but, rather, present a "queering" of traditional patriarchal masculinity:

> In the Greco-Roman world, the deeds that would render a man a suitable erotic object would have been phallic deeds par-excellence, deeds of value of one sort or another, while for the rabbis these deeds are precisely anti-phallic, masochistic challenges to the coherence and impermeability of the male body. Paradoxically, it is the penetrated body that constructs the penile ideal. . . . This male subject . . . is called upon and learns to recognize himself . . . not through an image of "unimpaired masculinity," but through an image of masculinity as impairment, as what would be interpreted in another culture as castration.[76]

Rather than a ritual exclusion of women, Boyarin suggests that circumcision be understood as a way for men to share in femininity *alongside* women.

The anthropologist Howard Eilberg-Schwartz shares Boyarin's perspective on the submissive and feminizing aspects of Jewish circumcision but has taken a contrary view on their overall significance. For him, Jewish

---

[74] Eva Kittay offers a feminist appraisal of Bettelheim's work on circumcision, suggesting (somewhat naively, in my opinion) that instead of circumcision, which does not ultimately resolve vagina envy, "the participation of men in the process of mothering should go a considerable distance in allaying men's envy" ("Mastering Envy," 154).

[75] Boyarin, "Freud's Baby," 131.

[76] Boyarin, *Unheroic Conduct*, 101–2.

masculinity is, in fact, driven by homophobia. The homoerotic implications of submission to a male deity required the ancient Israelites, and eventually the rabbis, to understand male worshippers as feminine in relation to God, in order to preserve a notion of heterosexual union:

> Circumcision was for the ancient Israelites a symbol of male submission. Because it is partially emasculating, it was a recognition of a power greater than man. The symbolism of submission to God is obviously related to the images of feminization of Israelite men in the Hebrew Bible. Both were symptoms of the same phenomenon. God was acknowledged as the ultimate male and in his presence human masculinity was seen to be compromised and put at risk.[77]

This form of religious gender-bending, argues Eilberg-Schwartz, was not embraced as an alternative model of masculinity but, rather, experienced as threatening, leading to the codification of a rigid gender hierarchy, and the scapegoating of women as "impure," in rabbinical Judaism. Where Boyarin sees queerness, Eilberg-Schwartz sees patriarchy and homophobia.

According to rabbinical law, newborn boys remain in a state of ritual impurity until their circumcision. Eilberg-Schwartz argues that ritual circumcision enacts "the passage from the impurity of being born of a woman to the purity of life in a community of men."[78] Lawrence Hoffman, a scholar of Jewish liturgy working in a similar vein, focuses on the blood symbolism in Jewish circumcision rites. For him, circumcision does not blur but, rather, shores up the difference between the sexes. (He views his work as "a ready contrast to [Boyarin's] attempt to blunt rabbinic androcentrism."[79]) He argues that circumcision blood is inserted into a system of symbolic difference with menstrual blood, where the former is holy and salvific and the latter impure and contaminating. In his analysis of rabbinical purity laws, Hoffman establishes a link between the rabbinical emphasis on mastery over bodily emissions, and sexist ideology: menstruation was implicitly represented as more involuntary, and therefore more impure, than seminal discharge. Shaye Cohen summarizes the feminist implications of Eilberg-Schwartz's and Hoffman's findings:

> Although Jewish women are Jews, they are Jews of a peculiar kind. The "normal" Jew for the rabbis, as the "normal" Israelite for the Torah, was

---

[77] Eilberg-Schwartz, *God's Phallus*, 161–2.
[78] Eilberg-Schwartz, *Savage in Judaism*, 175.
[79] Hoffman, *Covenant of Blood*, 23. Both these works are influenced by Douglas, *Purity and Danger*.

the free adult male. . . . The term "Jews" means men; Jewish women are the wives, sisters, mothers, and daughters of men, the real Jews. . . . Therefore it should occasion no surprise if only men are marked by circumcision—only men are real Jews in all respects.[80]

Against these scholars, Boyarin's "queering" of circumcision and rabbinical Judaism appears somewhat optimistic.[81] We will consider his views more closely in the next chapter.

Jewish versus Pagan Circumcision

Finally, an interesting opposition exists within the literature on the significance of Jewish circumcision in relation to tribal and polytheistic circumcision practices. Some authors argue that the former represents a radical break from pagan circumcision rites, whereas others posit continuity. Within this opposition, the question of rite's relationship to law and the symbolic order appears central.

Reik sees the underlying dynamics involved in Jewish circumcision as similar to pagan rites. He points out that the Abrahamic covenant is tied to the promise of fertility, linking Jewish circumcision to the sexual license granted "primitive" circumcised men.[82] By contrast, Bettelheim draws a sharp distinction between Jewish and tribal circumcision. Applying a developmentalist, ego psychological framework, he argues that among tribal peoples, circumcision involves the primitive attempt of the ego to organize and appease wishes from the id (primarily man's longings to experience femininity).[83] In Jewish circumcision, however, the more developmentally "advanced" agency of the superego enters the picture. Here Bettelheim agrees with other interpreters about the castrative nature of the rite: Jewish circumcision signals the emergence of "paternalistic monotheism," a psychosociological evolution in which the internalization of law, and

---

[80] Cohen, *Why Aren't Jewish Women Circumcised?* 572–3.

[81] Concern surrounding the male exclusiveness of the bris has given rise to "welcoming" ceremonies for newborn girls in Reform/progressive Jewish communities; however, these are usually understood as supplements to male circumcision rather than critiques of the practice. See Glick, *Marked in Your Flesh*, 254–6.

[82] Reik, *Ritual*, 157. Psychoanalyst Milton Malev endorses and expands on Reik's position in "Jewish Orthodox Circumcision Ceremony": "one cannot but be impressed by the congruence between [Jewish circumcision] . . . on the hand, and, on the other, the practices of savage peoples on the other side of the world" (517).

[83] Bettelheim, *Symbolic Wounds*, 88.

the subsequent emergence of castration anxiety, takes precedence over id-oriented gratification:

> Circumcision, which was the tool of man's greatest pride, might then have become [from paganism to Judaism] the means of degrading him to the status of a helpless subject of the supernatural god. Psychoanalytically, what had been energy used by the id for gaining magic power through manipulation of the genital was wrested from the id and arrogated as a source of energy by an externalized superego, which used it to restrain the id and weaken the ego by making them subservient to a superego representation.[84]

That Jewish circumcision takes place eight days after birth, in contrast to tribal circumcisions (which usually take place during puberty), suggests to Bettelheim this change in the rite's status—from a primitive homosocial event to the more sophisticated installation of prohibitive paternal authority.

Hoffman and Eilberg-Schwartz both emphasize the continuity between Jewish circumcision and its pagan counterparts. Eilberg-Schwartz addresses the civilized versus savage distinction upheld by many religion scholars between Judaism and more "primitive religions," which he argues is premised on a problematic "spiritualization" of the import of Jewish circumcision.[85] Whereas scholars typically understand the bodily imagery in tribal circumcision as part of a symbolic network of meaning, Jewish circumcision is viewed as a "sign" of covenant alone, an abstract marker linking the Jew to the written law. He demonstrates that the traditional Jewish rite is derived from the tribal practices of ancient Israelite religion, in which, as is the case in many tribal circumcision practices, the imagery of the blood and the phallic cut were linked to themes surrounding fertility and agriculture.[86] He argues that the Israelites likely practiced circumcision around puberty, as did their pagan counterparts, and that the commandment in Genesis to undergo circumcision on the eighth day was a subsequent revision introduced by the priestly class.[87] Hoffman echoes these arguments although he focuses more on the evolution of circumcision within the history of Judaism, especially the efforts of the priestly class and later the rabbis to make circumcision the centerpiece of a Jewish purity system.[88]

[84] Bettelheim, 131 and 133.
[85] Eilberg-Schwartz, *Savage in Judaism*, 1–28.
[86] Eilberg-Schwartz, 141–76.
[87] Eilberg-Schwartz, 146–8.
[88] Hoffman, *Covenant of Blood*.

From a Lacanian point of view, this tension between circumcision as a bloody, corporeal, "savage" rite, versus an abstract sign of civilized man's submission to paternal authority, seems to correspond to the tension between the imaginary (which pertains to the body and the image) and the symbolic (which pertains to language and law). Therefore, while I appreciate Eilberg-Schwartz's criticism of the scholarly tendency to "elevate" Jewish circumcision over pagan practices, from a psychoanalytic perspective we might consider these two poles of circumcision—the textual/legal versus the bodily—together.

The linkages between circumcision, blood, agriculture, and the genitals (including the question of the genital appearance of sexual difference) all concern the imaginary pursuit of understanding one's place in the world through narcissistic comparison. For example, those circumcision rites analyzed by Bettelheim as envious of female menstruation adhere to the following imaginary logic: *I see that certain people bleed out of their genitals, I struggle to understand what this means and why it does not happen to me, so I puncture my own genitals and thereby develop knowledge of a world outside my immediate experience.* Difference is managed and understood through the attempt to establish likeness in the imaginary. By contrast, the emphasis on circumcision as a form of paternal prohibition (and in Judaism, the link between circumcision, covenant, and textual law) foregrounds the symbolic register, the "beyond" to the world of imaginary correspondences and the problem of the subject's entry into a lawful social order mediated by language. Just as, in Lacanian theory, the subject encounters the symbolic only via its negotiation of the imaginary, so too in circumcision, we may understand the higher "spiritual" significance of the rite as inextricably intertwined with the physical act and all its associated imagery. The domains are distinct but knotted together. In its imaginary guise, circumcision appears as an attempt to mitigate, repudiate, overcome, or embrace the trauma of sexual difference; while, in the symbolic, it establishes a governing principle, by way of the phallus, to which all participants are bound.

Circumcision's Ambivalence

In his study of castration in Seminar Ten, after some idiosyncratic comments on the aesthetic superiority of the circumcised penis, Lacan remarks, "Circumcision embodies . . . the fact that something akin to an order may be brought into this hole, into this constitutive failing of primordial castration."[89]

---

[89] Lacan, *X*, 206; see also 90, where Lacan cites Nunberg as inspiration for his views on circumcision.

Here, he suggests that the function of circumcision is to provide some kind of "order," perhaps to compensate for the abyss of castration. A piece of the penis is sacrificed to represent the lack that founds the subject. In a sense, it is similar to Freud's thesis, yet it suggests a pacifying dimension of circumcision against Freud's emphasis on guilt and fear. Circumcision does not castrate you; rather, by symbolizing castration as a mark on the penis, it relieves the unbearable trauma of the more fundamental, "primordial castration."

Similarly, Luce Irigaray writes that Jewish circumcision "lies in the realm of the sign. What is cut away is only cut away in order to make a sign. . . . But almost the reverse of castrating, this excision is what marks the body's entry into the world of signs."[90] Castration represents the failure or limit point of language, whereas circumcision marks the possibility of the subject's embodied participation in language. Although both Lacan and Irigaray are here posing an opposition between circumcision and castration, I suggest we view the two as interdependent. Signification is possible only insofar as it incorporates a limit; language must be constitutively incomplete in order for us to go on saying different things. Likewise, to make use of signification, something of the body must also be incomplete; there must be an embodied experience of lack compelling us to engage in "the world of signs." More than solely symbolizing castration to mitigate its effects, circumcision marks— represents—this very moebius-like interrelation between lack (or castration) and signification.

Related to this is a complicated interplay of singularity and universality: the question of the subject's insertion into the symbolic and the nature of the wound thereby encountered. Is circumcision the "collective wound," the identifying mark, of a particular community or "symbolic order" (Jewish, Muslim, etc.)? Or does circumcision give a particular form to the universal entry into "the symbolic" as such? In an interview exploring his views on Jewishness, Derrida highlights this ambiguity:

> On the one hand, I insist on the singularity, the irrepressibility of the wound, circumcision, my own circumcision, which is irreplaceable, it's a wound which structures myself as an absolute singularity. But, on the other hand, I suggest that there are analogies between the Jewish circumcision and every kind of wound which constitutes a community. At the origin of any identity, or cultural identity or nationality, there is something like a circumcision, there is a mark on the body, an ineffaceable mark on the body and this wound is universal. So I postulate between the

---

[90] Irigaray, *Marine Lover*, 81.

two and I want to say both things at the same time. On the one hand it is absolutely irreplaceable and on the other hand there are circumcisions everywhere, even outside the Jewish or Islamic communities. That's the ambiguity of the mark on the body.[91]

Derrida's comments situate circumcision at the level of particular communal identity and universality at the same time. He moves between circumcision as something that "structures" him as an "absolute singularity," and as a wound which "constitutes a community." Singularity indicates something beyond the level of communal identification, something absolutely specific to an individual subject; Derrida's circumcision is his wound alone. Yet, for him, this singularity occurs against the backdrop of his communal constitution, his Jewish identity—which then extends further, into the conditions for the constitution of community as such. In Lacanian terms, Derrida appears to argue that circumcision illuminates how the encounter with castration and inscription into the symbolic order are simultaneously the universal conditions for subject formation *and* are undergone by each desiring subject in his or her ultimately singular way.

These problematics are also addressed in Lacan's remarks in Seminar Five, where he contrasts the mark a shepherd leaves on his flock of sheep with the mark of circumcision:

> It's indeed true that, in a certain way, circumcision presents itself as constituting a particular flock, the flock of God's chosen ones. Are we not merely rediscovering this? Certainly not. What analytic experience, and Freud, brought us at the beginning is that there is a close, even intimate relationship between desire and the mark. The mark is not simply there as a sign of recognition for the shepherd. . . . Where man is concerned, the marked living being has a desire which does not fail to have a certain intimate relationship with the mark.[92]

Unlike a simple identifying badge, circumcision, both Lacan's and Derrida's comments suggest, marks simultaneously one's communal identity *and* the individual desire that emerges out of the process of inscribing oneself *into* a community; both of these circulate around the subjection to a wound, at once singular and universal. As Reinhard Lupton writes, "Circumcision separates the individual from the nation in the very act of joining him to it, naming his strangeness *to* the symbolic in the moment of estranging him

[91] Cixous and Derrida, "Language of Others."
[92] Lacan, *V*, 290–1.

within it."[93] The cut traverses the imaginary, symbolic, and real: it imaginarily represents symbolic castration (referencing the penis as the imaginary origin of the symbolic phallus, as well as generating an identitarian mark that serves as the imaginary signified of a symbolic community) and in the process circumscribes the "hole" of the real. It both offers us the captivating image of the introduction of lack into the subject and repudiates this moment through the establishment of law and the invocation of the desired qualities of the Other sex—the attempt to eliminate the threat of difference.

These Lacanian reflections on circumcision bring us to my key argument regarding the moebius-like nature of the practice with respect to sexual difference. I propose we view acts of circumcision as fundamentally ambivalent, involving both a "masculine" attempt to secure the phallus and a "feminine" undermining of this pursuit or showing up of its fraudulence. In the former, circumcision mobilizes the logic of the phallus in an attempt to master the trauma of castration. The rite is inserted into a system of meaning that reassures the subject that something can be done with the trauma of the cut; it can be harnessed toward membership of a social order regulated by paternal law. (This corresponds to Eilberg-Schwartz's formulation, "One must have a [circumcised] member to be a member."[94]) Additionally, at the imaginary level, circumcision appears to appropriate and master enigmatic and threatening aspects of femininity. Circumcision thus transforms the penis into the phallus, an instrument of signification and social order, enabling members of the male sex to negotiate difference through the phallic pursuit of representing and mastering the unrepresentable. *Yet*, circumcision does this only by disavowing the phallus's emptiness. Thus, at another level, circumcision restages (and even valorizes) the very moment when the splitting of the subject takes place. The removal of the foreskin confronts men with the fundamental lack imposed by the symbolic order and the fraudulence of any subsequent claims to phallic wholeness (the same dilemma that faces women). In the final analysis, circumcision and its attendant significations can be seen as giving form to the originary signifying cut, and an attempt to respond to the problems it raises. This is not to negate specificity or context; for, in each case, circumcision (and the stances and controversies surrounding it) are, as the chapters of this book show, extremely particular. In any given moment in the history of circumcision, the problem of phallic (dis)possession plays itself out differently; yet, this irresolvable problem is always at play. Moreover, as is the case with signification as such, for any one

[93] Lupton, "Ethnos and Circumcision," 198.
[94] Eilberg-Schwartz, *Savage in Judaism*, 145.

meaning that circumcision accrues in a particular context, its inverse always threatens to emerge.

Viewing circumcision in this way helps us understand how the rite can hold such contradictory meanings for different groups of people; how, for example, it renders Jews into castrated women in anti-Semitic fantasy while at the same time appearing as a sign of "manliness" for many of its proponents.[95] Like the cut of sexual difference, circumcision symbolizes the moment at which both masculinity and femininity emerge as distinct, asymmetrical "solutions" to the structural antagonism of subjectivity.

Eric Silverman, in his psychoanalytically informed study of the symbolism of Jewish circumcision, reaches a similar conclusion. Inspired by Bettelheim, he interprets the Jewish rite as in part an envious appropriation of female parturitive powers; while its manifest purpose is to enhance and consolidate phallic masculinity, it carries with it the shadow of its opposite, the feminization of the male. He emphasizes how circumcision is mobilized, in both biblical texts and rabbinical literature, as a means of forging a patriarchal community bounded by law which nevertheless constantly threatens to undo itself; the "cut" paradoxically promises a sense of wholeness which, "like culture in Lacan's theory, inevitably fails."[96] Hence, he concludes, "circumcision dramatizes unease over separation-individuation through a symbolism that affirms yet blurs the normative boundaries between masculinity and motherhood."[97] Circumcision separates men from women and boys from mothers; yet, through its emphasis on father to son initiation, it induces its practitioners into the very maternal and feminine identifications that, he argues, it simultaneously repudiates. This ambivalence, Silverman claims, is the very source of its power; covenants "often derive their sacred character from otherwise immoral or taboo expressions of violence or intimacy."[98]

While Silverman limits his study primarily to the Jewish, religious context, we will examine how circumcision's ambivalence makes itself manifest in spaces beyond the solely religious, including medicine and politics. In the next, final sections of this chapter, I will discuss additional contemporary

---

[95] The crime of forced circumcision perpetrated by the Kikuyu ethnic group in Kenya against the Luo ethnic group is a recent, gruesome illustration of this point. For the Kikuyu, circumcision is understood as a rite of passage into manhood; however, when they forcibly circumcised Luo men (who did not ordinarily practice the rite), they intended it to humiliate and emasculate them—and sometimes they would castrate rather than circumcise them. See Auchter, "Forced Male Circumcision."
[96] Silverman, *Abraham to America*, 64.
[97] Silverman, "Anthropology and Circumcision," 423.
[98] Silverman, *Abraham to America*, xviii.

literature on circumcision and highlight how this psychoanalytic approach responds to its flaws.

Freud's Circumcision

We have looked at how Freud, and subsequent psychoanalysts, have interpreted circumcision. However, there is another important way that psychoanalysis and circumcision interact. Several scholars working in the fields of cultural studies, Jewish studies, and literary criticism have argued that circumcision occupies a key, but disavowed, place in Freud's life and thought, by consequence of the practice's centrality within fin de siècle European anti-Semitic fantasy.[99] This scholarship shares in common a concern with the profound, intimate links in the European imagination between circumcision, Jewishness, and femininity.

These links were, in fact, commented upon by Freud himself. In a famous footnote to his case study on little Hans, Freud writes:

> The castration complex is the deepest unconscious root of anti-semitism; for even in the nursery little boys hear that a Jew has something cut off his penis—a piece of his penis, they think—and this gives them a right to despise Jews. And there is no stronger unconscious root for the sense of superiority over women.[100]

Freud offers here a psychoanalytic interpretation of anti-Semitism and misogyny, arguing that the two emerge from the same unconscious "root." Both the Jew and the woman evoke the same fear of castration and provoke phobic and hostile treatment, by dint of the appearance of their genitals: the former, for having "something cut off from his penis," the latter, for not having a penis at all. Yet, the "cultural studies approach" to Freud I am referencing holds that his theories function as so many efforts to negotiate, repudiate, or transform his own imbrication within the symbolic coordinates of European racism and misogyny. As Eric Santner puts it in a critique of this scholarship, its thesis

> is that the founding concepts and terms of [psychoanalysis] were in large part determined by a kind of extended "masculine protest"—by

[99] Most scholars believe that Freud did not circumcise his sons (as was often the case with secular Viennese Jews), although there is some debate on this subject. See Bonomi, *The Cut*, 2–4.
[100] Freud, "Analysis of a Phobia," 36 n.1.

the struggle of a male, Jewish scientist-physician with a scientific and medical culture for which Jews embodied a condition of effeminate degeneration and abjection.[101]

In so doing, the cultural studies approach offers a somewhat diminished view of the contribution that psychoanalytic thinking (particularly the theory of castration) can make to the understanding of the libidinal economy of prejudice.

Sander Gilman is a key figure in this field, documenting the seemingly endless popular and medical literature linking the male Jew to feminization and illness that saturated fin de siècle European culture. Gilman argues that Freud constructed an identification as a masculine, secular, Enlightenment scientist by displacing anti-Semitic stereotypes about male Jews onto women. According to Gilman, Freud's notion of the "phallic phase" (in which the girl first understands her clitoris as a smaller penis before succumbing to full-fledged penis envy) was an attempt to displace the anti-Semitic image of the shortened, defective Jewish penis onto the clitoris; in Freud's time, a Viennese slang term for the clitoris was "the little Jew."[102] In Freud's case studies, Gilman further argues, circumcision-related themes and their bearing on Freud's own identity are regularly effaced. For example, Gilman claims that Freud "anglicized" his patient Ida Bauer by referring to her as "Dora," thereby disguising the fact that his discoveries were made chiefly via Jewish patients.[103] Freud, he argues, chose to associate the jewel case ("*schmuckkasten*") in Dora's dream with the female genitals, ignoring the term's obvious phonemic resonance to the Yiddish word "*schmock*," which means circumcised penis.[104] Additionally, Gilman argues that Freud chose to portray Daniel Schreber's psychotic delusions of undergoing castration and feminization as a reaction against Schreber's homosexuality, rather than "about acquiring the Jew's circumcised penis, the sign of the feminization of the Jew."[105]

For Gilman, Freud was thus insistently, unconsciously preoccupied with escaping the strictures of anti-Semitic stereotypes, which were encapsulated in the image of the Jewish penis. Freud accomplished this, on the one hand, by repressing those signifiers that would implicate him in anti-Semitic tropes wherever they appeared in his work, and on the other, by attempting

[101] Santner, *Private Germany*, 116.
[102] Gilman, *Freud,* 39.
[103] Gilman, *Jew's Body*, 60–103.
[104] Gilman, 88.
[105] Gilman, *Freud*, 155.

to displace the Jew/Gentile binary that underlay those tropes onto a male/
female one. Moreover, "in seeing the act of circumcision as 'primeval,' Freud
placed circumcision at the root of Western civilization,"[106] counteracting its
particularizing association with Jewishness and Jewish "degeneracy."

Using similar reasoning and historical material, Daniel Boyarin argues
that "knowledge of [his] own circumcision must inevitably produce in the
Jew a sense of inferiority vis-à-vis the Gentile, a sense of inferiority that Freud
himself shared."[107] Through an extended analysis of Freud's homoerotically
charged correspondence with Wilhelm Fliess and the subsequent breakdown
of their friendship, Boyarin develops the "queer" dimension of this argument.
Freud repeatedly characterized himself as taking an effeminate, passive,
and, indeed, hysterical position in relation to Fliess over the course of their
friendship. Boyarin argues that Freud was in the thrall of homophobic
panic—a reaction to the "discursive configuration imposed on him" that
"produced a perfect and synergistic match between homophobia and anti-
Semitism"[108]—when he simultaneously abandoned Fliess and constructed
his heteronormative Oedipal theory. "The Jew was queer and hysterical—
and therefore not a man," Boyarin writes. "The Oedipus complex is Freud's
family romance of escape from Jewish queerdom into Gentile, phallic
heterosexuality."[109] For Boyarin, this was not only a repudiation of anti-
Semitic fantasies about Jews but also a rejection of the alternative culture of
gender he argues is present within Judaism itself, epitomized by the figure of
the studious and sedentary *Yeshiva Bokhur*, a "queer" figure in contrast to the
active, phallic Gentile male.

Boyarin largely agrees with Gilman that *Moses and Monotheism* was
Freud's attempt to reinscribe Jewish identity into normatively gendered,
heterosexual masculinity, a function of "Freud's need to be manly, to discover
manliness at the origins of Jewishness, Moses, and the Bible."[110] Both Boyarin
and religion scholar Howard Eilberg-Schwartz also read this text as a
struggle with those feminine elements central to Jewish male worship itself.
As Boyarin writes:

> Renunciation of the fulfillment of desire, which is encoded in Freud's
> text as masculine, is occasioned by a submissiveness vis-à-vis the male

[106] Gilman, 83. In "Freud's Jewish Identity," Punzi suggests Freud's pride in circumcision
and Jewishness led him to implicitly inscribe the former in his "understanding of what it
means to develop as an individual with a socio-cultural history" (973).
[107] Boyarin, *Unheroic Conduct*, 239.
[108] Boyarin, "Freud's Baby," 129.
[109] Boyarin, 133–4.
[110] Boyarin, *Unheroic Conduct*, 257.

other, whether it be the "great man" Moses or the deity. But that very submissiveness, the mark of the religious person, was itself feminizing in the terms of nineteenth-century culture.[111]

For Eilberg-Schwartz, Freud's emphasis in *Moses* on Judaism's renunciation of images—of the corporeal body of God—as the model for instinctual sublimation, emerges out of his phobic avoidance of the homoerotic implications of submission to a male deity (made visibly manifest in circumcision).[112] This homophobia, Eilberg-Schwartz argues, is a product both of Jewish scripture itself—which, as we saw earlier, he understands as at once enacting and repudiating male homoeroticism—and the hostile social and political climate in which Freud found himself.

Jay Geller takes a more explicitly Foucaultian approach in *On Freud's Jewish Body: Mitigating Circumcisions*, focusing on the intensification of classificatory and disciplinary forms of racialization and gender codification in Freud's time, which were refracted through what he terms the "dispositive" of circumcision. Circumcision, he argues, is a contradictory symbol for racial identity insofar as it is an obvious product of culture rather than nature. It is this very contradiction that enables it to occupy such a central place in an anti-Semitic symbolic universe:

> Because it both pointedly encapsulated that which it would disavow— the misrecognition of constructed differences by which hegemony enacts itself—and remained inextricably attached to the (un)dead Jews, "circumcision" became both an apotropaic monument and a floating signifier that functioned as a dispositive, an apparatus that connected biblical citations, stories, images, phantasies, laws, kosher slaughters (*Schochets*), ethnographic studies, medical diagnoses, and ritual practices, among other deposits in that noisome landfill called Europe, in order to produce knowledge about and authorize the identity of *Judentum*—and of the uncircumcised.[113]

Geller does not see Freud's work as a "'masculine protest' against circumcision-induced inferiority" (*qua* Boyarin and Gilman). Rather, he sees the "feminizing representations of and allusions to (male) Jewish body parts and techniques that traverse Freud's corpus" as ambiguous traces of Freud's attempt to "mediate the double bind of Jewish existence while

---

[111] Boyarin, 254.
[112] Eilberg-Schwartz, *God's Phallus*, 39.
[113] Geller, *Freud's Jewish Body*, 11.

navigating through the crises of gender, sexual, racial (ethnic), class, and self-identity that were entangled in the European 'Jewish problem.'"[114] This adds a layer of complexity to Gilman's and Boyarin's reading of Freud's work as a repudiation of femininity/queerness—arguing that a more intricate and contradictory navigation of identity was involved—while maintaining the focus on anti-Semitic fantasies about circumcision as an occluded source of Freud's theories.

Eliza Slavet explores a more tangential concern in relation to the aforementioned authors in *Racial Fever: Freud and the Jewish Question*. In a chapter on circumcision, she examines Freud's explorations with theories of phylogenetic inheritance, arguing that the complicated significance of circumcision played a role in Freud's eventual prioritizing of cultural history over natural biology in his theory of the psyche. "Just as the instinct emerges as a 'concept on the frontier between the mental and the somatic,'" she contends, "circumcision emerges as a concept on the frontier between the realms of memory and heredity; spirituality and physicality; and culture, religion, and race."[115] In *Moses*, she argues, Freud was able to construct a theory of embodied racial (Jewish) identity that emphasized the unconscious transmission of cultural history over physically inherited racial characteristics in part through his focus on circumcision. Slavet's work challenges those authors who paint a more Lamarckian picture of Freud.

Finally, the psychoanalyst Carlo Bonomi uses Freud's relationship to circumcision in order to critically examine the development of psychoanalytic theory; however, he does so with a twist. Bonomi argues that, in their focus on the discursive and figurative aspects of castration and circumcision, these scholars have neglected to examine Freud's relationship to *actually existing medical genital surgeries*.[116] Bonomi believes Freud was more familiar with the use of genital surgeries as medical "cures" for nervous illness than he was willing to admit, drawing attention to Freud's early training under the prominent pediatrician Adolf Baginsky, who had theorized a relation between "genital irritation" and childhood hysteria.[117] Bonomi argues that Freud was so opposed to the implications of Baginsky's ideas—namely, that they might justify the use of genital surgery on children—that he repressed his knowledge of Baginsky's influence on his own theories regarding infantile sexuality.[118] (Freud also appears to have been at least vaguely aware of the

---

[114] Geller, 11–12.
[115] Slavet, *Racial Fever*, 100. (The nested quote is Freud's.)
[116] Bonomi, "Relevance of Castration."
[117] Bonomi, 562–6.
[118] Bonomi, 573–5.

growing popularity of medical circumcision in England and America and expressed skepticism about the practice.[119]) We will explore Bonomi's work in more detail in Chapter 4.

As mentioned at the beginning of this section, Eric Santner, in a book on Schreber, offers a compelling critique of the literature we've just reviewed on Freud's relationship to circumcision and anti-Semitism. Freud thought that Schreber's delusions of feminization were the consequence of his repressed homosexuality.[120] As Santner explains, Gilman, Boyarin, and Geller all make the case (with different emphases) that Freud unconsciously repudiated his own implication in queerness and femininity by failing to recognize the Jewish elements of Schreber's phantasmagoria (such as anti Semitic circumcision imagery) and focusing, instead, on Schreber's failed bid to heterosexuality.[121]

Santner contends that, in their respective interpretations of Freud's analysis, these authors mistakenly treat "that which is 'abjected' from a symbolic identity—in this instance 'queerness' and 'femininity'—*at the same ontological level* as the identity that is thereby constructed" (121, emphasis original). In other words, the authors believe that the femininity and queerness that both Freud and Schreber repudiate are no different in nature from one's positive symbolic identity:

> The claim is that when, at the end of the nineteenth century, a German man belonging to an elite . . . comes, for whatever reasons, to feel his identification with his status disturbed, he will automatically find himself in the symbolic position of the marginal figures of that culture—in this instance women and Jews—and begin, unconsciously and conflictually, to elaborate the consequences of his new set of identifications using whatever images and fantasies are ready to hand in the cultural "archive." (115)

Santner argues that this approach repeats what he sees as Freud's own failure vis-à-vis Schreber. Freud, Santner claims, was incorrect to interpret Schreber as homosexual on account of Schreber's delusionary hallucinations of feminization. That interpretation "domesticated" a more fundamental impasse. Schreber's psychotic experience of "abjection . . . of something

---

[119] See Bonomi, 574. Freud writes: "The analysis of cases in which circumcision, though not, it is true, castration, has been carried out on boys as a cure or punishment for masturbation (a far from rare occurrence in Anglo-American society) has given our conviction [of the castrative significance of circumcision] a last degree of certainty" (*New Introductory Lectures,* 87).

[120] Freud, "Psycho-Analytic Notes," 43.

[121] Santner, *Private Germany,* 138. Subsequent references given in text.

rotten within," emerged from his unique encounter, as a judge, with the impotence at the heart of symbolic authority as such, the lack of an "ultimate foundation" to secure a system of meaning and value—what psychoanalysis "theorizes under the sign of symbolic castration" (125; 141). Schreber discovered that his "own symbolic power and authority as a judge—and German man," had no ultimate, metaphysical basis; it was "founded . . . by the performative magic of the rites of institution," that is, through a purely performative and tautological act of language, invested with "jouissance," in which "it is so because it is said to be so" (124):

> It was the idiotic repetition compulsion at the heart of his symbolic function that Schreber experienced as profoundly sexualizing, as a demand to cultivate jouissance. That he experienced this sexualization as feminizing and "Jewifiying" suggests that at the advent of European modernity, "knowledge" of jouissance was ascribed to women and Jews, meaning that women and Jews were *cursed* with the task of holding the place of that which could not be directly acknowledged: that symbolic identities are, in the final analysis, sustained by *drive*, by performativity-as-repetition-compulsion. (125, emphasis original)

Freud, in constructing the discipline of psychoanalysis and its theoretical tenets, similarly had to encounter the tenuousness of symbolic authority:

> Freud's study of the Schreber material was conducted at a moment in the history of psychoanalysis when the symbolic authority of that new institution was being strongly contested from within the ranks as well as from without—at a moment of institutional stress that . . . made Freud particularly sensitive to the nature of Schreber's investiture crisis even though Freud never explicitly addressed it (17).

Thus, argues Santner, Freud's unconscious investments in phallic masculinity and "father figures" were not simply a defensive reaction to European anti-Semitism, but were more fundamentally a symptom of Freud's "cursed knowledge of jouissance" (125); that is, his "cursed knowledge" of the fact that symbolic authority is "purely performative," something held together not by a "Great Man" but by drive. Although Freud may have avoided this knowledge—believing, instead, in a mythic primal father as the originary source and guarantor of law—at the same time, the theory and practice he built are designed to stage an encounter with this impasse.

In my view, Santner's analysis marks a turning point in studies of the relationship between psychoanalysis and circumcision. For, rather than simply historicizing psychoanalysis by way of the repressed signifier of circumcision, Santner brings the most radical insights of psychoanalysis to bear on itself. While the cultural studies scholars imply that the sexist and homophobic resonances of Freud's theory of castration undermine the theory's validity—interpreting the theory of castration as Freud's flight from his own circumcision—Santner manages to both acknowledge the complex historical circumstances in which the theory was born *and* treat it as a serviceable and necessary concept for the very analysis *of* sexism, homophobia, and anti-Semitism. My own approach in the rest of this book is similar. While equating circumcision with castration reduces the latter to the level of the imaginary, controversies around circumcision can nevertheless help us appreciate the functioning of symbolic castration and the defenses to which it gives rise.

Historical Scholarship

My emphasis on the relationship between circumcision and phallic mastery also helps to analyze the extant historical scholarship on circumcision. Interestingly, recent historical monographs on the subject of male circumcision are almost all motivated by their authors' opposition to the practice. While these works offer useful historical data, they also foreground how encounters with the subject of circumcision, however apparently "objective," provoke phallic fantasies.

David Gollaher's *Circumcision: A History of the World's Most Controversial Surgery* covers a wide range, beginning in ancient Egypt and ending with a survey of contemporary medical views on circumcision. He argues that medical arguments for circumcision are the product of cultural biases. He does not cast the same skeptical eye on anti-circumcision perspectives, and, in fact, his own opposition to circumcision, which becomes more prominent toward the end of the book, is itself clearly bound up in cultural ideals. In a telling passage, he uncritically quotes a physician who claims, "Without the mobile sheath of the foreskin, the circumcised penis acts like a ramrod in the vagina. This is unnatural and has negative health consequences for women."[122] The poor evidence for this claim notwithstanding, it belies a heteronormative and naturalistic conception of sex that speaks more to fantasies of sexual harmony and its obstacles—the frustrated wish for phallic potency —than to the actual consequences of circumcision.

---

[122] Quoted in Gollaher, *Circumcision*, 121.

As the title suggests, Robert Darby's *A Surgical Temptation: The Demonization of the Foreskin and the Rise of Circumcision in Britain* takes an explicitly anti-circumcision stance: "The demonization of the foreskin as a source of moral and physical decay," he writes, "was the critical factor in the emergence of circumcision and its acceptance as a valid medical intervention."[123] Darby focuses on nineteenth-century British doctors who advocated circumcision. He argues that medical support for the practice emerged out of Victorian "anti-sensualism," a repressive attempt to curb masturbation and male sexuality, "partly the outcome of a powerful alliance between religion and medicine."[124] The book is tinged with apparent resentment at feminist appraisals of Victorian sexual mores that, in Darby's view, obscure the oppression of masculine sexuality: "The most serious sexual problem of the period was not how to keep women under the patriarchal thumb, nor even prostitution or venereal disease, but the male sex drive and how to control it."[125]

Leonard Glick's *Marked in Your Flesh: Circumcision from Ancient Judea to Modern America* offers a similar approach to Darby within the American medical context, though more focused on the practice's Jewish origin and resonance than its relationship to sexuality. After a thorough historical overview of the varied significance of Jewish circumcision and its place in Western culture—locating the rite at the heart of both Jewish identity and Christian anti-Semitism—he examines the unlikely rise of circumcision in Christian-majority America. References to Moses as a "great sanitarian" abound in nineteenth- and twentieth-century pro-circumcision medical literature by both Jewish and Gentile doctors: "In the imagination of these physicians, biblical heroes were reborn as medical visionaries and distinguished colleagues."[126] Glick argues that Jewish assimilation in America occurred in part through this transformation of the Jewish ritual, initially held in contempt by Christians, into a paradigm of sanitation. This involved the attempt by doctors (including Jewish doctors) to wrest control of the practice from mohels in the name of hygiene, thereby secularizing and medicalizing the rite. Although Glick treads more carefully than Darby in appreciating the place of anti-Semitism within the history of circumcision, both authors fail to analyze the fetishistic—and therefore not straightforwardly pro-Jewish— dimensions of the philo-Semitism surrounding medical circumcision. Indeed, at times, Glick, Darby, and Gollaher all make the rise of the practice

---

[123] Darby, *Surgical Temptation*, 4.
[124] Darby, 47.
[125] Darby, 13.
[126] Glick, *Marked in Your Flesh*, 179.

in the United Kingdom and the United States sound something like a Jewish conspiracy.[127]

Glick prefaces his book by confessing his regret over the fact that he had his three sons circumcised, announcing his desire for the Jewish community of which he is a part to let go of its mistaken attachment to the practice, referring to himself as a "scholarly activist" associated with the intactivist cause.[128] As with Darby and Gollaher, this anti-circumcision stance seems to preclude a more sophisticated analysis of cultural attitudes toward circumcision. In a concluding chapter on references to circumcision in popular American culture (such as TV sitcoms and "Jewish jokes"), Glick writes:

> Barely disguised beneath the banal humor . . . is the sense of anxiety that pervades so much of the discourse on circumcision. It seems that no amount of joking and banter obscures the simple fact that circumcision means cutting away part of the penis. Some jokes touch on the circumcision-equals-castration fantasy. I'll cite a number of examples—but don't expect to laugh.[129]

For intactivist scholars, circumcision boils down to a "simple fact," and it is no laughing matter. That the thought of circumcision generates castration anxiety, made manifest in jokes, means that the practice is self-evidently wrong. It is assumed that, when presented with the "reality" of circumcision as "violent," "anti-sensual," or "sexist," the reader will come to oppose the practice as a kind of inevitable triumph of scientific rationality. The analysis defensively stops at precisely the point where it might truly begin, as an inquiry into the unconscious dynamics surrounding circumcision and our attachment, or opposition, to it.

Gollaher surveys psychoanalytical and anthropological theories of the underlying motivations for circumcision but is largely dismissive, viewing them as extravagant and overreaching.[130] Darby's argument that medical circumcision emanated from the desire to repress male sexuality, begs the question of where such a desire comes from in the first place. His sole engagement with psychoanalysis takes the form of a crude Freudian reading of the poet A.E. Housman. The poet was circumcised at fourteen and shortly afterward wrote a melancholic poem about Rome, including the

[127] See Silverman's critical discussion of intactivist scholarship and its anti-Semitic overtones in *Abraham to America*, 179–82.
[128] Glick, *Marked in Your Flesh*, viii.
[129] Glick, 271.
[130] Gollaher, *Circumcision*, 53–72.

lines, "And here stands the shaft of a column/And there lies the wreck of a shrine."[131] Darby speculates, "it would be understandable if ruined shafts and broken columns had a particular poignancy for him at this time."[132] The poorly substantiated conjecture suggests more about Darby's own phallic preoccupations than Housman's.

None of these authors critically interrogate intactivism or consider the libidinal investments at stake in it. The anthropologist Eric Silverman offers a rare exception. Surveying the highly confessional nature of anti-circumcision activist literature, he concludes:

> For many opponents of the procedure, [male circumcision] is a potent symbol of anxieties that are not linked directly to the penis. Rather, the lost foreskin symbolizes a series of modern losses arising from historically specific anxieties. The anxieties concern the lost effectiveness of the political, economic, and judicial processes; pluralism; violence; contested notions of masculinity, motherhood, sexuality, and gender; the medicalization of birth; vulnerability before technological advances; notions of personhood similar to those raised in the abortion debate; and the hypercapitalist commodification of the body. Opposition to [male circumcision], widely hailed by the mythopoetic men's movement, also has revealed an enduring and disturbing antisemitism.[133]

In short, Silverman suggests that the loss of the foreskin is treated by intactivists as the culprit for the "lack in the Other," the failure of the symbolic order to secure meaning and consistency. His analysis rings equally true for scholarly writing on the subject.

Through this examination of the literature, I have made the case that circumcision confronts us with an impasse or irresolvable ambiguity around the question of sexual difference, provoking fantasies of phallic mastery. Circumcision stages both the attempt to secure phallic wholeness and the ultimate impossibility of such a project. The following chapters will examine particular cases where these problematics arise in social and political life.

---

[131] Quoted in Darby, *Surgical Temptation*, 296.
[132] Darby, 296. Evans offers a more convincing reading in "History around Housman's Circumcision."
[133] Silverman, "Anthropology and Circumcision," 435–6.

2

"Real Circumcision Is a Matter of the Heart"

Badiou's Paul and Boyarin's Jewish Question

At the turn of the twentieth-century, two major theoretical works were published on Saint Paul: *A Radical Jew: St. Paul and the Politics of Identity*, by historian of religion Daniel Boyarin, and the French philosopher Alain Badiou's *Saint Paul: La fondation de l'universalisme*.[1] Though the two authors would not encounter each other's work until many years later,[2] their arguments appear as if on opposite ends of the same pole. Both mobilize Paul and Pauline theology to investigate the idea of universalism and its place within philosophy and politics. Badiou's *Saint Paul* is a loving exploration of the saint which also functions as a sort of *précis* of Badiou's own embrace of universalism and its relation to the "event"; Paul's letters are made to serve as the historically situated demonstration par excellence of Badiou's universalist philosophy. Boyarin, on the other hand, turns a skeptical eye on Paul, arguing that his practice and advocacy of universalism form an originary source of a "phallogocentric" tradition that seeks to transcend all difference and that denigrates the feminine as the wellspring of impure particularity.

In a certain sense, the different perspectives of Badiou and Boyarin on Paul are paradigmatic of a much larger divide: between those who advocate an unapologetic, anti-identitarian universalism and those who prioritize cultural and historical specificity, wary of what such universalisms may exclude. In this instance, the boundaries between the theological, the political, and the philosophical are especially porous.

In this chapter, I will propose that the key to understanding the difference between Badiou and Boyarin—and thereby, to the larger divide their work represents—lies in their respective interpretations of Paul's stance on circumcision. In extending the new movement of Jesus followers to Jew and

---

[1] Badiou's book was translated, *Saint Paul: The Foundation of Universalism*. Subsequent references for these books are given in the text.

[2] See Caputo and Alcoff, *Paul*, for a dialogue with Boyarin, Badiou, and others on Paul.

Pagan alike, Paul stated that "a person is a Jew who is one inwardly, and real circumcision is a matter of the heart—it is spiritual and not literal."[3] The import of this was not lost on Freud, who prefigured our current authors when he argued in *Moses and Monotheism*, "Paul, who carried Judaism on, also destroyed it. . . . He abandoned the 'chosen' character of his people and its visible mark—circumcision—so that the new religion could be a universal one, embracing all men."[4] Whereas Badiou unreservedly embraces what he calls Paul's "indifference" toward the Jewish circumcision rite (23), arguing that it enabled a rupture from within the Pagan–Jewish divide of Paul's time, Boyarin views it as emblematic of a "Platonic" vision of transcendence premised on the rejection of the corporeal and the erasure of difference, paving the way for anti-Semitism and other forms of persecution. Circumcision functions here as a placeholder condensing a series of oppositions: between Badiou vs. Boyarin, Pauline Christianity vs. Judaism, and the "universalists" vs. the "particularists." By examining Badiou and Boyarin's respective positions on the Jewish rite and Paul's abrogation of it, I hope to shed light on these oppositions, illuminating their tensions and the possibility of rapprochement. For despite the two thinkers' important disagreements, they share the widely held desire to articulate and valorize a form of inclusive collectivity that rejects "totalization" and the subsumption of individuals into a transcendent ideology, each offering an interpretation of the significance of Paul's stance on circumcision that suits this aim. My argument will be made sharper by expanding on some of the insights articulated in the previous chapter, regarding the Lacanian theorization of sexual difference and the ambivalent nature of circumcision.

Who Was St. Paul?

Before we examine Badiou and Boyarin's arguments, we should review the basics of St. Paul and his relationship to Judaism. What is known about the saint derives primarily from the seven letters or "epistles" in the New Testament that biblical scholars, for the most part, deem authentically his own: Romans, 1 Corinthians, 2 Corinthians, Galatians, Philippians, 1 Thessalonians, and Philemon. These "authentic" letters comprise the earliest known books of the New Testament: the first epistle, Thessalonians, is dated to approximately 50 CE, whereas the first gospel, Mark, was written in approximately 70 CE.

---

[3]   Rom 2:29.
[4]   Freud, *Moses and Monotheism*, 88.

The New Testament attributes six other letters to Paul, all under various degrees of doubt among scholars regarding their authenticity.

The book of Acts offers the sole biography of Paul's life in the New Testament and is considered rife with exaggerations and fabrications. It is in Acts that we encounter the famous "road to Damascus" story: Saul of Tarsus, a Pharisee, was on his way to Damascus with a mandate to arrest the followers of Jesus, when suddenly he was blinded by a light from heaven, fell off his horse, and heard the voice of Jesus telling him to stop persecuting God. Subsequently, he became known as Paul and dedicated himself to preaching the "good news."

Unlike in the gospels, Paul has little to say about the "life and times" of Jesus. Rather, his letters, addressed to groups of followers and skeptics encountered on his travels through the Roman Empire, are aimed at convincing his audience of the salvation made possible "to the Jew first and also to the Greek,"[5] by the death and resurrection of Christ. Paul repeatedly reminds us of his Jewish credentials, notably through reference to his circumcision: he was "circumcised on the eighth day, a member of the people of Israel, a Hebrew born of Hebrews."[6] After meeting with church leaders in Jerusalem, he was "entrusted with the gospel for the uncircumcised, just as Peter had been entrusted with the gospel for the circumcised."[7] His mission, in other words, was to bring non-Jews into the fold of the new Jesus movement. This was not uncontroversial among the early followers of Jesus, most of whom were practicing Jews. Paul's letters regularly scorn Jewish Christ-followers who wanted Gentiles to undergo circumcision and conversion to Judaism in order to gain entry into their movement.[8] Jews need not renounce their laws and rituals, but Gentiles must be welcomed without the requirement to submit to these, Paul insisted:[9]

> Was anyone at the time of his call already circumcised? Let him not seek to remove the marks of circumcision. Was anyone at the time of his call uncircumcised? Let him not seek circumcision. Circumcision is

---

5. Rom. 1:16.
6. Phil. 3:5-6.
7. Gal. 2:7-8.
8. Nanos argues that these Jewish Jesus followers likely felt marginalized in the eyes of their fellow Jews, and may have worried about further endangering their status by welcoming Gentiles into their sect, without at least formally joining them to the Abrahamic covenant via conversion/circumcision ("Myth").
9. Paul's view on the status of Jewish law after Christ has been a long-standing subject of debate among theologians and philosophers, to which Boyarin and Badiou have contributed. See Westerholm, *Perspectives Old and New*; and Caputo and Alcoff, *Paul*.

nothing, and uncircumcision nothing. . . . Let each of you remain in the condition in which you were called.[10]

To make his case, Paul repeatedly deployed his extensive knowledge of the Hebrew Scriptures, arguing for universal brotherhood in Christ not in opposition to but from the position of his observance of Torah. Thus, far from opposing Judaism, Paul saw himself as its true adherent.

The following passage, from Romans, condenses the issues on Paul, Judaism, and circumcision fundamental to this chapter:

> Circumcision indeed is of value if you obey the law; but if you break the law, your circumcision has become uncircumcision. So, if those who are uncircumcised keep the requirements of the law, will not their uncircumcision be regarded as circumcision? Then those who are physically uncircumcised but keep the law will condemn you that have the written code and circumcision but break the law. For a person is not a Jew who is one outwardly, nor is true circumcision something external and physical. Rather, a person is a Jew who is one inwardly, and real circumcision is a matter of the heart—it is spiritual and not literal. Such a person receives praise not from others but from God.[11]

The crux here is the status of Jewish law in Paul's rendering. Paul treats "the law" as something other than the literal obedience of the Jewish commandments, such as the physical practice of circumcision. One can obey the "written code and circumcision" and still "break the law," and crucially, one can remain uncircumcised and still "keep the requirements of the law." He explains this by way of his frequently employed distinction between "spiritual" and "literal" circumcision: what matters is not circumcision "of the flesh," but circumcision "of the heart." Here, the law of circumcision is a synecdoche for law itself. Indeed, when Paul uses the Greek word for law, *nomos*, he often refers specifically to the law of circumcision, but with implications that extend to how Christ-followers ought to understand law in general. Additionally, the word Paul uses for circumcision, *peritome*, more literally means "cutting around"; when Paul refers to those who have been "cut off" from God, he is likely making a pun on the theme of circumcision.[12] Thus, in Paul, problems of universalism and law are tied to problems of circumcision and cutting.

---

[10] 1 Cor. 7:18-20.
[11] Rom. 2:25-29.
[12] Martin, *Epistle of Paul*, 141.

In the first line of this passage, Paul warns his audience against legal hypocrisy. The practice of circumcision is not enough to ensure that one is law-abiding. From a Jewish perspective, this point conveys nothing new. Jews had long before acknowledged that circumcision offers no immunity from all the other legal and practical requirements of worship. Nor even is the concept "circumcision of the heart" novel. Paul borrows the phrase from Jer. 4:4, "Circumcise yourselves to the Lord, remove the foreskins of your hearts." His truly novel gesture, rather, consists in his subtracting the "spiritual meaning" of Jewish law from the ritual practice altogether, seemingly eviscerating the bond between the Jewish spirit and the Jewish flesh. What is at stake in this moment, when Paul makes "true circumcision" available to all, Jew or Gentile? What becomes of circumcision, and Judaism, in Paul's rendering? By abrogating the centrality of the physical rite, has Paul set the stage for the suppression of the Jewish people? Or has he performed an act of revolutionary generosity?

In a debate with Badiou, Boyarin, and others, the biblical scholar Dale Martin locates the key to Paul's message in Paul's metaphor of the olive tree.[13] In Romans 11, Paul compares Gentiles to wild branches that God has offered to graft onto the cultivated olive tree of Israel (the Jews). The passage enjoins Gentiles to respect Israel, even those Jews who have been "cut off" from their tree (who have not accepted Jesus): "If you boast—well, you do not bear the root [i.e., Israel], but the root bears you."[14] Martin argues, following this passage, that Paul's "universalism" is one of expanding the Jewish community rather than transcending or superseding it. Paul's Christian-Judaism becomes, in Martin's reading, a liberal-pluralist "big tent." For Boyarin and Badiou alike, however, Martin's notion of Pauline Jewish expansionism is too simplistic. In different ways, they examine how Paul's grafting of the Gentile branches onto the tree of Israel does not merely affect the branches but changes something about the tree itself.

Badiou on Paul

"Paul's unprecedented gesture," writes Badiou, "consists in subtracting truth from the communitarian grasp, be it that of a people, a city, an empire, a territory, or a social class" (5). Badiou holds that the everyday order of things consists of a matrix of differential relations. Commodities,

---

[13] Martin, "Promise of Teleology," 100.
[14] Rom. 11:17 (Martin's translation).

nationalities, races, and so on function as "groupings" or "sets" of terms that demonstrate meaning or value in opposition to their different neighboring terms. These terms can be infinitely exchanged, regrouped, and re-related in a kaleidoscopic manner. Such an infinity constitutes, for Badiou, a "false universality" (7). Communitarianism reifies and makes visible this matrix of differences by attempting to subsume all possible forms of existence into positive identities opposed to one another.

However, the field of being is not exhausted by these positive articulations of difference. For Badiou, universal truth involves a moment of "subtraction" from a positive social order. A truth makes visible, and draws its vitality from, the failure of the social order to circumscribe the entirety of existence. Via this act of subtraction, something emerges that does not "fit" into the ordinary network of relations and which cannot be categorized or properly circumscribed.

While our commonplace conception of the universal involves elevating some particular thing into a master ideal, capable of containing and organizing the rest of the particulars, Badiou's notion of the universe does the inverse: it represents a point that no existing relation has yet incorporated, something that touches or borders on a void. This has both a negative and positive dimension to it. Universal truth is negative in the sense that it traverses and *negates* all of the extant forms of relation in a given order. It is positive in the sense that, via this very process, it produces something new and open to all. As Peter Hallward puts it, "Truth is nothing other than the local production of freedom from all relation, a situated production of radical autonomy or self-determination."[15]

This production of a universal truth constitutes an "event," and it requires subjects to name and declare their fidelity to it—despite the fact that its nature renders it meaningless within the terms of ordinary existence. Such an event does not simply "happen." Rather, subjects must declare, retroactively, that an event *has happened,* make an "interpretative intervention"[16] that ushers it into the world. The declaration of an event is a wager on nothing, a leap of faith; though Badiou declares his philosophy atheist, the idea is unmistakably inflected with theological overtones. For Badiou, St. Paul is not only an exemplar of this evental subject but a theoretician of the event in its universalist dimension:

> For me, Paul is a poet-thinker of the event, as well as one who practices and states the invariant traits of what can be called the militant figure.

[15] Hallward, *Badiou*, xxxi.
[16] Badiou, *Being and Event*, 181.

> He brings forth the entirely human connection . . . between the general
> idea of a rupture, an overturning, and that of a thought-practice that is
> this rupture's subjective materiality. (2)

In Paul's time, argues Badiou, the "Jew" and the "Greek" (i.e., pagan)
represented the major axis along which the pre-Christian social order was
divided. One side depended on its difference from the other in order to
exist, and neither side could conceive of a form of belonging that included
all, a truth that cuts through communitarian differences. Declaring salvation
through Christ was the means through which Paul subtracted from the Jew–
Greek totality something that neither side could lay claim to—that was, in
fact, senseless to both sides—and could therefore stand for universality.

Paul states, "For Jews demand signs and Greeks desire wisdom, but we
proclaim Christ crucified, a stumbling-block to Jews and foolishness to
Gentiles."[17] For Badiou, this Jew–Greek opposition is not just between two
historical groups, but between *"subjective dispositions . . .* or what could be called
regimes of discourse" (41, emphasis original). "Greek discourse," he claims,
stands for a way of relating to the world and the things within it as an organic,
natural totality. "Greek wisdom," which refers to the Greek philosophical
tradition, represents the impetus to understand and legislate one's place within
the natural order, to study each particular as part of a greater, self-enclosed,
ultimately harmonious Whole, "the matching of logos to being" (41). "Jewish
discourse," on the other hand, represents the inverse of Greek discourse, what
Badiou calls its "constitutive exception" (ibid.). Jewish discourse is predicated
on "that which lies beyond the natural totality" (ibid.): the miracle, the election,
the prophecy, and, of course, the covenant of circumcision. What connects all
these central concepts in Judaism is their exceptionality to Nature; Judaism
refuses the logic of Greek wisdom with its exact opposite:

> In the eyes of Paul the Jew, the weakness of Jewish discourse is that its
> logic of the exceptional sign is only valid *for* the Greek cosmic totality.
> The Jew is in exception to the Greek. The result is, firstly, that neither
> of the two discourses can be universal, because each supposes the
> persistence of the other; and secondly, that the two discourses share
> the presupposition that the key to salvation is given to us within the
> universe, whether it be through direct mastery of the totality (Greek
> wisdom) or through mastery of a literal tradition and the deciphering of
> signs (Jewish ritualism and prophetism). (42)

---

[17] 1 Cor. 1:22-23.

Both Jewish signs and Greek wisdom rely on the unifying principle of mastery. For Paul, "Christ crucified" is "a stumbling-block to Jews and foolishness to Gentiles"; it is universal *not* because it masters either the Jewish or Greek discourse, but because it *refuses* both sides' terms of legitimation, opening up a previously unforeseen form of belonging, in which, "There is no longer Jew or Greek, there is no longer slave or free, there is no longer male and female; for all of you are one in Christ Jesus."[18]

We can see in Paul's letters how he appears to illustrate and harness Badiou's notion of subtractive universalism by repeatedly invoking the power of weakness, foolishness, and absence against strength, wisdom, and presence. For example:

> God chose what is foolish in the world to shame the wise; God chose what is weak in the world to shame the strong; God chose what is low and despised in the world, things that are not, to reduce to nothing things that are, so that no one may boast in the presence of God.[19]

Paul's point seems to be that, in lieu of Christ, we must no longer rely on the ordinary means we have of sustaining identities and of separating truth from falsehood—that is, on that which is visible and available to us in society or our community's traditions. The qualities that are normally *devalued* across society, as markers of poverty, impotence, or ignorance, are now counterintuitively valued as the very location of divine truth.[20] Truth and salvation emerge *not* from what is given or discernible in the everyday world, nor from the impressive constructions of the wise, but from "what is low and despised in the world, things that are not"— we might say, from that which is "nearest" to the void, insofar as what is most despised is also unrepresented. The point is political as much as it is philosophical/theological: the unseen wretched of the earth (of which the suffering Christ is an exemplar) become, *ontologically,* the site of universal truth. Participants in this truth have nothing on which to ground their convictions but a leap of faith: belief in the resurrection. Thus, Paul links truth and universalism by claiming that what is true and salvific is simultaneously what is universally rejected, devalued, or obscured.

For Badiou, Paul's universalism occurs on multiple levels: he generated not just a socioreligious movement but a blueprint for universalism as such. Paul existed in a particular time and place, a "situation" in Badiou's terminology:

---

[18] Gal. 3:28.
[19] 1 Cor. 1:27-29.
[20] There is an apocryphal Christian belief that the saint chose to give up his regal Jewish name Saul for Paul, which means "little" in Greek.

he was a Jew living in the Roman Empire, in the time shortly following the death of Jesus. Declaring belief in the resurrection of Christ was a solution specific to his situation. The point, for Badiou, is not that we should believe in the "fable" of Jesus's resurrection. Rather, the way Paul harnessed the power of this fable, allowing it to transform him into a messenger of anti-communitarian universalism, involved an expertly deployed, formal logic of subtraction that we can apply to the situation of our own time. The formal quality of Paul's epistles is key:

> When one reads Paul, one is stupefied by the paucity of traces left in his prose by the era, genres, and circumstances. There is in his prose . . . something solid and timeless, something that, precisely because it is a question of orienting a thought towards the universal *in its suddenly emerging singularity*, but independently of all anecdote, is intelligible to us without having to resort to cumbersome historical mediations. (36, emphasis original)

Here, Badiou proposes a paradoxical relation between materiality, historicity, and the universal. Universal truth is "independent" of "anecdote" and "historical mediation," yet simultaneously occurs via the emergence of singularity, which suggests lived, historical experience; one of the challenges of fidelity to an event lies in sustaining "the twofold principle of opening and historicity" (25).

Circumcision in Badiou's Paul

Badiou does not address the meaning of the Jewish circumcision rite as such. Rather, he focuses on the reason Paul opposed those Jews who wanted Gentiles to undergo ritual conversion and circumcision. Within this context, Badiou claims, circumcision "indexes its function as a form of branding, of primary initiation" (19). The Jewish proselytizers required circumcision in order to symbolically demarcate themselves from Gentiles, solidifying their difference. (As Paul says to the Galatians, "Even the circumcised do not themselves obey the law, but they want you to be circumcised so that they may boast about your flesh."[21] In this instance, Paul accuses Jewish proselytizers of displacing righteousness with ethnic pride and

---

[21] Gal. 6:13.

competitiveness.) As such, Badiou admires Paul's claim that "circumcision is nothing, and uncircumcision is nothing."[22] He understands this as a form of "indifference to difference," of refusing to allow symbolic markers of difference—of which circumcision is paradigmatic—to "count." "It is not that communitarian marking . . . is indefensible or erroneous," writes Badiou. "It is that the postevental imperative of truth renders [it] indifferent (which is worse)" (23). Those participating in the new universality cannot constitute themselves on the basis of their symbolic difference from others, circumcised or uncircumcised.

Although Badiou thinks Paul's "indifference" to circumcision is intended to dissolve the ordinary criteria for insider/outsider, a new outsider does nevertheless emerge: those who fail to fully adhere to Paul's notion of universality and continue to believe in the importance of circumcision. "For [Paul] (and we shall grant him this point)," writes Badiou, "a truth procedure does not comprise degrees. Either one participates in it, declaring the founding event and drawing its consequences, or one remains foreign to it" (21). All are welcome to participate in the universality of the event, which distinguishes it from a particularist project for which exclusion is foundational. Yet, those who refuse the event are identified as such. This is demonstrated in moments when Paul appears to lose his temper:

> Beware of the dogs, beware of the evil workers, beware of those who mutilate the flesh! For it is we who are the circumcision, who worship in the Spirit of God and boast in Christ Jesus and have no confidence in the flesh.[23]

Following this, I propose that in Badiou's Pauline logic, circumcision functions as a symbol of regression into communal particularism. After Paul, circumcision *indexes the refusal of the event.* We might say it becomes a dialectical antithesis to Pauline universalism: something which emerges as a problem only after the event, yet on which, in a negative way, the whole universal project rests. This raises two questions, unanswered by Badiou: first, what place is left for the particular, historical circumstances from which a universal truth emerges? Second, how might one respond to those Jews who said, and continue to say, "No" to Paul—who continued to follow Jewish law, and practice circumcision, both before and long after Christianity transformed the Roman Empire?

---

22 1 Cor. 7:19.
23 Phil. 3:2-3.

Boyarin on Paul

For Daniel Boyarin, the key to understanding Paul's universalism lies in the dichotomy Paul establishes between the flesh and the spirit, epitomized by Paul's claim that "real circumcision . . . is spiritual and not literal." Boyarin understands this as an allegorical reading of the Hebrew Scriptures that positions the (Jewish) letter as the particular, concrete signifier of an abstract, universal signified, (Christian) spirit:

> Paul was motivated by a Hellenistic desire for the One, which among other things produced an ideal of a universal human essence, beyond difference and hierarchy. This universal humanity, however, was predicated (and still is) on the dualism of the flesh and the spirit, such that while the body is particular, marked through practice as Jew or Greek, and through anatomy as male or female, the spirit is universal. (7)

Christ made the spirit available to all, but the consequence, in Boyarin's reading, is that the letter of the Torah, and its many associated terms—all connected to the particularity of the embodied Jew—are transcended or superseded. As Paul says, "for the letter kills, but the Spirit gives life."[24] Instead of cutting the flesh, literally inscribing Jewish identity onto the body of the male Jew, post-Pauline Christianity turned to baptism, forgoing the bodily ritual in favor of a simple, figurative rite—bloodless and without physical trace. "In one stroke," writes Boyarin, echoing Freud's point in *Moses and Monotheism*, "by interpreting circumcision as referring to a spiritual and not corporeal reality, Paul made it possible for Judaism to become a world religion" (230).

Boyarin is skeptical of this project (as he understands it) and its political implications. "For Paul," he writes, "the only possibility for human equality involved human sameness. . . . If Paul is not the origin of anti-Semitism (and I hold that he is not), it may certainly be fairly said that he is the origin of the 'Jewish Question'" (156). He argues that the rabbinical tradition of Judaism, which emerged largely in the wake of Christianity, "is in part a reaction formation . . . or, at the very least, a typological antithesis" to Pauline universalism (8), and deserves special consideration for how it returns to questions of materiality, the body, and sexuality allegedly denigrated by Pauline Christianity.

Unlike Badiou, who understands Paul's discourse as a radical break from everything that preceded it, Boyarin situates Paul within a longer

---

[24] 2 Cor. 3:6.

philosophical tradition. Paul, he contends, emerged from a lineage of Jewish thinkers inspired by Hellenistic, and specifically Platonic thought. These pre-Pauline Jews were also concerned with universalism, as they wanted to demonstrate that Judaism made a worthy contribution to cosmopolitan Hellenic society. Before Paul, Hellenic Jews already practiced an allegorical reading of the Torah, "founded on . . . a dualistic system in which spirit precedes and is primary over body" (14). For them, the "text" of the Torah, like the material body, was the *means through which* the transcendental spirit could be discerned and experienced. As imperfect humans, tainted by the passions of the flesh, we cannot escape the substandard realm of corporeal life, but, they reasoned, the Torah provides the key to channeling our flesh into spirituality. Read allegorically, the Torah became a compendium of metaphors gifted by God to help man transcend the flesh.

The Hellenic Jew Philo of Alexandria (25 BCE–50 CE), for example, wrote that he was interested in "the hidden and inward meaning which appeals to the few who study soul characteristics rather than bodily forms" (cited in Boyarin, 79).[25] He attempted to lay bare universal truths hidden underneath the particular practices commanded by Jewish law. For instance, he claimed that the excision of the foreskin during circumcision corresponded to "the excision of pleasures which bewitch the mind";[26] the bodily act pointed to the spiritual transcendence of the body. He wrote approvingly of the fact that the ancient Egyptians, "abounding in all kinds of wisdom," also practiced circumcision, seeing it as further proof of the universal value of Jewish law.[27] Maimonides (1135 CE–1204 CE) offered a similarly ascetic interpretation of circumcision, referring to a "weakening of the organ in question."[28] Despite the fact that the two thinkers lived in different times and places, their merging of Jewish theology with Greek philosophy, Boyarin argues, seems to have influenced them both to generate "rational and universal reasons for being circumcised" based on allegorical logic (26). Circumcision was praiseworthy because, among other reasons, it supposedly reduced man's interest in, and capacity for, sensual pleasure—a theory which would make circumcision potentially as valuable for the Gentile as for the Jew, that is, universal.

---

[25] Philo's work would eventually become more significant to Christian theologians than Jews. Given Boyarin's arguments about rabbinical Judaism (discussed later), this is unsurprising.

[26] Philo, "Special Laws," 105.

[27] Philo, 105. Boyarin notes than in an early anti-Jewish Christian polemic, *The Epistle of Barnabas,* the fact that circumcision was practiced by pagans is used as proof *against* the validity of Jewish ritual. What for the cosmopolitan Philo proved Judaism's righteousness, for anti-Semitic Christians underscored Judaism's moral bankruptcy ("Carnal Israel," 486).

[28] Maimonides, *Guide of the Perplexed,* 609.

There was also a misogynistic hue to this allegorical technique, familiar to contemporary feminist criticism: for Philo, man stood for pure mind and woman for impure matter, "For just as the man shows himself in activity and woman in passivity, so the province of the mind is activity and that of the perceptive sense passivity, as in the woman" (cited in Boyarin, 21). In his reading of Genesis, Philo interprets the birth of Adam prior to Eve as linked to the priority of "Mind" over "Sense-perception." Eve was created from Adam's rib "to be a helper and ally" to Adam, who was formerly pure Mind—yet the union of the two also signaled the lamentable breakdown of man's spiritual purity: "For when that which is superior, namely Mind, becomes one with that which is inferior, namely Sense-perception, it resolves itself into the order of the flesh which is inferior." "It is here," writes Boyarin, "that a historical vector begins that will ultimately end up in phallogocentric versus as-a-woman reading."[29]

Though Philo and other Hellenic Jews saw the material practices of Judaism as necessary *starting points* for accessing spirit, Paul, argues Boyarin, went a step further. Whereas Hellenic Jews saw "circumcision of the flesh" as a way *toward* "circumcision of the heart," Paul would argue that, thanks to Christ, we now can skip the former. Circumcision of the heart, the spiritual signified, is available sans fleshly signifier:

> For the less radical Philo, the body remained significant but was significantly downgraded vis-à-vis the spirit, both the body of sexuality and the body of language/history. Both the carnal and the spiritual were meaningful, but in a severely hierarchical way. For the more radical Paul and most of the Fathers, the body was devalued much more completely, retaining significance primarily as a pointer to spirit and the spiritual/universal sense.[30]

Earlier Platonic Jews would never abandon Jewish law, but "Paul came to oppose the Law because of the way that it literally—that is, carnally—insisted on the priority and importance of the flesh, of procreation and kinship, symbolized by the mark in the flesh, par excellence, the penis" (Boyarin, 68–9). Paul may not have advocated asceticism, but his radical allegorical project opened the door for corporeal renunciation. He may have "tolerated" the physical practice of circumcision, but his tolerance "deprives differences of the right to be different, dissolving all others into a single essence in which matters of cultural practice are irrelevant and only faith in Christ is significant" (Boyarin, 9).

---

[29] Boyarin, "Carnal Israel," 477.
[30] Boyarin, "Carnal Israel," 482–3.

Boyarin versus Badiou

A selection from Romans on Paul's position on the flesh and the spirit will allow us to juxtapose Badiou and Boyarin's differing interpretations:

> For God has done what the law, weakened by the flesh, could not do: by sending his own Son in the likeness of sinful flesh, and to deal with sin, he condemned sin in the flesh, so that the just requirement of the law might be fulfilled in us, who walk not according to the flesh but according to the Spirit. For those who live according to the flesh set their minds on the things of the flesh, but those who live according to the Spirit set their minds on the things of the Spirit. To set the mind on the flesh is death, but to set the mind on the Spirit is life and peace. For this reason the mind that is set on the flesh is hostile to God; it does not submit to God's law— indeed it cannot, and those who are in the flesh cannot please God.[31]

For Boyarin, this passage exemplifies Paul's Platonic stance toward Jewish observance (111–15). Jewish law (principally, the law of circumcision) is "weakened by the flesh"; man is bound to commit sin even as he attempts to follow the "just requirement of the law," because legal observance takes place within the corporeal domain, where the sinful ways of the flesh reign. The sacrifice of Christ has rescued man from this predicament, providing the opportunity to relinquish investment in the particular, and particularizing, bodily practices of Judaism and directly access the universal spirit.

Badiou offers a very different take, imploring us to "forget the Platonic apparatus of the soul and the body. . . . Paul's thought ignores these parameters" (68). Whereas Boyarin interprets the flesh/spirit, death/life dichotomies in precisely these terms, Badiou argues that they refer, rather, to two "way[s] of being in the world" (ibid.). The flesh, Badiou claims, corresponds to ordinary relationality, participation in the everyday matrix of differences. Spirit, on the other hand, corresponds not to the *transcendence* of one's socio-symbolic situation but, rather, to the universal void *within* any "fleshly" situation that has the potential to fundamentally disrupt and reconfigure it. The division is thus not between the "pure" subject and his/her "impure" physical body, but a division *within* the embodied subject as such:

> The death about which Paul tells us, which is ours as much as Christ's, has nothing biological about it, no more so for that matter than life.

---

[31] Rom. 8:3-8.

> Death and life are thoughts, interwoven dimensions of the global subject, wherein "body" and "soul" are indiscernible (which is why, for Paul, the Resurrection is necessarily resurrection of the body—that is to say, resurrection of the divided subject in its entirety). Grasped as thought, as subjective path, as a way of being in the world, death is that part of the divided subject that must, again and always, say "no" to the flesh and maintain itself in the precarious becoming of the spirit's "but." (68)

It is not a matter of *abandoning* flesh for spirit but of experiencing spirit as an *immanent*, universal potential, an excess *inherent to* the flesh. Badiou interprets Paul's phrase "walk not according to the flesh but according to the spirit" as a call for the subject to "maintain itself in the precarious becoming of spirit's but," refusing to delimit oneself within particularity by actively participating in the excess of the event.

Importantly, though they have such divergent readings of Paul, Badiou and Boyarin end up *sharing* an opposition to Platonic dualisms and totalizing logics of transcendence. Badiou writes, "It is John who, by turning the logos into a principle, will synthetically inscribe Christianity within the space of the Greek logos, thereby subordinating it to anti-Judaism. This is certainly not the way that Paul proceeds" (43). Just like Boyarin, Badiou argues that Greek logocentrism provides the ideological frame for anti-Semitism. The disagreement rests on whether one should ascribe this philosophy to Paul.

Contra Boyarin, Badiou thinks that Paul's critique of the law is not rooted in any notion of corporeal transcendence but is, rather, an attack on the "closed particularities (whose name is 'law')" (64). Is this, we might ask, a fair assessment of the significance of the law in Judaism? Does circumcision function solely as a form of communitarian bondage, or might it serve other purposes, perhaps unforeseen by Paul?

The Rabbinical Alternative

Regardless of whether Boyarin is correct to locate Paul within a Platonic allegorical approach to the Torah, he persuasively argues that rabbinical Judaism constitutes a unique nonallegorical alternative, emblematized in the midrash, one of the major sources of rabbinical thought. Midrash is the name for a diverse collection of narrative, exegetical and legal texts that addresses various intricacies, paradoxes, and contradictions in the Torah. Midrashic authors connect seemingly disparate sections of scripture to generate new narratives, apocryphal stories, and interpretations that fill in apparent gaps.

In sharp contrast to Platonism, argues Boyarin, midrash refuses the dualisms of "inner-outer, visible-invisible, body-soul."[32] "Accordingly," he writes,

> if Philo's allegory is the restoration of the visible text (body) to its source and origin, to its spiritual, invisible meaning (spirit), midrash is the linking up of text to text to release meaning—without any doctrine of an originary spirit that precedes the body of the language of the Torah.[33]

In Paul's time, the rabbinical movement had not yet consolidated, and Greek-allegorical versus proto-rabbinical approaches to the Torah existed side by side. However, as the borderlines between Judaism and Christianity were drawn in the centuries after Paul, Platonic allegory would become increasingly foreign to Judaism, and rabbinical Judaism would eventually become synonymous with Judaism as such. Boyarin does not think this was an accident: the rabbis, he argues, crafted a Judaism that is at least in part a response, a developed alternative, to (their interpretation of) Paul and the religion he helped generate. Contemporary Judaism, in other words, is the theological "No" to Paul and Christianity. While Philo's gloss on the Torah read the feminine as the bodily supplement to the masculine spirit, and Paul's approach allegedly relied on a division between the literal Torah text and its greater spiritual truth, rabbinical Judaism

> thematizes neither a supplementarity for the woman nor for its own materiality and physicality as text. Man and woman, body and spirit, language and meaning are inseparably bound together in it from the beginning. It escapes the logic of the supplement entirely because the culture resists the Platonic metaphysics of signification.

Key to understanding the difference between rabbinical Judaism and other approaches to the Hebrew Bible is the significance that the former attributes to circumcision. For the rabbis, circumcision is not (or at least not solely) an identitarian marker of affiliation, Boyarin claims. Rather, the rite becomes a complex, nonallegorical "technique of the body," that *literally* joins the Jew's body to God, in the bloody, historical moment of the act. "The cut in the penis completes"—note, Boyarin does not use the word *symbolize*—"the inscription of God's name on the body" (37). Not a "pointer" to a greater signified, circumcision is intricately interwoven in practices of reading and religious observance that knot together the Jew, the law, sexuality, kinship,

---

[32] Boyarin, "Carnal Israel," 477.
[33] Boyarin, "Carnal Israel," 480.

history, the body, and divinity. Thus, while Paul may have understood the practice in the context of Hellenic Jewish allegory (in Boyarin's reading)—or advocated "indifference" toward it based on its "function as a form of branding" (in Badiou's reading)—the rabbinical approach invested the practice with an entirely different meaning, concerned less with identity than with an embodied approach to spiritual practice.

Boyarin develops his argument from rabbinical texts on circumcision, especially those inflected by mysticism, which spend significant time elaborating on the physicality of the rite. One midrashic text, for example, refers to circumcision as the inscription of the divine Hebrew letter, *yod*, onto the flesh.[34] The actual shape of the head of the circumcised penis is thought to resemble—or more literally, reveal—this letter. Here, the body is not transcended but sanctified, transformed into a holy object. The Jewish studies scholar Elliot Wolfson, whom Boyarin draws on, shows how in the Kabbalah, the act of physical opening that imprints the *yod* onto the flesh is understood in a theurgical sense, corresponding to an opening in the divine realm itself.[35] This opening, according to the *Zohar* (the definitive midrashic text of Jewish mysticism), allows the circumcised Jew to experience visions of God.[36] The opening/inscription of circumcision also brings together, as Derrida would notice, the sacred and the text.[37] The opening of the penis, and the opening of God, take place via the *letter*. The sacred is thus experienced, or disclosed, through a process of reading/writing that blurs together the physical, the textual, and the holy, elegantly communicating Judaism's unique emphasis on biblical study. Particularity matters here, but not in an exclusionary sense; the opening to something "other" is not defended against but, rather, incorporated into the founding act of Jewish constitution.

Another example of the relationship between nonallegorical midrashic reading practices and a rabbinical approach to embodiment vis-à-vis circumcision offers a fascinating contrast to Paul. In Romans 4, Paul argues that before his circumcision, Abraham was already "justified"[38] by virtue of

---

[34] See Wolfson, "Circumcision."

[35] Wolfson, 82–5.

[36] Wolfson, 82–5.

[37] See, for example, Bennington and Derrida, "Circumfession."

[38] Rom. 4:2. Campbell proposes the translation "liberated." Campbell opposes the so-called "justification theory" that has dominated popular and scholarly interpretations of Paul, which sees Paul as arguing that faith in Christ, as opposed to works (obedience to Jewish laws), is necessary for "justification." He argues that an accurate translation of Paul shows that the saint was concerned neither with "Jewish legalism" nor the individual beliefs necessary for salvation but, rather, with preaching the unconditional availability of salvation, which was due not to individual faith in God but to *God's faith* in humanity (*Deliverance of God*).

his faith in God. He builds his case from a sequence of events in Genesis. In Genesis 15, which takes place before Abraham's circumcision, God tells Abraham that despite his old age, he will be fertile. Paul quotes from Genesis Abraham's response to God's unlikely promise: "Abraham believed God, and it was reckoned to him as righteousness."[39] Paul argues that it was Abraham's faith in God alone, rather than circumcision or the fulfillment of any Jewish laws, that made him righteous: "How then was [Abraham's righteousness] reckoned to him? It was not after, but before he was circumcised. He received the sign of circumcision as a seal of the righteousness that he had by faith while he was still uncircumcised."[40] In a Boyarinian reading, circumcision functions here as the material signifier of a preexisting spiritual signified.

One of the earliest midrashic texts, written after Paul, appears inspired by, yet a radical departure from, the saint's interpretation. Written in the voice of Abraham, it is a perplexing fragment at first sight:

It is written, "This, after my skin will have been peeled off; but I would behold God from my flesh" (Job 19:26). Abraham said, After I circumcised myself many converts came to cleave to this sign. "But I would behold God from my flesh," for had I not done this [i.e., performed the act of circumcision], on what account would the Holy One, blessed be He, have appeared to me? [As it is written] "The Lord appeared to him etc."[41]

Common to midrash, the author of this fragment generates a narrative that does not appear in the actual biblical text. In this case, it is the speech of Abraham logically deducing that circumcision was the cause of his theophany. The author observes that, in Genesis 17/18, Abraham undergoes circumcision immediately prior to his vision of the Lord. The last line of Genesis 17 reads, "Thus Abraham and his son Ishmael were circumcised on that very day; and all his household, his home born slaves and those that had been brought from outsiders, were circumcised with him." The first line of Genesis 18 reads, "The Lord appeared to [Abraham] by the terebinths of Mamre; he was sitting at the entrance of the tent as the day grew hot." A modern reader would likely not find any causal connection between these two lines, as Genesis 18 is clearly the beginning of a new story; but the logic deployed in midrash eschews such concern over narrative linearity, treating "all parts of Scripture as a self-glossing text."[42] The author of this midrash

[39] Gen. 15:6, quoted by Paul in Rom. 4.3.
[40] Rom. 4:10-11.
[41] Cited in Wolfson, "Circumcision," 192.
[42] Boyarin, "Carnal Israel," 479 n. 12.

further justifies his argument by appropriating a verse from the book of Job (an entirely different book from Genesis): "This, after my skin will have been peeled off; but I would behold God from my flesh." Again, narrative linearity is disregarded. In the relevant surrounding passage of Job, the issue of circumcision does not appear in any explicit way. Yet in the specific line quoted, this author links the peeling off of the skin to the removal of the foreskin, and the vision of God "from my flesh" to theophany experienced via circumcision. The passage thus exemplifies the relationship between midrashic intertextuality, corporeality, and circumcision.

The difference between Paul and the rabbis here is stark. Whereas Paul emphasizes Abraham's pre-circumcision righteousness, the midrash we quoted emphasizes the good things that happen to Abraham *after* his circumcision. Both Wolfson and Boyarin contend that in this midrash, "The emphasis on Abraham's circumcision . . . can only be seen as a tacit rejection of the Christian position that circumcision of the flesh had been replaced by circumcision of the spirit (enacted in baptism)."[43]

Rabbinical Circumcision and Femininity

Importantly, Boyarin also focuses on the feminine—or feminizing—aspect of the rabbinical approach to circumcision. Boyarin examines a midrash on the *Song of Songs* that, via gender-bending word plays, implies that the male Jew must be feminized by circumcision in order to receive a vision of the divine. The author of the midrash performs an exegesis of the verse "O, Daughters of Zion, go forth, and gaze upon King Solomon."[44] The author understands the "Daughters of Zion" to represent the nation of Israel and "King Solomon" to represent God.[45] In order for the Daughters of Zion to include the *male* members of Israel, he deploys a series of puns on the Hebrew words. King Solomon becomes one who "requires perfection" (the Hebrew *Schelomoh* = Solomon, *Schelemut* = perfection), and the Daughters of Zion become the *circumcised* members of Israel (*Tsiyyon* = Zion, *ts/y/n* = "to be marked," that is, circumcised). Circumcision removes the male Jew's imperfection, turning him into a *daughter* of Zion in order for him to view God (cited in Boyarin, 128).

---

[43] Wolfson, "Circumcision," 194.
[44] Song of Sol. 3:11.
[45] Although such an interpretation involves a kind of "decoding," Boyarin does not view it as allegorical; the rabbis understood the poem to refer to real, historical events, not abstract spiritual ideals.

Boyarin further substantiates his argument by reference to a blessing recited in traditional Jewish circumcision rituals. The blessing is taken from Ezek. 16:6, where God discovers Israel—explicitly figured as female child—"wallowing in [her] blood." God says to her, "Live in your [feminine] blood." This phrase is repeated verbatim by the ritual circumciser to the male newborn, suggesting a powerful link between femininity, menstrual blood, and the act of circumcision.[46]

These examples suggest to Boyarin that rabbinical Judaism offers an alternative gender culture that eschews the Platonic hierarchy of (masculine) mind versus (feminine) matter and reverses the Western devaluation of the "passive" role; circumcision is "counter phallic, cutting an image of manhood that is distinctive and contrary to dominant notions of male identity by incorporating desirable qualities associated with women into an ideal of masculinity."[47] In the previous chapter, we examined other examples, both in Judaism and cross-culturally, in which circumcision was related to feminization. Many authors made an opposite conclusion, interpreting the rite as a misogynistic appropriation of feminine bodily functions or an attempt to install a rigid gender hierarchy. Boyarin briefly considers these possibilities for Judaism, arguing that he is not "trying to discredit such an interpretation but rather to suggest an alternate reading, both of which may be functioning in the culture at the same time" (464 n. 64). In response to Eilberg-Schwartz's arguments that ancient Israelite circumcision functioned to exclude women from procreation, Boyarin argues that in the rabbinical context, "[circumcision] may . . . have been understood not as exclusion of the female so much as inclusion of the male in filiation," and that "the persistent reference to the foreskin as a blemish may be understood as a reading of circumcision as an operation that renders men more like women by removing that blemish" (68). In other words, for Boyarin, the feminizing aspects of circumcision do not displace women but, rather, offer an opportunity for men to share in femininity *alongside* women. As we will explore in a moment, I suggest that we hold on to Boyarin's interpretation, however much it may obscure the reality of gender oppression in rabbinical Judaism, because I think it is valid as one side of the ambivalence inherent to circumcision.

To summarize: in Boyarin's exposition of rabbinical Judaism, circumcision becomes, first, the paradigmatic representative of a tradition that values the living corporeal body and its connection to material history and procreation;

---

[46] Boyarin, "Carnal Israel," 495–6.
[47] Silverman, "Anthropology and Circumcision," 425.

and second, it involves a practice of receiving (visually, physically and textually), and submitting to, divine penetration—with all the gendered implications that this phrasing invokes.

Sexuation, Circumcision, and the Judeo-Christian Neighbor

Is this "feminine" rabbinical approach to Judaism outlined by Boyarin strictly in opposition to Badiou's theory of universalism, or is there a possibility for rapprochement between these two thinkers and their respective views on Paul and circumcision? Revisiting our Lacanian approach to sexual difference and circumcision will help to answer this question. Lacan's theorization of "sexuation" in Seminar Twenty has been taken up by post-Lacanian thinkers to understand different forms of social organization.[48] I suggest that Badiou's vision of Pauline universalism can be understood as a proposal for a mode of collectivity that corresponds to Lacan's theorization of feminine sexuation, and a *critique* of the dominant, "masculine" form of social organization, implied in Paul's anti-communitarian critique of Jewish legal observance.[49] At the same time, I propose that Boyarin's embrace of rabbinical Judaism—particularly his emphasis on the feminizing aspects of the circumcision rite—*also* locates, within Jewish collectivity, a feminine alternative to the masculine paradigm, which addresses some of the pitfalls of a Badiousian–Pauline approach without falling into the communitarianism Badiou rightly laments.[50] The opposed conclusions Boyarin and Badiou make about Paul ultimately rest on their different understandings of circumcision as alternately a masculine or feminine act.

In his "formulas of sexuation," Lacan distinguishes between masculine and feminine subjectivity, and modes of enjoyment, in terms of their different relations to the "phallic function," the castrative nature of language. The formulas illustrate the ways that a subject may organize his/her relationship to the symbolic order given the inevitability of castration and, as we will see, the potential social consequences of this.

---

[48] Lacan, *XX*. On the formulas of sexuation, see Copjec, *Read My Desire,* 201-236. On the implications of sexuation for political theory, see especially, McGowan, *Enjoying What We Don't Have*; and Žižek, Santner, and Reinhard, *Neighbor.*

[49] Zupančič makes a similar argument on the relation between Badiou's universalism and Lacan's theory of feminine sexuation, with a different emphasis, in "Perforated Sheet."

[50] Reinhard theorizes a Badiousian–Jewish universalism, also linked to feminine sexuation, in "Universalism."

For masculinity, Lacan offers two propositions: "All 'x's' are submitted to the phallic function," and "There is at least one 'x' that is not submitted to the phallic function."[51] Intended to be read together, the two propositions indicate the contradiction encoded into masculine subjectivity. We can translate the "x" to "man." On the one hand, all men are castrated, barred access to the "outside" of language. On the other hand, men are confronted, at the level of their subjectivization, with the idea of the possibility of an exception to castration, one who is "not submitted to the phallic function." This appears, in masculine fantasy, as that which is tantalizingly forbidden, the possibility of an unlimited jouissance, represented in Freud's myth of the primal father of the horde. What makes one a man is not that one ever becomes this uncastrated Man, but the illusion that one might. As Zupančič writes, for masculinity, "the inaccessibility of [full] enjoyment is the very *mode of enjoyment*."[52]

Femininity involves a different problematic with regard to castration. The two propositions Lacan offers for femininity are: "There is not one 'x' that is not submitted to the phallic function," and "Not-all 'x's' are submitted to the phallic function." The first establishes the universality of castration for women; if there is a woman (an 'x'), she is castrated. However, the second proposition, rather than posing, in positive terms, the possibility of an exception to castration, instead offers the much more ambiguous notion of the "not-all." Although this is a contested area of Lacanian thought, the proposition is convincingly read to mean that femininity does not rely on the posited existence of an uncastrated subject (as masculinity does), but, rather, negates the consolidating power of castration: every single woman is, indeed, castrated, but that's "not all." It is not that there exists an exception to castration, a promised land of phallic completion, from which women are barred. Rather, a feminine subject confronts the lack inherent to language *without* (the promise of) *exception*. If masculine enjoyment is about the possibility of (an always deferred) gratification, feminine enjoyment is about its impossibility. As a consequence, a feminine subject's enjoyment is not fixed to the fantasy of an inaccessible fullness but occurs contingently in the vicissitudes of her singular experience of lack.

Darian Leader offers a clinical example of the differing relations to language between men and women. Stammering, he notes, is a problem

---

[51] These as well as the feminine formulas appear in Lacan, *XX*, in the mathematical shorthand deployed in formal logic, with the addition of Lacan's symbol Φ for the "phallic function" (78). I restrict my discussion to the top portion of Lacan's formulas, as the bottom portion is less relevant for our purposes, and have translated the shorthand into plain English.

[52] Zupančič, "Perforated Sheet," 291 (emphasis original).

typically found in boys and men (including Moses, the great law giver, whose speech impediment is often referred to in the Bible), suggesting a difficulty in assuming one's position as a bearer of language, an anxiety surrounding the castrative experience of uttering the word. Yet "if a boy is paralyzed at the level of the syllable," writes Leader,

> many women complain of not being able to finish not words but sentences. Men often take advantage of this to finish their sentences for them, but to do that is to miss the point. Not to finish a sentence may often indicate a hesitancy to be pinned down by words, to show that one is not equivalent or identical with a particular linguistic representation, to be something more than what one says.[53]

Leader suggests here that femininity functions in closer proximity to the nature of signification itself—that is, its inherent ambiguity. Whereas men struggle with this fact, women take a certain pleasure in it or resist the attempts of men to seal language—and its speakers—off. Here we see a different relation to castration than that inhabited by men. Women, Leader suggests, do not so much tremble before the threat of castration but, rather, may mobilize the possibilities it opens up. This perspective puts a new spin on the so-called "riddle of femininity." Rather than a problem to be solved once and for all, Leader suggests that femininity has a stake in perpetuating the impossibility of a "final solution," in ensuring that something about the feminine subject always remains a riddle.

The formulas of sexuation present a further development of Lacan's theory of the phallus, as examined in the last chapter. Although they clearly emerge from the problematics of Freudian castration—circulating around the question of whether individuals (presume to) have or not have the phallus, with all the complicated penile resonances involved therein— they formalize this problem in ways more conducive to examining social/ discursive structures, allowing us to move from individual men and women to the ways that a society (comprised of both men and women) constitutes and regulates itself in relation to lack.

---

[53] Leader, *Why Do Women Write More Letters*, 131. Leader's interpretation is not as far-fetched as it may sound. The organization Action for Stammering Children writes on their website that a biological "cause" of stammering has yet to be found, and that, while as many girls as boys experience stammering in early childhood, "By the age of ten, the ratio of boys to girls who stammer may be as high as 4 or 5:1" ("When Does It Begin?"). From a psychoanalytic perspective, this may suggest that different post-Oedipal relations to speech are organized by sexual difference.

Lacan's formulas for masculinity, it has been argued, illuminate the libidinal economy of communitarian or nationalistic social bonds. In such situations, members function "as a unified group . . . with the imaginary integrity of mutual love precisely in order to deny the castration that each individual . . . suffers."[54] A positive identity marks one as belonging to others, obscuring the traumatic lack that underwrites the desire for identification. Shared laws, to which all members are bound, constitute the borders of the community; transgression symbolically represents the prohibited "outside."

This denial of castration—formalized in the posited exception to castration—comes to haunt the group, presenting itself as a reminder of "mythical lost plenitude."[55] The community may react by scapegoating those deemed to possess an "excessive, traumatic enjoyment,"[56] projecting their fantasy of forbidden jouissance onto others; alternately, they may feel induced to violate the law in order to access the greater pleasures they presume to lie on the other side. Žižek's work is largely concerned with the ways that postmodern societies mobilize shared transgressions that, far from undermining the social bond, constitute the libidinal basis of communal identification.[57] We are most under the spell of the law not when we obey its prohibitions but when we participate in the carnivalesque "escape valves" to which the police (in whatever form they take) turn a blind eye.

Post-Lacanian thinkers have argued that this masculine logic is homologous to the Nazi political theorist Carl Schmitt's notion of the sovereign.[58] Schmitt held that every political society must be constituted by a rigid distinction between friend and enemy (insider and outsider), as well as a sovereign who both institutes the legal/political order and is

---

54 Reinhard, "Universalism," 50.
55 Reinhard, 50.
56 Reinhard, 50. Freud makes a similar point in *Civilization and its Discontents*: "It is always possible to bind together a considerable number of people in love, so long as there are other people left over to receive the manifestations of their aggressiveness" (113). His cynicism on love leads him to a Boyarinian position on Christian universalism: "In this respect the Jewish people, scattered everywhere, have rendered the most useful services to the civilizations of the countries that have been their hosts; but unfortunately all the massacres of the Jews in the Middle Ages did not suffice to make that period more peaceful and secure for their Christian fellows. When once the Apostle Paul posited universal love between men as the foundation of his Christian community, extreme intolerance on the part of Christendom towards those who remained outside it became the inevitable consequence" (113). A different but no less psychoanalytic theorization of universal love is made possible by Lacan's formulas of sexuation.
57 See Dean's helpful discussion in *Zizek's Politics*, 135–77.
58 See, for example, Reinhard, "Political Theology"; and McGowan, *Enjoying What We Don't Have*, 155–6.

himself exempt from its rules.[59] The sovereign occupies this position of the exception to castration: he simultaneously causes the formation of a closed society and stands outside it. In moments of crisis, Schmitt argued, the sovereign's exceptionality makes itself visible via the declaration of a "state of exception," which invariably involves waging war against one's enemies.[60] Lacan's formula for masculinity, emulated in Schmitt's theory, involves a kind of societal "completion" or "totalization," a phallic political order of "friends," constituted through opposition to its "enemies" and its dependence on the sovereign, the one who is exempted from castration/the law. The imperative to draw boundaries between friend and enemy, and to wage war when these boundaries appear to dissolve, is a form of disavowal against the inherent, traumatic permeability of the social structure itself.

I propose that Badiou's Pauline opposition to communitarianism is implicitly a critique of this masculine form of social bond, which functions to disavow castration (in Badiou's terminology, the void of being) and otherness. Paul's opposition between Greeks and Jews constitutes a Lacanian imaginary rivalry—the "two aspects of the same figure of mastery" in Badiou's terms (42)—locked in a perpetual antagonism in order to deny their shared castration and the porousness of their respective boundaries. Žižek, drawing on Lacan, has sharpened this line of thought by calling attention to the superegoic dynamic outlined in Paul's critique of the law.[61] As Paul states in Romans:

> If it had not been for the law, I would not have known sin. I would not have known what it is to covet if the law had not said, "You shall not covet." But sin, seizing an opportunity in the commandment, produced in me all kinds of covetousness.[62]

Identification with communal law produces the desire to transgress, trapping the subject in a restrictive, guilt-ridden, and unagential mode of enjoyment: "Now if I do what I do not want, it is no longer I that do it, but sin that dwells within me,"[63] says Paul. Circumcision, in Badiousian logic, comes to represent the mark of one's entrapment within this identitarian program. The ritual removal of the foreskin situates man within the discourse of Jewish

---

[59] Schmitt writes: "The specific political distinction to which political actions and motives can be reduced is that between friend and enemy," in *Concept of the Political*, 26; and "The sovereign is he who decides on the exception," in *Political Theology*, 5.

[60] Schmitt, *Political Theology*, 6; and *Concept of the Political*, 32–5.

[61] Žižek, *Ticklish Subject*, 148–51; see also Lacan, *VII*, 80–4. For a comparison of Žižek and Badiou on Paul, see Kotsko, "Politics."

[62] Rom. 7:7-8.

[63] Rom. 7:20.

signs. Far from castrating him, it pacifies the trauma of castration, offering
the Jew a positive identity to assert against the uncircumcised other and the
promise that one's alienation in language can be mitigated by the observance
of Jewish law. A pound of flesh becomes a relatively small price to pay.

By contrast, Boyarin appears to read Paul as an *exemplar* of totalizing
masculine logic, evidenced in his statement, "Paul was motivated by a
Hellenistic desire for the One." Paul, according to Boyarin, preaches an
allegorical approach to the Torah that attempts to overcome or transcend the
material signifier, the markers of one's "fleshly" incompletion.[64] His Platonic
gesture, as Boyarin sees it, involves rejecting all those Jewish practices
that place emphasis on castrated, embodied experience, and exhorting his
followers to embrace, instead, these practices' "spiritual signified." Baptism
replaces circumcision because it represents spirituality without the flesh,
divinity before the *cut*. Paul's vision of society, which now encompasses
Jew and Gentile, has Schmittian consequences: first, cultural/ethnic/sexual
difference will be subsumed under a positive unifying logos, negating
specificity and history. Second, those who refuse to take on this new principle,
who fail to embrace the supersession of the flesh (by continuing to practice
circumcision, among other things), will become the hated enemies of the
Christian order of friends. Paul does not expressly wish these consequences,
but their take-up in post-Pauline Christianity is inevitable because of the
(masculine, Schmittian) logic he develops and deploys.

Lacan's feminine formulas, on the other hand, offer a different way of
thinking the social. A collectivity that corresponds to the feminine axis
of sexuation cannot be organized around the fantasy of completion, denial
of castration, and identitarian enmities these generate. Rather than the
problem of *having* (an identity, gratification, wholeness) and the barriers to
it that the masculine social order is preoccupied with, feminine collectivity is
paradoxically constituted along the universal fact of *not having*. Consequently,
there is no fantasied outside to "glue" together this type of social bond:

> Rather than viewing the social order in terms of friend and enemy, inside
> and outside, or rule and exception, the logic of [feminine structure]

---

[64] It is interesting to note the correspondences between allegory, masculine sexuality, and
metaphor. Freud argued that masculine sexuality abides by the principle of substitution:
the prohibited mother is replaced with a mother-substitute. In feminine sexuality, on
the other hand, Freud thought that a woman need not repress her libidinal attachments
to her father, and consequently her choice of partner could more obviously resemble
him. Lacan's linguistic reading of Freud suggests that (masculine) psychic substitution
is a metaphoric process—one signifier replaces another—unlike metonymy, where the
connections between signifiers are less severed. Allegory operates primarily along a
metaphoric axis, and therefore, in a Lacanian sense, a masculine one—corresponding to
the Lacanian reading of Boyarin I offer here.

posits that there are only enemies, only outsiders, and only exceptions. According to this idea . . . we can't erect a firm distinction between inside and outside because those inside—friends—are defined solely in terms of what they don't have, and this renders them indistinct from those outside—enemies.[65]

Badiou's interpretation of Paul imagines him, I believe, as an advocate of such a collective. What hold together a universalist collective, in Badiou's thought, are not any shared positive properties (laws, ritual markings, philosophical positions) but a commitment to the name of a void—a "not having"—that traverses a given situation, something that renders "indifferent" the common differences that mark inside and outside, friend and enemy. As we saw earlier, Paul's notion of "Christ crucified" unified his followers *not* because of anything positive that it offered, but because it was "a stumbling-block to Jews and foolishness to Gentiles"; it stood for a lack that neither side was able to avow.

McGowan argues that this is the only authentic form of universalism. The universal "is not a quality that multiple particulars possess in common. The universal is what particulars share not having. The shared absence of the universal rather than the shared possession of it bonds particulars together."[66] The subsumption of particular individuals into a supposedly "universal" totality will invariably exclude "at least one"—making it, in the final analysis, a form of particularism. "Lacan shows that the only possible universality is that of the not-all. The universality of the all is faked, just like masculine potency."[67]

However, though Boyarin conceives of rabbinical Judaism as *opposed* to the Pauline collective, I propose that his theorization *also* speaks to the universalism of the "not-all," made evident in his discussion of circumcision. In Boyarin's version, the ritual is less about "branding" the Jew in opposition to the Gentile than it is a matter of performatively embodying one's constitutive relation to otherness or "not having." Circumcision becomes itself an act of Badiousian "subtraction," the opening of a void within the organic body. An intimate part of the self is marked by a lack, subjected to an originary wound imposed by the Other. Whereas the typical masculine strategy is to disavow or try to fill in this void, in Boyarin's reading of circumcision it becomes the ineradicable origin-point of the (Jewish) self, linking man to a divinity beyond him. That the rabbinical approach to the rite invokes symbolic signifiers of femininity—menstrual blood, sexual receptiveness, and so

[65] McGowan, *Enjoying What We Don't Have*, 159.
[66] McGowan, *Universality and Identity Politics*, 23–4.
[67] McGowan, 245 n. 10.

on—suggests, in Boyarinian/Lacanian logic, an attunement to this feminine relation to castration, releasing the logic of feminine subjectivity from an exclusively anatomical referent.

Boyarin's remarks on the Jewish diaspora underscore this universalistic dimension to Jewish collectivity:

> Diaspora cultural identity teaches us that cultures are not preserved by being protected from "mixing" but probably can only continue to exist as a product of such mixing. All cultures, and identities, are constantly being remade. Diaspora Jewish culture, however, lays this process bare, because of the impossibility of a natural association between this people and a particular land, thus the impossibility of seeing Jewish culture as a self-enclosed, bounded phenomenon. (243)

The rabbinical Jewish culture that took shape after the rise of Christianity (and crucially, before the emergence of the Israeli state), when Jews no longer asserted collective control over a physical territory, while wedded to particular forms of self-representation, nevertheless became profoundly permeable to the "neighbor." As McGowan explains, modern anti-Semitism is not a universalism directed against the particularity of the Jewish "race," but more fundamentally an ideology of racial particularism directed against this universalist dimension of Jewishness: "According to the fantasy proffered by key Nazi figures, Jews have no distinct racial identity of their own but are parasitical on other races. For them, Jewishness is not a race but a nonrace, which gives it its universalist hue."[68] This must be distinguished from older forms of Christian anti-Semitism, argues McGowan, which treated Jewishness as a particularist refusal of Christian universalism.[69]

Referring to the Hebrew Bible's injunction in Leviticus, Paul says to his followers, "the whole law is summed up in a single commandment, 'You shall love your neighbor as yourself.'"[70] In a famous passage of the Talmud, the Rabbi Hillel offers a similar interpretation of the commandment to an aspiring convert, but with a Jewish twist: "That is the whole Torah; the rest is just commentary. Now go and study it."[71] Here, the universalist injunction "love thy neighbor" is accepted as the core of Jewish law, but it is not enough to simply be told so: it must be grounded in study and practice. The stance

---

[68] McGowan, 95.
[69] In Chapter 4, we will explore how Otto Weininger's anti-Semitic work made explicit these fantasmatic links between Jewishness, femininity, and nonidentity.
[70] Gal. 5:14.
[71] B.T. Shabbat 31a.

toward the Torah advocated here is neither the masculine fantasy of eventual gratification tied to superegoic legal observance nor a communitarianism predicated on the shoring up of identity (stances that Paul and Badiou vehemently critique). Rather, study of the Torah is presented as *the particular means through which a Jew is able to participate in the universalism of neighbor-love*. If the rabbis were wary of Christianity's anti-Jewish logocentrism, they responded not by entrenching identitarian difference but by generating a sophisticated Jewish subjectivity foundationally related to otherness. (Again, this is to put to one side the various forms of exclusion that developed within rabbinical Judaism, which could be seen as "masculinist" betrayals of neighborliness brought on by the inherent difficulty of such a project.) As Julia Reinhard Lupton put it, circumcision "is a question not of choosing the world or the nation, but of opening up to the world precisely by obeying the ritual laws distinguishing the nation."[72]

Boyarin's own account of this process lacks a theorization of its universalist dimension. The final chapter of his book, "Answering the Mail: Towards a Radical Jewishness," contains an anemic defense of cultural pluralism, understood as an antidote simultaneously to the erasures enacted by Platonic idealism as well as the racism perpetuated by ethnic exclusivism. His vision of "A Diasporized (Multicultural) Israel" ultimately rests on an all-embracing Whole: the multicultural, politically correct Nation, able to subsume the foreskinned and foreskinless alike. Convinced that universalism can only mean the coercive production of sameness in the service of a particular ideology presented as "universal," Boyarin winds up endorsing a sanitized version of the very thing he critiques: a "universalist" ideology of humanity, or tolerance. As the masculine formulas of sexuation—and Boyarin's own critique of universalism—make clear, this "universal" will always exclude at least one.

Badiou offers a more robust theory of universalism, which does not involve the idealization of a particular term, but a moment of subtraction from all the terms that circulate in a given situation, leading to the invention of something new and open to all. Within this theorization, the possibility for such a subtraction, for an encounter with the void, is the constitutive condition of universality. Boyarin's analysis of the circumcision rite can therefore be understood, in Badiousian logic, as a ritualized demonstration of the foundational place of universality within Jewish subjectivity.

One may question whether Badiou's exposition of universalism via Paul achieves its purported aims or merely sneaks a totalitarian anti-difference

[72] Lupton, "Ethnos," 196.

ideology through the backdoor. The two authors' respective interpretations of Paul present us both options. For Badiou, Paul opened a previously unforeseen mode of thought and a radically inclusive form of belonging; for Boyarin, this universality was predicated on the suppression of Jewish difference and the body.

Regardless of the accuracy of his interpretation, Badiou's gloss on the saint seems to more closely represent Paul's experience. For Boyarin, Paul is basically a smart political philosopher, who manipulates the theoretical tools at his disposal to craft a universalist ideology applicable to his surroundings. "Paul was a Jew who read the Torah in a particular way, a way prepared for him by his culture and the perceived requirements of his time," writes Boyarin. "The culture was the culture of allegory, and the requirement was to produce Judaism as a universalizable religion."[73] Badiou, on the other hand, understands Paul as the subject of a transformative event, who did not rationally and self-consciously manipulate his discourse, but was overcome by an irrepressible, paradigm-shattering truth; his experience forced him to reject the various modalities of thought (which would include Jewish Platonism) that dominated his situation.

Any reader of Paul cannot help but notice something in him that exceeds intellectual prowess: his uncompromising stance, his sudden abandonment of his former life to take up that of an itinerant preacher, his willingness to risk persecution and death from his own kinsmen, not to mention his immense staying power among believers centuries later. Furthermore, Paul himself tells us that he was suddenly overcome by a vision of God that transformed his relation to the world; he preached the gospel not to share his philosophical "wisdom" (a term he explicitly rejects), but because he simply could not contain the glory of revelation. This is the stuff of religious experience, and the Badiousian phrase "fidelity to an event" feels intuitively more applicable than, say, "ancient cultural critic." Christianity domesticated Paul, argues Badiou, turning him into a revised vector of Greek anti-Judaism, precisely *because* it incorporated him into the extant ideology. To integrate Paul into intellectual history, as Boyarin may be accused of doing, is to lose the sui generis rupture that his discourse effects.

Yet, the question remains whether Badiou's Pauline "indifference" to Judaism, and narrow reading of the circumcision rite, is symptomatic of a failure to engage with the role of embodied representation, and history, in a universalist cause. Badiou claims that his universalism does not avow the destruction of particularity but openly relies on difference to "verify" itself.

[73] Boyarin, "Carnal Israel," 503, n. 83.

He writes, "Only by recognizing in differences their capacity for carrying the universal that comes upon them can the universal itself verify its own reality" (106). Yet, he seems to contradict this when he fails to recognize any place for the particular, historical origins of Paul's movement: "In [Paul's] eyes," he writes approvingly, "the event renders prior markings obsolete, and the new universality bears no privileged relation to the Jewish community" (23). As Hallward asks, "What kind of despecification does [Badiou's universalism] involve?"[74] In this regard, Boyarin's development of the feminine rabbinical "alternative" vis-à-vis circumcision can be seen, contrary to his own exposition, as not exactly *opposed* to Badiou/Paul so much as a dialectical advancement, addressing the universalist collective's necessary grounding in the particularity of subjective life.[75]

It is an interesting contradiction that the feminine structure we have identified in Badiou emerges from Paul, a man, and that it emerges in Boyarin's Judaism through circumcision, a rite that exclusively concerns men. On the one hand, this contradiction can be understood as "queering" the relationship between anatomical sex and sexual difference. On the other, it may simply reiterate the exclusion of women from the social, consigning the feminine to a shadow that can achieve the fullness of representation only in a male register.

As we saw in the previous chapter, circumcision can be understood to embody both a masculine defensive response to phallic lack/dispossession, and a feminine demonstration of the fundamentally illusory nature of the phallus itself. Boyarin's reading of circumcision develops this latter option, while Badiou (via Paul) implicitly adheres to the former reading. The difficulty in deciding which reading of circumcision is correct corresponds to the constitutive ambivalence or tension within circumcision itself. In a sense, both Boyarin and Badiou mobilize the figure of circumcision to explore the social consequences, possibilities, and contradictions inherent to sexual difference as such.

---

[74] Hallward, *Badiou*, 28.
[75] This may offer a different way of considering the Jewish antecedents of Marxism (as the universalist, materialist political movement par excellence).

3

The Circumcision Cure

Circumcision's Nineteenth-Century Medicalization

East London, 1865. The previously rogue discipline of surgery is now experiencing tremendous growth and newfound authority, thanks in part to the efforts of Mr. Jonathan Hutchinson, a prolific English surgeon with a knack for building and strengthening medical institutions. Hutchinson has just helped to organize the publication of the second volume of the *Clinical Lectures and Reports of the London Hospital*, which contains early forms of the contemporary medical journal article. Esteemed colleagues, such as Hughlings Jackson,[1] an English neurologist of equal stature to Jean-Martin Charcot,[2] have contributed articles, bestowing prestige on the London Hospital and helping to bridge the long-standing divide between doctors and surgeons.[3]

One paper in particular commands our attention: "Circumcision as a Remedial Measure in Certain Cases of Epilepsy, Chorea, &c," by Nathaniel Heckford. In addition to his surgical work at the London Hospital, Heckford had founded the East London Hospital for Children, considered a "Small Star

[1] Jackson (1835–1911) is best known for his pioneering research on epilepsy. His work included uniquely detailed case studies of unusual motor disorders, earning him continued esteem for his clinical observation and descriptive skills. He was also interested in philosophy, and developed theories about the organization of the human mind and its capacity for "regression" to primitive states that influenced thinkers such as Freud. See Critchley and Critchley, *Jackson*. On Jackson's influence on Freud, see Sulloway, *Freud*, 270–5. The complicated relationship between "physicalist" theories of nervous disorder offered by thinkers like Jackson, and psychoanalytic theories, is one of the preoccupations of this and the next chapter.

[2] Charcot (1825–93) is also known as "the father of neurology." His use of hypnosis to study and treat hysteria had a major influence on Freud, who named his first son after him. There exists a wide body of feminist scholarship on the history of hysteria, particularly as it relates to Charcot's demonstrations of hysterical women at the Salpêtrière hospital. See, for example, Didi-Huberman, *Invention of Hysteria*.

[3] I thank Jonathan Evans, archivist at the Royal London Hospital, for explaining the historical significance of this text to me and pointing me to a number of additional valuable materials while I was conducting the research for this chapter.

in the East" by Charles Dickens for its free treatment of the youngest of the East End's impoverished residents.[4]

Heckford opens with a clarification of the euphemism in the title of his paper: "It is evident that by 'certain cases' I refer to those in which masturbation is the supposed cause. I think we may safely assume that this vice is a frequent agent in the causation of the above-named and allied maladies." To illustrate this, he introduces the notes of a case from Hughlings Jackson, his colleague. Jackson was treating a woman for epilepsy, and the patient "took the opportunity of asking [his] advice about her child," a "delicate" fifteen-month-old boy who kept his legs in a "peculiar position": "The right leg was almost always placed . . . high up over the other, and he kept moving it in a sawing way towards the pelvis. The penis was in the way of friction, and was quite stiff when I examined it." In addition to the child's distressing behavior, the mother explained to Jackson that he was "frequently crying, so much so that her neighbors fancied she was beating him."[5]

Jackson identified "congenital phymosis" in the boy and asked Jonathan Hutchinson to circumcise him. After the operation, the boy stopped the "peculiar" motion and was apparently "improved very much in health," although Jackson notes he did not follow up to see if the cure was permanent.[6]

"The inferences to be drawn from the above statement of facts are, I think, obvious," writes Heckford.[7] To the contemporary reader, the inferences Heckford drew may not seem so obvious. For, Heckford did not think that Jackson merely relieved some local pain from a tight foreskin that was making the boy cry and rub his penis. Rather, he engaged with a complex theory of the nervous system, in which masturbation and genital "irritation" were held to generate massive physiological disturbances that could manifest in epilepsy and other serious disorders.

Heckford illuminates the kind of inferences he drew from Jackson in his following case study, a patient of his own. He describes an eight-year-old boy, "of fair complexion, blue eyes, light hair, and delicate appearance," who suffered severe "spasmodic movements . . . he was unable to feed himself or walk without help, and his speech was also much affected." After an unsuccessful treatment consisting of "bark and arsenic," Heckford reexamined him:

> The mother now drew attention to some "swelling on the groins." On examination I found . . . a congenital phymosis, the prepuce being

[4] Dickens, *Uncommercial Traveller*; see also Granshaw and Porter, *The Hospital in History*.
[5] Heckford, "Circumcision," 58–9.
[6] Heckford, 59.
[7] Heckford, 59.

considerably thickened by the constant irritation of retained secretions. She said that he was constantly "pulling his privates about," and that she frequently punished him for the habit. The penis at these times was always in a state of erection. This state of things by itself required operative interference, but it appeared to me that the chorea [movement disorder] was probably in a great measure due to the same cause. I therefore circumcised him on December 22nd . . . and at the same time ordered all medicine to be discontinued.[8]

Immediately, the boy's spasms reduced. "Eight months afterwards," Heckford writes, "there had been no return of chorea, his health had greatly improved, and he had been completely cured of his former bad habit. His mental condition also progressed to a corresponding degree; instead of being dull and spiritless, he had become sharp, intelligent, and boisterous."[9] Heckford's paper details four other cases where circumcision appeared to heal his young patients' fits and improve their overall constitution with varying degrees of success.

A number of interesting themes emerge from this summary of a nineteenth-century medical paper on circumcision—replete with some of the founding figures of modern medicine—that reach far beyond the question of scientific accuracy. The fear of infantile erotism is palpable; the sight of a child's penis in a "state of erection" appears at least as distressing to the physician and worried parent as any recognizable disease ("This state of things by itself required operative interference"). The problem of sexual difference manifests, with the implication that these "fair" and "delicate" boys may be insufficiently masculine, or that their apparent innocence may hide a more sinister character. The proper parenting of children is called into question ("her neighbors fancied she was beating him"). Problems of speech—"much affected" in Heckford's aforementioned case—are referred to, though unelaborated. Finally, the reader may detect echoes of the better-known nineteenth-century medical interest in hysterical women, whose seemingly intractable symptoms, sometimes also treated with genital interventions, eventually led to the birth of the "talking cure."

So far, we have brought psychoanalytic theories of castration and sexual difference to bear on ritual and religious circumcision practices. Over the course of the next two chapters, we will draw on these theories to illuminate the unusual early history of *medical* circumcision. Here, we will first examine how circumcision became established as a curative medical procedure,

---

[8]   Heckford, 60–1.
[9]   Heckford, 61.

interrogating the complex theory of the nerves used to justify it. Then, we will read closely the work of nineteenth-century circumcision proponents, interrogating how their writing addresses anxieties surrounding race, sex, and gender bound up in this moment as a particular response to the fundamental quandary of sexuality.

The "circumcision doctors," as I will refer to them, transformed circumcision from a Jewish ritual into a medical procedure in an attempt to gain phallic mastery over the threat of castration.[10] Their work is attested to in the dozens of papers they published in British and American medical journals, which I have examined.[11] Their writing is marked by a particular, anxious investment in the sexual innocence of the child. In her study of children's literature, Jacqueline Rose emphasizes how the notion of childhood innocence functions "not as a property of childhood but as a portion of adult desire":

> The child can be used to hold off a panic, a threat to our assumption that language is something which can simply be organised and cohered, and that sexuality, while it cannot be removed, will eventually take on the forms in which we prefer to recognise and acknowledge each other.[12]

By localizing sexuality to a piece of the genitals that could be excised, the circumcision doctors hoped to eliminate its threat through precise surgical intervention. Yet, their attempt at phallic mastery regularly called forth the shadow of its opposite.

Lewis Sayre

As far as the medical archive attests, Heckford's circumcision paper did not attract much attention, perhaps because he himself "confessed" that, in the other circumcision treatments he documented, "the results are not

---

[10] Some of these circumcision advocates were, in fact, surgeons, rather than doctors; in the nineteenth-century the two professions were separate (see Loudon, "Surgeons"). Although the doctor-surgeon divide is an important aspect of the history of medicine, it is not particularly relevant for this chapter.

[11] These texts were located primarily in the British Library, the Royal London Hospital archives, the Wellcome Library, and online (in digitized versions hosted by various institutions and university libraries). Some were published in medical journals that still exist, such as *The Lancet*, others in smaller, often regional journals that eventually ceased publication. The recent historical monographs on circumcision I discussed in Chapter 1 also explore many of these texts; however, they do not bring psychoanalysis to bear on them.

[12] Rose, *Peter Pan*, xii and 10.

very startling."[13] Yet, five years later, in 1870, the American surgeon Lewis Sayre published a strikingly similar but more optimistic paper, "Partial Paralysis from Reflex Irritation, Caused by Congenital Phimosis and Adherent Prepuce."

Sayre opens his paper by quoting a letter he received from the surgeon J. Marion Sims. Some readers will recognize Sims as the so-called "father of modern gynecology," notorious for having conducted experimental operations on enslaved African American women (we will return to this subject):

> Dear Sayre: Please let me know at what hour you can come to my house to see the son of Mr. M–, of Milwaukee. The little fellow has a pair of legs that you would walk miles to see. Yours truly, J Marion Sims.[14]

Sayre rushed to Sims's office and discovered "a most beautiful little boy of five years of age, but exceedingly white and delicate in appearance, unable to walk without assistance or stand erect." He first tried a treatment for paralysis standard at the time, applying electric currents to the affected limbs. While passing the electrodes over his body, the boy's nurse suddenly exclaimed, "Oh doctor! Be very careful—don't touch his pee pee—it's very sore." The physician was shocked to discover the boy's penis in a state of "extreme erection":

> The body of the penis was well developed, but the glans was very small and pointed, tightly imprisoned in the contracted foreskin, and in its efforts to escape, the meatus urinarius had become . . . puffed out and red . . . ; upon touching the orifice of the urethra he was slightly convulsed, and had a regular orgasm. This was repeated a number of times, and always with the same result.[15]

Sayre was so confident that the "irritation" caused by the tight foreskin was the source of the boy's paralysis that he immediately arranged to circumcise the boy in front of an audience of medical students. (We might again think here of Charcot's famous demonstrations of hysterical theater at the Salpêtrière.) As with Heckford's first case, there was a miraculous recovery:

> From the very day of the operation, the child began to improve in his general health; slept quietly at night, improved in his appetite, and, although confined to the house all the time, yet at the end of three weeks

[13] Heckford, "Circumcision," 63.
[14] Sayre, "Partial Paralysis from Reflex Irritation," 205.
[15] Sayre, 206.

he had recovered quite a rosy color in his cheeks, and was able to extend his limbs perfectly straight while lying upon his back. . . . He left for his home in the west about the first of April, entirely recovered; having used no remedy, either iron, electricity, or other means to restore his want of power, but simply quieting his nervous system by relieving the imprisoned glans penis as above described.[16]

Again like Heckford, Sayre tried the procedure on other boys suffering similar symptoms, this time, however, with consistently impressive success.

It does not seem that Sayre ever read Heckford's paper.[17] If we are to rely on Sayre's account, he stumbled independently upon the idea to circumcise (though based on a shared conceptualization of the body which we must examine). Sayre eventually became famous on both sides of the Atlantic, primarily for his innovative work in orthopedics. He was a tireless medical organizer, reformer, and sanitation advocate and held a number of prestigious professional positions, including president of the American Medical Association.[18] Though circumcision was not the cause of his celebrity, he continued to practice the treatment and publicized his cases widely (including in the opening sections of his *Lectures on Orthopedic Surgery and Diseases of the Joints*, which became a standard medical reference). Given his prestige, he was taken seriously, if sometimes challenged by colleagues. References to and discussions surrounding "the kind of cases Dr. Sayre cures"[19] abound in the Anglo-American medical literature of the time. One doctor wrote that "as soon as the frequency and gravity" of Sayre's cases "come to be fully understood," his circumcision discoveries "will rank among the most important in the whole range of surgical science."[20] We owe the medicalization and routinization of circumcision in no small degree to his work.[21]

There are dozens of papers discussing Sayre's circumcision cure, by both supporters and detractors, published in prominent nineteenth-century British

---

[16] Sayre, 207.
[17] The medical literature of the time surrounding Sayre's work occasionally discusses the origin of this circumcision cure. In 1872, Richard Barwell published "Infantile Paralysis" in the *Lancet* with many similar conclusions to Sayre (and Heckford). He later discovered Sayre's work and wrote to him, "acknowledging [Sayre's] priority of observation and description, but fully confirming the views expressed" (Sayre, "Spinal Anaemia," 256). Earlier physicians who theorized connections between nervous disorders and the genitals are also mentioned in the literature, but Heckford never again appears in this connection.
[18] See Zampini and Sherk, "Sayre."
[19] Quoted in Sayre, "Paralysis from Peripheral Irritation," 306.
[20] Quoted in Sayre, "Spinal Anaemia," 274.
[21] On "medicalization" as a sociological phenomenon, see Conrad, "Medicalization and Social Control."

and American medical journals and books. Many of these papers include additional case studies written by medical practitioners who emulated Sayre's technique. Proponents argued that circumcision led to miraculous recoveries from a laundry list of symptoms, from paralysis and seizures to vaguer problems like malaise, clumsiness, poor digestion, and bedwetting. In all of these papers, there features the distinctive nineteenth-century style in which the subject of sexuality is both taboo and extremely charged, seeming to ooze out of every word in the kind of pornographic moralism often mocked today when discussing "the Victorians." Stephen Marcus argues that this particular style of scientific writing "shares . . . in common with pornography itself":

> a mass of unarmed, unexamined and largely unconscious assumptions; its logical proceedings are loose and associative rather than rigorous and sequential; and one of its chief impulses is to confirm what is already held as belief rather than to adapt belief to new and probably disturbing knowledge.[22]

In the decades that followed, justifications for circumcision shifted from an emphasis on curing nervous disorders to promoting hygiene and sanitation, influenced by the development of germ theory and particularly the discovery of penicillin.[23] Smegma, the mucus sometimes found inside the foreskin, was thought to harbor dangerous germs, and therefore a circumcised penis was believed to be "cleaner" and less likely to make one ill than an uncircumcised one.[24] Today, proponents argue (using more rigorous but no less culturally freighted medical science) that circumcision is preventative of various STDs, penile cancer, and urinary tract infections, as discussed in the book's introduction. Although these later justifications for circumcision are also worthy of analysis, here I wish to put the magnifying glass on this earlier and more neglected period surrounding Lewis Sayre's cure. This is because in these nineteenth-century papers—prior to the advent of germ

---

[22] Marcus, *The Other Victorians*. Foucault mockingly refers to Marcus's book in the first chapter of *History of Sexuality, Vol. 1*, entitled "We 'Other Victorians.'" He implies Marcus has fallen prey to the repressive hypothesis, the naive presumption that power seeks to repress sexuality rather than proliferating it for disciplinary purposes (4). In my own reading, Foucault's argument is a straw man: Marcus is not concerned with the "repression" of sexuality but, rather, with documenting the logical operations of fantasy in both the professional "non-pornographic" texts and the explicit pornography of the Victorian era.

[23] See Gollaher, *Circumcision*, 82–92. On germ theory, see Worboys, *Spreading Germs*. On why medical circumcision persists in the United States but has declined in the United Kingdom, see Carpenter, "On Remedicalisation."

[24] Gollaher, *Circumcision*, 82–92.

theory and modern, statistical medicine—the phantasmagoria surrounding circumcision and sexuality are particularly manifest, allowing us to better appreciate fantasmatic dimensions of circumcision in general.

Reflex Theory: Sex and Sexual Difference

How did Heckford and Sayre, apparently unacquainted, come to such similar conclusions about the relationship between the genitals and paralysis/epilepsy? The key lies in a once popular but now forgotten medical paradigm known as "reflex theory," and its associated diagnosis, the "reflex neurosis," which justified and underlay their findings. As the medical historian Edward Shorter explains, reflex theory's central proposition was that "nervous connections running via the spine regulated all bodily organs, including the brain, quite independently of human will."[25] An "irritation" in one part of the body, it was believed, could generate physiological disturbances in another part of the body, serving as an explanation for mysterious and otherwise undiagnosable ailments. As one critic of Sayre put it at the time, a reflex symptom is "dependent upon irritation of some peripheral nerve, either of the internal or external tissues, which is attended by no structural alterations of the nervous centres visible to the microscope, and which is relieved by the removal of the irritation."[26] The theory thus enabled doctors to render mysterious symptoms into reassuringly "organic" ailments responsive to physical intervention. Sayre and his followers argued that the foreskin was particularly prone to irritation, and that such irritation would induce a varying array of physical and behavioral problems that often appeared sexual in nature. In so doing, they followed a well-worn path of treating threatening manifestations of sexuality as if they were discrete (and potentially eliminable) physical disorders. As Steven Marcus observes, Victorian sexual medical theory is a form of "fantasy physiology" that "expresses to the full the unconscious psychology that created it."[27] Here, I will sketch out a history of reflex theory and its concerns to see how it was eventually taken up by the circumcision doctors.

Although fastened on to by the circumcision doctors, reflex theory was initially developed primarily as a way to account for, and intervene in, the "nervous" troubles of women, part of the replacement of the earlier "humoral" paradigm in medicine. Illnesses such as hysteria, which were formerly understood as disturbances of the humors, were now considered "nervous

[25] Shorter, *From Paralysis to Fatigue*, 40.
[26] Gray, *Genital Irritation*, 2.
[27] Marcus, *The Other Victorians*, 23.

disorders" or "neuroses" (from the Latin root, "of the nerves").[28] It was thus intensely bound up in nineteenth-century views on women and sexual difference. The theory lasted between approximately the 1820s and the end of the nineteenth-century, when its ideas would be discredited by advances in the study of germs as well as alternative approaches to the treatment of hysteria (such as psychoanalysis). By the mid-nineteenth-century, the theory was on the decline in the European Continent, its early proponents gradually abandoning the core ideas and associated treatments; in the States, however, doctors like Sayre breathed new life into it, appropriating its language (and shifting its patients) to justify the circumcision cure.[29]

Shorter argues that many of the illnesses that reflex theory sought to cure were those which we would now understand as psychosomatic. Although these illnesses were sometimes labeled "hysterical," reflex theory posited a somatic etiology for the hysteria (an "irritation" or "reflex neurosis"), in keeping with the popular medical belief that discrete anatomical pathologies, visible or invisible "lesions," could explain all forms of illness.[30]

"Spinal irritation" was the first diagnosis generated, in the 1820s, from this way of thinking. Proponents of this diagnostic category believed that various paralyzes and other dysfunctions might be caused by irritation of the nerves in the spine. The sufferers of "spinal irritation" were almost exclusively young women who were thought to exhibit widespread "irritability." Later in the century, the theory expanded from its focus on the spine; now, irritation in any organ of the body could affect any other organ, including the brain. "It was this simple logic," writes Shorter, "that gave reflex theory its breathtaking capacity to inspire meddlesomeness among doctors."[31]

The ovaries, rather than the spine, became a main locus of irritation, the "neural node affecting innumerable aspects of female physiology," as medical historian Chandak Sengoopta explains.[32] Held responsible for all

---

[28] On the shift, from the late-seventeenth-century onward, to nervous-based theories of hysteria, see Aranuad, *On Hysteria*, chp. 1; and Scull, *Hysteria*, chp. 1. On the relation between nerves and subjectivity within nineteenth-century literary and scientific discourse, see Salisbury and Shail, *Neurology and Modernity*.

[29] Unfortunately, there exists no definitive study of the history of reflex theory. Scholarship that references the topic tends to focus on its application to women and the surgeries on the female genitals it justified, without significantly analyzing the theory itself. See, for example, Moscucci, *The Science of Woman*, 104–5; and Rodriguez, *Female Circumcision*, 21. A broader examination of reflex theory occurs in Shorter's *From Paralysis to Fatigue*, chps. 2–3; see also Sengoopta, *Most Secret Quintessence*, chp. 1. The subject also emerges in discussions of Wilhelm Fliess's "nasal reflex neurosis" and Freud's relationship to Fliess, which we will examine in the subsequent chapter. See, for example, Sulloway, *Freud*, 147–50.

[30] See Davidson, *Emergence of Sexuality*, chp. 1.

[31] Shorter, *From Paralysis to Fatigue*, 40.

[32] Sengoopta, *Most Secret Quintessence*, 3.

the complicated work involved in producing and regulating "femininity," the ovaries were thought to be especially prone to generating internal irritation—to *irritating themselves*, as it were, with consequences for the rest of the body. (We might read this as a nerve-centered revision of the "floating womb" responsible for hysteria.) Ovarian irritation, in this model, was not about external stimuli impinging on the body (caused by a railway accident, for example), but about an *internal disequilibrium*, a "design flaw" in the seat of the female sex that rendered women especially delicate and illness-prone—linking to older humoral conceptions of disease as imbalance.

Doctors inspired by reflex theory fastened on to correlations between the (mal)functioning of the female genitals and the appearance of nervous illness to make their case. For example, they argued that hysterical women's symptoms worsened during menstruation and pregnancy, and that the surgical removal of cysts from the female genitals often led to improvements in overall constitution and the lessening of nervous troubles.

Thus, reflex theory, the theoretical origins of the circumcision cure, was closely related to the problem of sexual difference as manifested in nineteenth-century views on men and women, superimposing this difference onto a mind/body dualism. "Masculinity, most nineteenth-century thinkers and medical experts would have agreed, was only partly biological, femininity almost wholly so," explains Sengoopta.[33] Men possessed the transcendent qualities of intellect and rationality, and these functions suffered disruptions from the body only in contingent cases of illness. Women, on the other hand, were constantly subject to the capricious whims of their reproductive organs. Thought to perform so much complicated and precarious biological labor in the female organism, the ovaries diminished women's capacity to transcend their bodies and fully inhabit the field of will and rationality. To put it in psychoanalytic terms, symbolic castration was treated as a matter of one's subjection to the body: men had the capacity to avoid castration and possess willful, phallic self-mastery, whereas women were permanently confined to castration due to their excessive immersion in the flesh.

From Ovaries to Foreskins

Most of the original physicians who constructed the doctrine of reflex theory offered mild, nonsurgical recommendations for the treatment of reflex neuroses. For example, Moritz Romberg, who argued in 1853 that hysteria

---

[33] Sengoopta, 29.

was "a reflex-neurosis dependent upon sexual [i.e., genital] irritation," reported a cure using "injections of an infusion of rue . . . into the vagina, hip-baths, with an addition of the mineral waters of Franzensbrunn."[34] However, statements such as the following make it easy to see how their theories opened the door for more drastic surgical interventions: "The principle upon which our treatment must be based, is the removal of the main condition of the disease, the exalted state of the reflex functions."[35]

Not unlike the strange coincidence with Heckford and Sayre, in the summer of 1872, the first recorded "ovariectomies" for the cure of reflex neuroses occurred both in Germany and the United States, by surgeons who had not exchanged their work with one another. Eventually nicknamed "Battey's operation," after the American surgeon who performed it and understood medically as female "castration," the procedure enjoyed considerable popularity in the newly fashioned discipline of gynecology, and was widely discussed in medical journals throughout the Western world. Particularly notable was that the operation was performed on women *without visible signs of genital disorders*. Apparently healthy genitals were thought to disguise underlying irritations that were the source of nervous troubles. One estimate holds that, by 1906, 150,000 women had their "normal" ovaries removed.[36]

Around the same time, the British medical community found themselves in a heated debate over the practice of "clitoridectomy," the surgical extirpation of the clitoris. This was ignited by the English surgeon Isaac Baker Brown's 1866 publication, *Curability of Some Forms of Insanity, Epilepsy, Catalepsy, and Hysteria, in Females*, where he argued that masturbation was the cause of women's nervous diseases and advocated clitoridectomy as a cure.[37] The medical community ultimately found themselves opposed to Baker Brown's cure, and the surgeon was disgraced and stripped of his medical license. In the circumcision papers by Sayre and his followers, Baker Brown occasionally surfaces and sympathetic views toward his practice are sometimes advanced.

For these early reflex theorists, the problems of hysteria and other nervous disorders lay in the functioning of adult, female sex organs, and the surgeries their ideas spawned would target the genitals of grown women. However, the circumcision doctors offered something new. Just as reflex theory was

---

[34] Romberg, *Manual*, 99 and 92.
[35] Romberg, 92.
[36] Cited in Sengoopta, *Most Secret Quintessence*, 16. On "Battey's operation," see also Masson, *A Dark Science*; and Shorter, *From Paralysis to Fatigue*, chp. 4.
[37] See Moscucci, "Clitoridectomy"; Shorter, *From Paralysis to Fatigue*, 66; and Darby, *Surgical Temptation*, chp. 7.

on the decline, they shifted the focus to childhood and infancy and made the *foreskin*, rather than the ovaries, a privileged genital irritant. With this transformation, the question of infantile sexuality, and its relationship to self-mastery, entered the frame.

What Does Circumcision Cure?

Here is a follower of Sayre describing the onset of symptoms experienced by boys with phimosis:

> In children previously brisk and cheerful, there is a striking change of temper, they are now peevish, fretful and discontented. The mental energies fail; the child is inattentive and forgetful at school; and there are disturbances of appetite and of sleep. But in a certain proportion of these cases the evidence exhibited will be of a more serious character. The nervous system will be undermined to such an extent as to result either in chorea, or in some varied forms of reflex or peripheral palsy.[38]

To a contemporary reader, this description seems perplexing. Although we can imagine that a child's experience of penile pain, caused by constrictive foreskin or some other problem, would generate distress that might manifest in unusual physical behaviors, it is hard to understand how phimosis could be held responsible for such wide-ranging health effects. Yet, in the context of reflex theory, this was perfectly reasonable: the intricate interconnectivity of the nerves meant that a "local" problem like phimosis could upset major functions of the body such as motor coordination.

What were these children actually suffering from? Remarkably, not a single case study that I have found on the subject—involving boys as old as fifteen—mentions any verbal complaint from the patient himself, whether about his supposedly irritated penis or anything else. We do see mention of the *loss* of voice, however. Here is the case of a seven-year-old boy described as "truly piteous," from a doctor in Georgia:

> Charlie, a sprightly, intelligent lad up to six weeks since, was taken with general pains and peculiar nervousness; the pain soon localizing itself in knees, ankles and fingers, accompanied . . . with some swelling in these parts. On the third day of attack, could not walk. . . . Upon fourth day he

---

[38] Chapman, "Nervous Affections," 314–15.

lost his faculty of speech. From this date it was evident that his mind was impaired; did not understand when addressed; desisted from all effort to speak, even when spoken to by his parents. . . . When lifted up in bed he would immediately fall back, remaining in a perfectly passive state. At no time of attack was there fever. He was vigilant and restless at night, apparently suffering from pain in fingers and ankles. . . . Appetite poor; could not masticate his food, and swallowed milk and mush, administered by his father, with some difficulty.[39]

The doctor ran a battery of medical tests—although he does not mention any sustained attempt at conversation with Charlie—and did not find anything. Then, he examined the penis, which he discovered "in a state of semi-erection," the glans "tightly encased." "I felt that I had found the key to his symptoms," he writes, "and determined to act upon this hypothesis." He made an incision into the foreskin "to relieve the imprisoned glans" and clean out the inner secretions. The boy, he reports, immediately improved. After follow-up a few months later, the doctor concludes, "It is now clear that the cure is perfect. . . . The idiotic and blank expression of his face has disappeared, and intelligence, with the rosy hue of health, has resumed its place upon the little face of Charlie."[40]

The discovery of the penis "in a state of semi-erection" appears to have provided this puzzled doctor with the thrill of certainty. Via the theory of the reflexes, the doctor linked the boy's mysterious, out-of-control behavior to the presence of the erection. Something unknown—the source of the boy's "peculiar nervousness"—was reassuringly linked to a physiological (and therefore knowable) event. Yet, while an erection can be observed, the cause of an erection is never so clear. Erections depend on subjective experience and fantasy, and to know something about this requires engaging with language, which is never transparent. Erections, in other words, bring us directly into a confrontation with symbolic castration. It does not seem a coincidence, then, that speech is avoided or, in Charlie's case, disappears. To confront the patient's suffering at the level of speech would mean inviting the question of desire, of that which exceeds the doctor's mastery of the body. "Once you recognize language," writes Rose, "then you also have to acknowledge its potential (Freud would say essential) disorder."[41] Rather than doing this, a physical cause for the erection—irritation caused by phimosis—was produced. Through circumcision, the penis was substituted for the phallus:

---

[39] Richardson, "Congential Phimosis," 143.
[40] Richardson, 146.
[41] Rose, *Peter Pan*, 60.

the problem was with the organ, not with its potential psychic implications as manifested in speech.

Another case, by a different doctor, follows a similar pattern:

> Case 6: Is a strange case of over-development of the sexual organs. Boy, aged eight years, rather small for his age, poorly nourished and very nervous.

> . . . At the time of examination the penis was very irritable, erecting at the slightest touch and presenting every appearance of a fully developed organ in the state of very strong erection and large enough for an average boy of fourteen years.

> Under chloroform the organ relaxed and showed the prepuce to be quite redundant. I circumcised, slitting the foreskin well back to make it loose, and cut the frenulum. The result was marked and immediate, the peculiar nervous wiggle left him at once, and the boy has since gained rapidly in general nutrition, and is growing rapidly.[42]

Here again, the presence of a "very strong erection" on a "fully developed organ" both evoked a fear of childhood sexuality and provided the doctor with a physical explanation through which he could disavow the possibility of desire. It is interesting that the doctor understood an "irritable" penis to be one which "erected at the slightest touch." From the doctor's description (and absence of the patient's testimony), we cannot discern whether the patient actually experienced any penile pain; "irritation" appears indistinguishable from pleasure.

These cases suggest that the complicated nature of "reflex theory" as a justification for circumcision—with its extravagant claims about the invisible relations between the nerves—attempted to give a purely physicalist account of that which actually exceeds the physical, reducing sexuality to the observable and manipulable functioning of the genitals. The foreskin symbolically functions here as the site of nontransparency in the patient, its excision akin to removing a veil over medical knowledge of the child. "If we do not know what a child is," writes Rose, "then it becomes impossible to invest in their sweet self-evidence, impossible to use the translucent clarity of childhood to deny the anxieties we have about our psychic, sexual and social being in the world."[43]

[42] Beaty, "Peripheral Irritation," 34–5.
[43] Rose, *Peter Pan*, xvii.

In this context, Charlie's silence may be read as a symptomatic manifestation of the circumcision doctors' own refusal to listen. While we should not attempt retrospective diagnosis (especially without the presence of his words), if we believe the doctor's claim of Charlie's recovery, we can surmise that *something happened* to him in relation to circumcision. There was a "miraculous" alleviation of so many unusual symptoms that exceeded any contemporary account of phimosis or other recognizable disease. Perhaps there was a relief of a painful disfigurement, but might there also have been an additional "symbolic" element? Something that could not be said with words but was spoken through the body, which responded to the knife? Charlie's apparent recovery, in other words, may not have been due to the physical benefits of circumcision on his phimotic penis but may, rather, have been a transferential response to an authoritative figure's intervention into his body. The same dynamics appear at play in the subsequent case of the eight-year-old boy. Through medical circumcision, the obscure play of desire was both enacted and disavowed.

Masturbation and Infantile Sexuality

The circumcision doctors' extension of reflex theory from adult women to young boys, and their promotion of the diagnosis of foreskin-induced genital irritation, occurred within the context of the sudden and dramatic rise in concern over masturbation and childhood sexual activity that began in the eighteenth-century.[44] Before then, both childhood eroticism and masturbation were rarely considered a problem, "even by those whom one might expect to be most concerned" such as Christian clergy, theologians, and moralists.[45] However, at the beginning of the eighteenth-century, an anonymous author published the first anti-masturbation treatise of its kind, "Onania or the Heinous Sin of Self-Pollution and All Its Frightful Consequences," what Thomas Laqueur called "masturbation's primal text."[46] The publication met with tremendous success, ushering newfound interest into the topic

---

[44] Although girls' sexuality "was equally suspect" within wider society (Fishman, "Childhood Sexuality," 278), there are very few cases in the literature where the genital irritation theory and any analogous surgery was applied to them. (However, see Dawson, "Circumcision in the Female.") I am not able to account for this discrepancy, but I suspect that the additional ritual significations attached to male circumcision (discussed later), and the lack of any equivalently significant female genital procedure in the Judeo-Christian context, may have played a role.

[45] Fishman, "Childhood Sexuality," 270.

[46] Laqueur, *Solitary Sex*, 31.

---

while also being considered a work of quackery by much of the medical establishment. Subsequently, in 1760, celebrated Swiss physician Simon-André Tissot published an account of the medical dangers of masturbation which was received with greater professional acclaim.[47] In so doing, Tissot supplemented moral concern over the practice, couched in the language of sin, with professional medical concern, understood in terms of disease.[48] By the middle of the nineteenth-century, as René Spitz has documented, surgical treatments such as circumcision became a preferred means of cure for the "solitary vice."[49]

This medicalization of masturbation coincided with the evolution of "spermatorrhea," the nineteenth-century name for the multifarious adverse health effects thought to arise from "excessive" semen loss. As Darby has uncovered, the doctor Claude-Francois Lallemand (1790–1893) was a key figure in transforming medical concern over semen loss from an ancient to a modern disease category and making masturbation the prime culprit.[50] In his three-volume work on the subject, published between 1836 and 1842, Lallemand effected a synthesis between earlier Galenic concern for the stability of the bodily humors and more contemporary "nerve force theory"—a close relative of reflex theory—which was concerned with the nervous "shocks" that could arise from muscle spasms such as orgasm.[51] The boundary between "excess" (in the form of nervous excitement) and "loss" (in the form of seminal discharge and consequent disease) is blurred here, in a seeming exemplification of the Lacanian concept of jouissance. Fear of this condition captured the public and the medical imagination, with one observer commenting that no other disease produced "more intense mental anxiety" in men at the time.[52] "Building on the masturbation phobia of the eighteenth century," writes Darby, "[Lallemand's] theories turned normal male sexuality into a life-threatening disease that required constant watchfulness and drastic remedies; focused attention on the genitals (the foreskin in particular) as the

---

[47] Tissot, *Onanism*.
[48] Laqueur, *Solitary Sex*, 40.
[49] Spitz, "Authority and Masturbation," 499. Spitz finds that, while surgical interventions against masturbation gradually gave way to "educational measures" in the twentieth-century, it was not until approximately 1940 that doctors finally recognized that masturbation was not medically harmful (504). A 1938 article in the *British Medical Journal* has a surgeon recommending circumcision as a "justifiable measure in confirmed masturbation when there is reason to believe that the long foreskin is a source of irritation," suggesting that these nineteenth-century views died very slowly (Walker, "Circumcision," 1377).
[50] Darby, "Pathologizing Male Sexuality."
[51] Darby, 292–3.
[52] Quoted in Darby, 298.

source of many illnesses, some real, some imaginary; and identified the hope of cure in painful and mutilating procedures on them."[53]

The campaign against masturbation, and fear of spermatorrhea, was finally combined with the middle class's "new interest in childhood and . . . eagerness to intervene in the lives of children, in order to protect them."[54] Children, it was now believed, were not supposed to have erotic thoughts or behavior, and if they did, it was sinful and/or medically pathological. Childhood masturbation thus became a focal point of medico-moral concern. Consequently, "the campaign against childhood sexuality, especially masturbation . . . [was] transformed into a crusade," what Foucault memorably called "the war against onanism."[55] Akin to the "sodomite," Foucault explains, the nineteenth-century masturbator became "a personage, a past, a case history," his identity "written immodestly on his face and body because it was a secret that always gave itself away."[56] Athol Johnson, writing in the first volume of the *Lancet*, gives a typical description of the child masturbator, which is similar to those found in the case studies of circumcision cures:

> The irritability of the mind and body, the peevishness, the alteration of the habits and general tone, together with the deterioration of the mental faculties occasionally observed in children, may . . . be attributable to [masturbation]. The disturbance of the nervous system is attended usually with some derangement of digestion and nutrition. . . . The appetite becomes capricious, the muscles get weak and flabby, there is general wasting, and, in some cases, a decided state of marasmus.[57]

Johnson enjoins parents to be vigilant for signs of the vice even in their babies, who, he explains, may move their thighs convulsively to generate genital pleasure. "The face of the infant at the time," he writes, "becomes injected and covered with sweat, the eyes are brilliant, and the child is abstracted from objects around."[58]

Crucial to our study is *how* doctors conceptualized incidents of childhood sexual behavior and precisely what it meant for masturbation to be "medicalized." For many medical practitioners, childhood and adult masturbation were different in nature because children were not supposed

[53] Darby, 298.
[54] Fishman, "Childhood Sexuality," 275.
[55] Fishman, 276; Foucault, *History of Sexuality*, 104.
[56] Foucault, 43.
[57] Johnson, "On an Injurious Habit," 345.
[58] Johnson, 345.

to possess a sexual "instinct" until after puberty. The Victorian physician and moralist William Acton encapsulates professional views of childhood asexuality:

> In a state of health no sexual impression should ever affect a child's mind or body. All its vital energy should be employed in building up the growing frame, in storing up external impressions, and educating the brain to receive them. During a well-regulated childhood, and in the case of ordinary temperaments, there is no temptation to infringe this primary law of nature. . . . The first and only feeling exhibited between the sexes in the young should be that pure fraternal and sisterly affection. . . . Thus it happens that with most healthy and well-brought up children, no sexual notion or feeling has ever entered their heads, even in the way of speculation.[59]

Acton did not himself promote circumcision, yet he endorsed the theory of foreskin-induced genital reflex irritation. ("[The foreskin] affords an additional surface for the excitement of the reflex action."[60]) The theory was: if children *were* engaged in masturbation, this was possibly—hopefully—a matter of some physical irritation they were trying to relieve through mechanical rubbing. In his 1860 textbook, *The Surgical Diseases of Children*, the English surgeon and circumcision advocate J. Cooper Forster argued that when "onanism" occurs in young children, "it must be regarded as a purely physical disease."[61] However, danger lay in the possibility that such innocent acts would inadvertently generate feelings of pleasure which could lead to sexual pathology. Hence, the circumcision advocate Frank Lydson posed an opposition between prepubertal "genital titillation," induced by irritation, and "true masturbation," while warning that the former may lay the ground for the adoption of the latter after puberty.[62] And in his *Psychopathia Sexualis,* Krafft-Ebing argued that it is important to "differentiate" between cases of masturbation

> in which, as a result of phimosis, balanitis, or oxyuris in the rectum or vagina, young children have itching of the genitals, and experience a kind of pleasurable sensation from manipulations occasioned thereby . . . and those cases in which sexual ideas and impulses occur in the child

[59] Quoted in Marcus, *The Other Victorians*, 13.
[60] Quoted in Marcus, 15.
[61] Forster, *Surgical Diseases*, 197.
[62] Lydson, *Surgical Diseases*, 548.

as a result of cerebral processes without peripheral causes. It is only in this latter class of cases that we have to do with premature manifestations of the sexual instinct. In such cases it may always be regarded as an accompanying symptom of a neuropsychopathic constitutional condition.[63]

It was understandable for children to experience bodily genital pleasure; however, it was a sign of serious mental illness if such physical pleasures were accompanied by sexual "ideas and impulses." For these nineteenth-century doctors, it was not just "sexual activity" at stake, but the place, and time, of eros in the life of the mind.

For Sayre and many of his followers, "genital irritation" would *induce* children to touch their genitals, not necessarily for erotic pleasure but as an "innocent" attempt to relieve the irritation; this would inadvertently generate further irritation, exacerbating the symptoms. Circumcision would remove the source of irritation and hence cure the supposed root cause of all the symptoms. The identification of a "reflex irritation" therefore *de-eroticized* boyhood sexual behavior, treating it as a purely mechanical problem and, furthermore, exonerating the child from moral disapprobation.

Sayre, for example, showed himself eager to help children avoid the charge of the vice. Upon being presented with a paralyzed boy whose father "feared he was guilty of masturbation, and was very anxious that I should talk to him seriously upon the subject," Sayre reports, "I found [the patient] unusually intelligent on the subject, strictly truthful and honest in all his statements, and perfectly free from the vice of masturbation."[64] Another circumcision advocate writes:

> Masturbation in a child under the age of puberty is not provoked by internal emotions. It is downright cruelty to punish a little child for masturbating. It would be as reasonable to punish one for crying with a grain of sand in the eye, or for being fidgety with ants under his clothing.[65]

Thus, potential incidents of childhood eroticism—in which mind and body, fantasy and physical sensation, were combined—were transformed into purely physical and discrete pathologies. The children were not engaging in vice but self-medicating, as it were, in response to local irritation. Paradoxical

[63] Krafft-Ebing, *Psychopathia Sexualis*, 55–6.
[64] Sayre, "Partial Paralysis from Reflex Irritation," 207.
[65] Dawson, "Circumcision in the Female," 121.

though it may seem, we could think of Sayre and similar reflex theorists as crusaders for science and the secular enlightenment. The children weren't sinners; they were, through no fault of their own, physically impaired.

Some circumcision doctors *were* willing to discuss the link between masturbation and sexual pleasure, however. Frank Lydson, for example, writes, "An evil that frequently results [from phimosis] is masturbation. The irritation beneath the prepuce induces the child to pull at the penis in an attempt to obtain relief. Pleasure sensations having been once experienced, the child is likely to become a confirmed masturbator."[66] Drawing on nerve force theory, Lydson likened the sexual orgasm to "an epileptic attack," warning that "it is only mature individuals who can bear" such an experience "without . . . injury."[67] Even here, the sensation of pleasure is quickly subsumed into a physicalist medical model, disavowing other registers in which children may experience the erotic.[68] Other doctors listed "seduction" by an older child, parent, or nanny, as a major factor alongside mechanical irritation, which might induce a child to masturbate and awaken a precocious, illness-generating sexuality. Forster turns this particular theory on its head, arguing that "the same physical conditions which induce [childhood masturbation], may lead to dreams upon the part of children . . . which . . . may have their share in the extraordinary and almost unaccountable charges sometimes made by them against their friends or guardians."[69] Here, the content of dreams, arguably the domain of fantasy par excellence, gets re-inserted into mechanistic bodily processes. (We will return to the "seduction theory" in the next chapter.)

Other circumcision doctors maintained the focus on the "vice" of masturbation as the source of nervous disorder, viewing genital irritation as only a contributing factor. For them, circumcision was more a punitive masturbation prophylactic than a relief of suffering. Heckford, for example, noted that in some cases the return of symptoms might be due to the "non-eradication" of masturbation. After discovering that one of his circumcised patients "returned to his former habit," he recommended a change in his technique: "In operating . . . it is desirable to remove the prepuce freely, and

---

[66] Lydson, *Surgical Diseases*, 80.
[67] Lydson, 553.
[68] Lydson justifies his claim regarding the epileptic nature of the orgasm by reference to the male rabbit, which, "after each act of copulation, falls over upon his side, the whites of the eyes being turned up, and the limbs in a clonic spasm" (553). A YouTube search for "rabbit mating" confirmed this assertion. The comedy of Lydson's argument notwithstanding, we can detect a certain logical rigor involved in these theories regarding nervous disorder and sexuality, albeit one which would not withstand contemporary scientific scrutiny.
[69] Forster, *Surgical Diseases*, 198.

to delay as long as possible the process of healing."[70] Johnson detailed this medical sadism more plainly:

> In [unsuccessful] cases we must, I believe, break the habit by inducing such a condition of the parts as will cause too much local suffering to allow of the practice being continued. . . . [Circumcision] should not be performed under chloroform, so that the pain experienced may be associated with the habit we wish to eradicate.[71]

Another circumcision doctor understood the physical "cause" of masturbation as an initial entry point into more serious sexual pathology, explaining his work as simultaneously medical and moral:

> Case 2: Shows at what an early age a child with local irritation may acquire the habit of masturbation.

> Boy aged six. Had been detected by his kindergarten teacher acting strangely. After some suspicious movements a strange look would come over his face, after which he would become limp, pale and languid for some time.

> A close watch was kept, and it was found that he was not only himself masturbating, but had taught his four-year-old brother the art; and these strange looks and actions were evidently connected with a distinct sexual orgasm.

> Examination showed prepuce normal in length but adherent over the whole top of the glans. To combine mental with physical reformation, these adhesions were broken without an anaesthetic (a very painful procedure both for the patient and everyone else within a block); for a while he was better, but after some weeks was detected in his old habit, and it was found that the prepuce was again adherent. Again the work was done, eliciting loud assurances that he would be good, and as far as I was ever able to learn he kept his promise.[72]

John Harvey Kellogg, the inventor of corn flakes, promoted both the cereal and circumcision for what he thought to be their libido-diminishing effects.

[70] Heckford, "Circumcision," 64.
[71] Johnson, "On an Injurious Habit," 345.
[72] Beaty, "Peripheral Irritation," 33–4.

His book *Plain Facts for Old and Young*, which he allegedly worked on during his honeymoon in lieu of consummating his marriage,[73] is essentially a long restatement on nineteenth-century reflex theory-based views on the dangers of masturbation. He too took psychology into consideration when promoting circumcision:

> A remedy [against masturbation] which is almost always successful in small boys is circumcision, especially when there is any degree of phimosis. The operation should be performed by a surgeon without administering an anaesthetic, as the brief pain attending the operation will have a salutary effect upon the mind, especially if it be connected with the idea of punishment.[74]

These examples suggest that through the moralistic infliction of pain, reflex theorists were led to consider the *psychical* aspects of circumcision, despite their theory's avowed focus on the physical. One note from a medical review argued that those who *opposed* medical circumcision because they did not believe in the theory of the reflexes ignored "the mental effect of the operation, always a potent factor in any remedial appliance."[75] Landon Gray, one of Sayre's most astute and thorough critics—who published an article in 1882 addressing the flaws of scientific reasoning and medical observation in each of Sayre's reported circumcision cures—nevertheless conceded that circumcision "may prove to be a useful therapeutic measure in certain cases," on the grounds that such surgeries may make "impressions" upon the nerves that produce symptomatic relief.[76] The language is reminiscent of Freud and Breuer's early work on the traumatic mental "impressions" they believed to lie at the source of hysteria; yet, while the former write of relieving such impressions through the talking cure, Gray wishes to impose them: "Your nerve cannot itself be directly reached except by great violence," Gray explains.

In fact, the psychical trauma that childhood circumcision might inflict would concern a later generation of psychoanalysts. In a 1939 letter to the *British Medical Journal*, Winnicott criticized a circumcision advocate, arguing that the procedure was usually medically unnecessary, "built on the gravestones of superstitions," and that he had "seen a great deal of acute

---

[73] See McLaren's (brilliantly entitled) essay, "Porn Flakes: Kellogg, Graham, and the Crusade for Moral Fiber."
[74] Kellogg, *Plain Facts*, 205.
[75] Anonymous, "Circumcision in the Neuroses," 270.
[76] Gray, *Genital Irritation*, 23.

distress in mothers and babies during the weeks following circumcisions."[77] Winnicott's perspective on the effects of the procedure was precisely the inverse of the reflex theorists; he wrote that circumcision led to "sexual excitement during the changing of dressings and prolonged priapism," causing the "artificial awakening of genital sensuality."[78] In a 1952 article, Anna Freud wrote that the child's ego is sometimes unable to cope with surgical operations, which "lend . . . a feeling of reality to . . . repressed fantasies, thereby multiplying the anxieties connected with them"; she cautioned against the "castration fears" "aroused" by circumcision.[79]

The reflex theorists' wish to cause children pain begs the question: Was "genital irritation" the problem or the solution? Could it have been both? As we examine these papers closely, we see that the boundaries separating irritation from pleasure, disease from cure, and psyche from body, were contradictory and ill-defined. While the circumcision doctors attempted to master manifestations of childhood sexuality by treating them as physiological dysfunctions amenable to surgery, the unmasterable problems of fantasy and the erotic imagination continued to rear their head.

Masculinity and Sexual Difference in the Circumcision Cure

This nineteenth-century paranoia surrounding childhood masturbation was linked in important ways to the attempt to secure sexual difference. "Boys of studious and retiring habits are most apt to be masturbators and to suffer severely from its effects," writes Lydson. He contrasts the young lover of the great American outdoors with his degenerate, bookish, and likely urban-dwelling counterpart:

> The active, robust, manly boy who indulges in out-of-door athletic sports, hunting and so on, has an outlet for what has been aptly termed the "effusive cussedness" of boy-nature, and is not apt to study his sexual apparatus. . . . The "mother's boy," of all, requires watching.[80]

Here, too much intellectual curiosity becomes a conduit for sexual curiosity. This state of affairs is enabled by the coddling mother who, permitting

---

[77] Winnicott, "Circumcision," 86–7.
[78] Winnicott, 87.
[79] Anna Freud, "The Role of Bodily Illness," 74–5.
[80] Lydson, *Surgical Diseases*, 552.

her boy to stay indoors, denies him the appropriate outlet for his "effusive cussedness." Somewhat ironically, the solution the doctor offers for the libidinally dysfunctional bookworm—typically a Jewish caricature—is to circumcise him.

As this example suggests, the circumcision doctors often understood their patients as failing to embody and enact certain masculine ideals.[81] Physicians and parents appear visibly anxious to manage and, if necessary, subtend the masculinity of their young patients. Through circumcision, they hoped to ward off the threat of phallic dispossession that the boys' manifestations of desire and nervous illness called forth. The procedure therefore appears as a kind of secularized rite of passage, or trial of masculinity, ushering boys into their proper sex role.

One doctor, treating a "momma's boy" for bedwetting, reportedly discovered a "redundant prepuce, with contracted orifice" on the patient, who, he notes, "took but little interest in the sports of childhood."[82] The day after the operation, he received word from the father, "that his son 'seemed to be quite another boy.'"[83] The father's choice of phrasing, like the doctor's description of the patient, speaks to gendered concerns beyond the mere problem of bedwetting. A nearly identical description occurs in one of Sayre's cases, a fifteen-year-old boy treated for "nervousness and fainting fits." Sayre writes that six weeks after the operation, "He sleeps quietly all night, has had only two nocturnal emissions, has increased in flesh and strength, has become buoyant in spirits, and in fact is, as his father says, 'a perfectly changed boy.'" In these and other cases, the fathers express the most enthusiasm about the cure, apparently eager to wrest their boys out of maternal dependence.

Another follower of Sayre considered that the infliction of pain by circumcision would cure more than just masturbation: "When no lesion exists, the simple stripping of the glans will convert many a feeble, puny, ill nourished, wakeful, irritable boy into a healthful and happy child."[84] Here, the entire theoretical premise that justified genital surgery as a cure for nervous disorder is seemingly discarded. Never mind the penile irritant triggering the reflex symptoms; if the boy is not quite right, utilize the knife.

Problems surrounding sexual differences are also evoked in the striking illustrations that occasionally accompany the circumcision cases.[85] One such

[81] This was of particular concern in the nineteenth-century, within the wider context of imperial expansion and settlement. See Hall, *White, Male and Middle Class.*
[82] Dr. Otis, quoted in Sayre, "Spinal Anemia," 270–1.
[83] Sayre, 270–1.
[84] Dr. De Forest Willard, quoted in Sayre, *Deleterious Results*, 21.
[85] On the cultural anxieties encoded into medical illustrations of sexual disease, see Palfreyman, *Visualising Venereal Disease.*

image (Figure 1) depicts a three-year-old boy with a contorted gait. The doctor notes that he had perfect control of his limbs while seated, but when walking, he assumed the awkward posture and moved clumsily, often falling down. One is particularly struck by the disembodied hand in the illustration, which grasps the boy by the tips of his fingers apparently to hold him upright for the audience. The viewer is given the impression that, were the hand to let go, the boy would simply collapse, as if his body were too weak to withstand the effects of gravity. Whose hand is this? Though ostensibly intended to represent the hand of the doctor, who performs the minimal intervention necessary to demonstrate to his audience the full extent of the boy's illness, the decorporealized image enables a wealth of associations in the viewer. In contrast to the embodied and enfeebled child, the hand is pure function, steady and precise. We might draw here a distinction between the body, as subject to death and decay, and the symbol, as permanent and immortal. Absent an identifying body image, the hand signifies not just the doctor but the abstract qualities with which he is endowed—authority, certitude, and power. Yet, the hand also portrays a certain ambivalence in its putative owner. Touching only the bare minimum of the boy's skin, it is as if the hand is dangling away from itself a fetid, loathsome object, which threatens to contaminate it—one can imagine the doctor simultaneously closing his nostrils with his other hand and looking away. All of these associations work to consolidate the idea that the boy is not, or has not yet been, initiated into a higher order of abstract masculinity, one undefiled by corporeality. Moreover, he is unable to even begin the process, in dire need of specialized assistance.

The doctor who authored this case was, in fact, a critic of Sayre. The patient was formerly circumcised by Sayre and pronounced cured but subsequently came under this doctor's care in the state pictured, his father adamant that Sayre's operation "amounted to nothing."[86] The doctor concluded that circumcision as a treatment for paralysis or spasms "may be efficacious in a very limited class of cases" but thinks Sayre has vastly overstated its medical utility.[87] This is a case that exceeded the doctor's capacity to cure; he admits that his initial medical optimism faded after a number of medicines he prescribed failed to help. Perhaps this may explain the note of ambivalence or disgust we identified in the image. The doctor is helpless to treat this type

---

[86] Hammond, *Muscular Incoordination*, 14. The father wrote a contradictory letter to Sayre a few weeks earlier, reporting that the operation had cured his son. Quoted in Sayre, "Paralysis from Peripheral Irritation," 306–7.

[87] Sayre, 15.

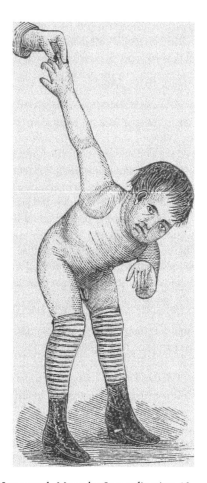

Figure 1 From Hammond, *Muscular Incoordination*, 12.

of sickness. Sayre is mocked for his overconfidence. The boy represents the medical man's folly, or alternately, his next unsolved mystery.

We could contrast this with a different image from Sayre's repertoire (Figure 2). This is a much more successful case, at least according to Sayre's report. The boy suffered from paralysis and frequent prolapse of the rectum. For a year, his ability to walk steadily degenerated, and eventually, he was unable to stand without support. Sayre diagnosed him with phimosis and "constant priapism" (persistent erection). In the image, there is again the appearance of the defective, half-naked boy against the background of impersonal medical men who seem to embody authority and expertise. Yet,

Figure 2 From Sayre, *Lectures*, 19.

there is none of the ambivalence of the previous illustration. Instead, the hands of the doctor—who is clothed in priest-like robes—touch the boy's head in a quasi-religious, somewhat menacing manner, as if he were about to release some kind of magical, transformative energy from his fingertips into the boy's body. Another hand, presumably that of an assistant, holds the boy's leg, clutching a fold of skin that oddly resembles an adult-sized penis (perhaps indicating the sexual maturation that awaits?). The hands of both the doctor and the assistant are simultaneously supporting the boy, who is said to be unable to stand on his own, and displaying him to the audience.

The boy seems to be playing his role as well, pulling up his medical gown to display his small, phimotic penis. Again, we have the sense that the boy is due for an initiation into a higher order of masculinity. This time, however, it is clear that the doctor will successfully facilitate this rite of passage. Two days after his circumcision, Sayre reports, the boy slept quietly and could stand unsupported; by twelve days he had made a full recovery, walking and running normally and suffering no further rectal prolapsus.[88]

This example sheds further light on the circumcision doctors' peculiar understanding of the childhood erection. The presence here of the "priapic" signifies not virility but weakness, a lack of control. If the experience of male impotence is typically thought of as a kind of failure calling into question the subject's masculinity, here it is the persistent erection that signifies something broken and perhaps feminine. Crucially, the erection is portrayed as uncontrollable, coming from without—a sign of the child's weakness of will. (The symptom of rectal prolapsus, of a hidden orifice suddenly becoming all-too-visible, further underscores associations with femininity.) Sexuality is for men to master, not be mastered by. Infantile sexuality may appear particularly threatening insofar as it reminds those who seek mastery of their own passive position in relation to forces outside the ambit of the ego. Through circumcision, doctors sought to "phallicize" the penis, and, by extension, its young owner. Yet, they worked not simply with biological material but with symbols, making their attempt to overcome castration indissolubly linked to the symbolic order, the cause of castration itself.

Myths and rites of passage are often thought of as necessary tools through which otherwise mysterious and anxiety-provoking life events can be managed. In the nineteenth-century, when the religious significance of rituals was increasingly eroded and replaced by secular knowledge, might it be the case that a procedure that was deeply suffused with ritualistic connotations— yet went under the guise of a medical treatment—could fill in the gap left in secularization's wake?[89] Typically, rites of passage are understood to be universal for a given sex within a community—not merely an intervention for certain misfits. Yet, in the circumcision papers, the nature of the "illness" in question is so amorphous—from the shape of one's foreskin to a varying set of troublesome behaviors—that it appears it could accommodate just

---

[88] Sayre, *Lectures*, 18–22.
[89] My hypothesis regarding unconscious manifestations of religious rituals under secularization is further underscored by Greenblatt's observation that Hughlings Jackson's neurological work "completed the nineteenth-century's 'secularization' of the cerebral hemispheres," given that, as I mentioned earlier, Jackson himself experimented with circumcision (*Jackson*, 377).

about any boy, eventually becoming so general as to justify us calling the "cure" a rite of passage.

"You Had Better Make a Jew of Him": Universalizing the "Mosaic Rite"

Indeed, many of Sayre's followers, impressed by the "miraculous" effects of the procedure, were increasingly considering whether *all* boys might benefit from circumcision. They argued that incidences of genital irritation were much more widespread than commonly assumed, and, as a prophylactic against masturbation, the "trifling" operation would be beneficial to all boys, regardless of the visible presence of foreskin-related problems. However, this raised a difficult question: Did the universalization of circumcision imply the "Judaization" (and potentially, feminization) of the masses—or had doctors successfully wrested the operation from its religious-racial domain? The debate that ensued over the legitimate reach of medical circumcision was thoroughly imbued with the contradictory ideas and anxieties surrounding the "Jewish question" in Anglo-American society.

Sayre himself vociferously objected to the overextension of circumcision to cases that did not demonstrate his criteria for genital irritation and associated nervous disorders. Interestingly, he referred to the "indiscriminate performance of the operation" as an "unjustifiable mutilation," perhaps suggesting that he did not think very highly of that group of people whose identity is represented by the mark of circumcision.[90] This suspicion is further confirmed in Sayre's criticism of the technique of a colleague, who "made the mistake of cutting off the integument in a circle, the same as the Jew does."[91] Another doctor, also warning against "enthusiasts," who "look upon circumcision as a panacea," writes of a colleague who "made such slaughter among the innocents that the mothers of his section of the city ceased bringing their male children to him."[92] The language evokes anti-Semitic blood libels and related mythology. Sayre promoted circumcision as a miraculous cure that could be applied to so many vaguely defined cases that one senses a desire to implement it universally, to Judaize the masses; yet as soon as this wish became manifest, it was repudiated.

---

[90] Sayre, *Deleterious Results*, 8.
[91] Sayre, "Paralysis from Peripheral Irritation," 307.
[92] Gray, *Genital Irritation*, 7.

It is a classic psychoanalytical observation, fundamental to the analysis of racism, that the loathed object is also an object of desire, representing the conflict one experiences over the more fundamental prohibited and repressed object. An obsessional strategy for managing one's relationship to this ambivalent object is to divide it into an admired and a hated part, disavowing their inherent relation and distancing oneself, although never sufficiently, from the latter. Such is the strategy at work in one of Sayre's followers, Dr. Willard, when he attempts to differentiate religious circumcision, which he condemns, from his own surgical practice:

> It is idle to class this operation among Mosaic sanitary laws. It was ordered long before the time of Moses, not upon hygienic, but upon religious grounds, as a distinctive mark. Its adoption by other nations was undoubtedly due to the fact that their superstitious minds easily accepted the theory that by thus mutilating themselves, the acknowledged blessings showered in past times by the Almighty upon this "peculiar people" might be secured to themselves, since this was the only outward and visible sign of difference. Such barbaric sacrifices are not infrequent, and those who practice this rite are certainly not noted either for their morality or cleanliness.[93]

We are offered here a speculative history that separates out "Mosaic sanitary laws" from the "barbaric sacrifices" adopted by unclean and immoral people who "mutilat[ed] themselves" through circumcision in the hope of attaining divine favor. Willard firmly believed in Sayre's findings on reflex neurosis but, like Sayre, argued against the overapplication of circumcision. His position on Judaism here is somewhat unclear. It seems he is criticizing those "other nations" who *mimicked* the ancient Hebrews by practicing circumcision, while acknowledging that the original Jews, who had "blessings showered" on them "by the Almighty," were appropriately following divine law. Yet, who are these "other nations" he does not name? He may be referring to the existence of tribes that practice circumcision—perhaps studied by the anthropologists of the era—whom he accuses of foolishly copying the Jews. However, his critique seems equally pointed at those ritually circumcising people who have a place in the surrounding society: living Jews. We should recall the Christian anti-Semitic belief that living Jews were the illegitimate heirs, and pathetic imposters, of the mighty Hebrews of the Old Testament.[94]

---

[93] Quoted in Sayre, *Deleterious Results*, 20.
[94] See Biddick, *Typological Imaginary*, 9.

In this line of reasoning, Moses is adopted as a proto-Christian doctor, while the mark of his people belongs to a bygone era, superseded by Christianity, but perversely reconstructed by "superstitious minds."

Willard's invocation of Moses was not unusual. Those doctors who promoted universal circumcision were readily proclaiming the medical wisdom of Moses and the advantages of the Jews in relation to circumcision. Indeed, many of the doctors in favor of circumcision (some but not all of whom were Jewish) were avowedly philo-Semitic, often in an exoticizing way. In the same discussion of Sayre's work in which Willard's remarks appear, another doctor argues that the widespread prevalence of reflex irritations justifies "the radical [i.e., universal] application of the Mosaic rite of circumcision." "I believe thoroughly in the Mosaic law," he writes, "not only from a moral but also from a sanitary standpoint."[95] From across the Atlantic, Jonathan Hutchinson, the surgeon we mentioned at the beginning of this chapter, offered precisely the kind of circumcision history that Willard sought to dispel: "It is surely not needful to seek any recondite motive for the origin of the practice of circumcision. No one who has seen the superior cleanliness of a Hebrew penis can have avoided a very strong impression in favour of removal of the foreskin."[96] A more evocative association occurs in the following doctor's advice to a colleague, while treating a fifteen-month-old boy suffering from "swollen joints": "In view of the history given and the appearance of the child, I said to the mother, Undo his diaper, please, which seemed to surprise her considerably. . . . After viewing the condition, I turned to the doctor, and said, 'You had better make a Jew of him.'"[97]

Doctors like Willard thus found themselves in the awkward position of defending what they viewed to be a medically useful procedure, while striving to separate it from its ritualistic and Jewish associations. But would it not be easier for Willard to simply reject Sayre's genital irritation theories?[98] Here we enter into the finer details of obsessional logic. Willard advocated circumcision as a last resort in cases of reflex disturbance, "in itself mutilatory, but, like amputation, [sometimes] a necessity."[99] Ideally, he believed, genital

[95] Quoted in Sayre, *Deleterious Results*, 21.
[96] Hutchinson, "Circumcision," 15.
[97] Ohr, "Genito-Reflex Neurosis," 64.
[98] Some of Sayre's opponents alleged that Jews suffered from *more* nervous disorders than non-Jews *because* of circumcision. For example, George Beard, popularizer of the diagnosis of neurasthenia, is cited in a medical discussion of Sayre's cure expressing skepticism: "Dr. Beard thought that the Jews were quite subject to nervous troubles, despite the absence of a prepuce. He was of the opinion that circumcision might actually do harm" (Gray, "Reflex Disturbances," 577).
[99] Quoted in Sayre, *Deleterious Results*, 20.

irritation should be relieved by "stripping" the prepuce from the glans, to which it is sometimes adhered. For infants up to two years old, Willard's procedure "is performed by manipulating the penis for a moment until slight rigidity occurs" and then breaking up the adhesions with the thumbs or a probe.[100] Like nearly all the doctors of his time, Willard considered masturbation dangerous; he viewed his genital care regimen "as the greatest safeguard, not only against reflex irritations, but also against masturbation."[101] Yet, his recommendation involved the doctor *inducing, by masturbation, an erection in the patient.* In his treatment, both the disease and the cure are inscribed by the doctor onto the patient in the same moment. It is the same with Willard's comments on religion: circumcision is affirmed as medically useful while, at the same time, its unavoidable ritualistic associations are dramatically denigrated. Willard was fighting fire with fire. Yet, he had to compulsively disavow the implications of his *pharmakon*—namely, that the poison he was trying to avoid (masturbation and the Judaizing implications of circumcision) was simultaneously the very material of his cure.[102]

A doctor writing in 1915, apparently not troubled by circumcision's Judaizing implications, faced Willard's problem head-on:

> The prepuce is one of the great factors in causing masturbation in boys. Here is the dilemma we are in: If we do not teach the growing boy to pull the prepuce back and cleanse the glans there is danger of smegma collecting and of adhesions and ulcerations forming, which in their turn will cause irritation likely to lead to masturbation. If we do teach the boy to pull the prepuce back and cleanse his glans, that handling alone is sufficient gradually and almost without the boy's knowledge to initiate him into the habit of masturbation. . . . Therefore, off with the prepuce![103]

The obsessional is seduced by that which he wishes to eradicate, driven into increasingly mad propositions to manage this circuitry of desire.

For both Willard and Sayre, it was important not to think of circumcision as in itself desirable, but as a technical procedure with desirable aims. Yet, as the pro-circumcision remarks I have quoted demonstrate, many others admired circumcision as a surgical improvement of the penis, not only unperturbed by its Jewish associations but sometimes even welcoming of them. "Moses was a good sanitarian," writes one doctor, "and if circumcision

[100] Sayre, 19.
[101] Sayre, 19.
[102] Derrida, *Dissemination.*
[103] Robinson, "Circumcision," 390.

was more generally practised at the present day, I believe that we would hear far less of the pollutions and indiscretions of youth; and that our daily papers would not be so profusely flooded with all kinds of sure cures for loss of manhood."[104] Another way to manage the encounter with something disturbing is to exoticize it, endow it with magical properties.

The report of an Irish-American father on his son's circumcision is particularly striking in this regard. The father appeared before a medical audience, on Sayre's request, to tell his story. His son would not sleep for more than a few hours at a time and would experience "paroxysms of laughter and crying . . . like hysterics," in the father's words. He noticed that his son had erections but did not initially think they were of concern. Suspecting "worms," he took the boy to a homeopath, who prescribed unhelpful remedies. In the quoted text, he seemed to enjoy sharing with the audience his initial experience of quackery at the hands of the homeopath. The audience laughed at his tale, reflecting their keenness to solidify their legitimacy against those they considered charlatans. Finally, the father "mustered up" his "courage" and took the boy to Sayre, who operated on the foreskin. The boy improved rapidly. The father concludes, "His health is first-rate, and he is getting so docile that we hope to train him, bye-and-bye, *so that he will act like a white man's child*, in three or four years."[105]

The connections this father drew between circumcision and the ascension to whiteness are striking. Sayre's operation seems not only to have cured his troublesome boy but to have provided the son a place in Protestant America that the father himself, as an Irishman, had possibly been denied. What's more, the boy's newly improved behavior may have served to elevate the parents as well, who would now be seen as capable of raising a "white man's child." Sayre's reputation is affirmed through the father's self-legitimizing tale of struggle and eventual triumph, an all-American classic. Far from disfiguring the boy and, by extension, his family, circumcision became a totemic object that domesticated their otherness. We might think here of those Jewish American entertainers whose use of blackface helped them assimilate into American society.[106]

This racialized embrace of circumcision becomes more disturbing in the work of circumcision advocate Frank Lydson. Lydson earned his surgical reputation by transplanting slices of human testicles into his patients' scrotums.[107] One of his celebrated cases involved transplanting the testicles

---

[104] Chapman, "Nervous Affections," 317.
[105] Sayre, "Paralysis from Peripheral Irritation," 308 (emphasis mine).
[106] See Rogin, *Blackface*, for this history. Also see Ignatiev, *Irish*, on how Irish-American assimilation was predicated upon anti-black racism.
[107] See Lederer, *Flesh and Blood*, 168–9.

of an executed African American prisoner into a 72-year-old white prisoner. "Before operation [the white prisoner] was naturally reticent," reads the medical report, "but now is positively emphatic. Summing the whole demeanor 5 days after operation, he has more 'jazz and pep' and the increased energy of a man many years younger than he."[108] The phrase "jazz and pep" is replete with associations to black American culture. It is as if receiving the black man's testicles turned the old white patient black, or rather endowed him with the desired properties of stereotyped blackness (strength, virility). More strikingly, after the procedure, the patient reportedly gained, for the first time, an ability to appreciate jokes.[109] Lydson also performed a transplant on himself, reporting that it increased his "physical efficiency and especially physiosexual efficiency."[110]

Race and Mastery: The Case of Sims

As these previous examples suggest, nineteenth-century medical circumcision appears against the backdrop of the medicalization and sexualization of racial oppression, and the legacy of American slavery. This returns us to J. Marion Sims, the doctor mentioned at the beginning of the chapter, who requested Sayre's expertise in the case of a paralyzed boy that led to Sayre "discovering" his cure.

Sims is a notorious figure in the history of medicine.[111] He claimed to have discovered the first effective surgical technique to cure a debilitating childbirth complication called vesicovaginal fistula through a series of experiments, performed without anesthesia, on enslaved women suffering from it. We now know the condition is caused by the very forms of deprivation

[108] Stanley, *Men at Their Worst*, 109–10; cited in Lederer, *Flesh and Blood*, 168–9.
[109] Lederer, 168–9.
[110] Cited in Tilney, *Transplant*, 30–1. Freud underwent a similarly "vitality-restoring" testicular procedure in 1923, electing to have a half-unilateral vasectomy in line with the voguish medical procedure known as the "Steinach operation." According to his biographer Ernest Jones, Freud hoped "the rejuvenation such an operation promised might delay the return of [his mouth] cancer" (Jones, *Freud, v. 3*, 104; see also Stepansky, *Freud*, 137–8. I thank Dany Nobus for alerting me to this). Freud's close follower, Princess Marie Bonaparte, underwent clitoral surgery as an attempted cure for frigidity (see Cryle and Moore, *Frigidity*, chp. 8).
[111] For an overview, see Sartin, "J. Marion Sims"; also McGregor, *From Midwives to Medicine*. Washington's *Medical Apartheid* brought Sims's record into popular consciousness. Hallman's "Monumental Error" corrects some inaccuracies in the literature; see also Hallman, "J. Marion Sims," which unearths evidence that Sims may have served as an agent for the Confederacy during stints in Europe where he claimed to be practicing medicine.

and abuse that characterize chattel slavery, including malnourishment, poor living conditions, and giving birth at a young age.[112] Sims went on to establish the Woman's Hospital in New York, the first of its kind in the United States and was elected president of the American Medical Association in 1876. In addition to his work on fistula, he was also, along with his colleague Robert Battey (mentioned earlier), a vocal proponent of the surgical removal of apparently healthy ovaries to cure epilepsy, hysteria, and other conditions.[113] Although Sims does not appear to have written about the circumcision cure himself, his medical itinerary and the justifications he proposed for "ovariotomy" show him working within the same reflex theory coordinates as the circumcision doctors; and his letter to Sayre suggests that he saw nervous problems afflicting women and boys as linked through a genital etiology that called for surgical intervention. Once celebrated as the "father of gynecology," Sims has since fallen into disrepute for the unethical nature of his work and his exaggerated claims of originality.[114] Opposition to his legacy and its whitewashing culminated in a 2018 protest at a monument dedicated to him in Central Park—linked to the wider interrogation of Confederate monuments and the Black Lives Matter movement—which led New York mayor Bill de Blasio to order its removal.[115]

Through the historical figure of Sims, we can see clearly how the nineteenth-century surgical removal of genital tissue is articulated to questions of childhood, femininity, and race. The figure of the slave-master casts a disturbing shadow over the circumcision doctors' attempted mastery over these questions. As Sheldon George argues, chattel slavery established "whiteness" as a master race in relation to the slave configured as lacking object, enabling a "fantasy of being that race guaranteed to the master," and providing forms of enjoyment to slaveowners "bound most fundamentally to the master's own masking of lack through the surpluses allowed by a coordination of capital and fantasy."[116] We can see these dynamics at work in Sims's charged description of the moment he "discovered" a technical solution to the problem of how to view (and thereby treat) the inside of a vagina. After instructing an enslaved woman suffering from fistula to bend knee-to-chest, and applying a metal spoon to her vaginal opening, he writes, "I saw everything, as no man had ever seen before."[117] In Sims's "language

---

[112] See Wall, "Obstetric Vesicovaginal Fistula."
[113] See Sims, "Remarks on Battey's Operation."
[114] Hallman, "Monumental Error." Defenses of Sims's work persist; see, for example, Wall, "Medical Ethics."
[115] Neuman, "City Orders Sims Statue Removed."
[116] George, *Trauma and Race*, 23–4.
[117] Sims, *The Story of My Life*, 234.

of discovery," writes C. Riley Snorton, "divided flesh was defined by its characteristic accessibility, its availability for viewing, exploration, and other modes of unrelenting, unmitigated apprehension."[118] Through nineteenth-century surgical exploration and cutting—in which the circumcision cure is deeply implicated—femininity, childhood, and enslaved blackness become interlinked sites of abjection and the underside of phallic mastery in the latter's drive for total knowledge.

Remondino and Cockshut's Christian Cut

Perhaps the most bizarre combination of racism and a philo-Semitic embrace of circumcision occurs in the baroque writings of Peter Remondino, a decorated Californian surgeon who referred to Sayre as the "Columbus of the prepuce" in his popular 1891 book, *History of Circumcision*. Remondino refers to opponents of circumcision as suffering from the "narrow and benighted point of view of the Congo Negro."[119] In a paper intended as a reply to circumcision disbelievers, he deplores the case of a patient reported, in a medical journal, to have died from penile cancer:

> Had [the patient] been fortunate enough either to have been born a Jew or a Turk, or to have fallen into the hands of an energetic and persistent advocate of circumcision when a child, [he] would not only have been spared some long eight months of atrocious suffering, but would then in all probability have lived to a very comfortable age.[120]

In Remondino's eyes, not only is it right to emulate the Jews' (and Turks') practice of circumcision, but it is degenerate, and downright criminal, that Christians have renounced it. "Saint Paul undoubtedly did humanity, especially Christian humanity, great wrong in every way when he failed to retain circumcision as a religious rite," he writes.[121] He substantiates his claim with a quote from a Scottish Presbyterian patient whose nervous disorders he treated with circumcision:

> I have been brought up and educated to look upon Saint Paul, the founder of Christianity, with awe and admiration, but, by God, Sir, if I

---

[118] Snorton, *Black on Both Sides*, 23.
[119] Remondino, "Circumcision and its Opponents," n.p.
[120] Remondino.
[121] Remondino.

had Saint Paul here now, Sir, I would shoot him, yes, Sir, I would shoot him. He had no biblical warrant nor no business to summarily abolish circumcision as he did.[122]

Here, Remondino supplies us with a surprisingly contemporary perspective on the theological divide over circumcision that we examined in the previous chapter. The religious significance of circumcision in which Paul intervened is made superfluous to the rite's medical utility. This is comparable to how contemporary scientists laud the cognitive benefits of religious identification while eschewing the theological questions that make religion meaningful in the first place ("New study proves prayer increases serotonin!"). Such an approach does not appropriate religious ritual so much as sanitize it, transforming circumcision from a bloody and potentially castrative rite into a civilizing force. As James Boon comments, "In Remondino all circumcision that can be surveyed—anywhere, anytime—is enlisted in the ranks of a unified species of the practice—reduced to medical benefits and ratified by rationality."[123]

In this respect, I will draw these examples to a close with the unfortunately named R. W. Cockshut, whose twentieth-century defense of circumcision in the *British Medical Journal* adds a surgical twist to the notion of the "civilizing mission" and the sacrifice of pleasure that Freud considered the "discontent" of civilization:

I suggest that all male children should be circumcised. This is "against nature," but that is exactly the reason why it should be done. Nature intends that the adolescent male shall copulate as often and as promiscuously as possible, and to that end covers the sensitive glans so that it shall be ever ready to receive stimuli. Civilization, on the contrary, requires chastity, and the glans of the circumcised rapidly assumes a leathery texture less sensitive than skin. Thus the adolescent has his attention drawn to his penis much less often. I am convinced that masturbation is much less common in the circumcised. With these considerations in view it does not seem apt to argue that "God knows best how to make little boys."[124]

Cockshut's perspective received a more violent articulation in an 1899 newspaper article in favor of the American colonization of the Philippines, which exclaimed: "There is no dilly-dallying with these uncircumcised, uncivilized,

---

[122] Remondino.
[123] Boon, *Verging on Extra-Vagance*, 65.
[124] Cockshut, "Circumcision," 764.

unthankful and treacherous cutthroats; the sooner soldiers are sent there in sufficient numbers to finish up the business, the better it will be for Christianity and human progress."[125]

To promote medical circumcision forced one to encounter its various religious, racial, and sexual associations. The ways in which this occurred revealed the variety of masculine strategies—some more stable than others—to confront, and attempt to overcome, symbolic castration.

Turning the Screw, Twisting the Knife

It is tempting to reduce the medical texts we have examined to bygone relics of Victorian prudery, madness, and sadism. More challenging is to read the desires, anxieties, and contradictions visible within this particular moment in the history of circumcision as particular attempts to navigate something fundamental about the human condition. Jacqueline Rose writes:

> Freud is known to have undermined the concept of childhood innocence, but his real challenge is easily lost if we see in the child merely a miniature version of what our sexuality eventually comes to be. The child is sexual, but its sexuality (bisexual, polymorphous, perverse) threatens our own at its very roots. Setting up the child as innocent is not, therefore, repressing its sexuality—it is above all holding off any possible challenge to our own.[126]

While we may no longer circumcise children for the same reasons we did in the nineteenth-century, childhood remains invested with notions of innocence, purity, and transparency that anxiously ward against the threatening nature of sexuality.

The circumcision doctors attempted to master the mysterious, sexualized behaviors of their patients by localizing the danger onto the foreskin. A dangerous and protean vice—infantile sexuality—became metonymically linked to a piece of excess skin, which could be snipped off. Yet, in the process, they found themselves driven to commit the very acts they wished to eliminate, from masturbating the patient (in order to better perform the operation) to advocating circumcision universally (with all its "Judaizing" and feminizing implications). Their "knowledge" of childhood nervous

---

[125] Cited in Silverman, *Abraham to America*, 182.
[126] Rose, *Peter Pan*, 4.

illness became a fetish, in which the presence of infantile sexuality was both sustained and disavowed.

Here, we may be reminded of Henry James's Victorian horror story, a perennial favorite of psychoanalytic criticism, *The Turn of the Screw* (published in 1898, around the same time as the circumcision texts), in which a young governess is driven to paranoiac madness and possibly murder in her search for knowledge of whether the two children she cares for have been subjected to "dreadful passages of intercourse."[127] With great dexterity, James's story conveys how the attempt to secure innocence from "contamination" puts one squarely in the realm of the very evils one wishes to combat. In her essay on the work, Shoshana Felman offers a Lacanian interpretation of the consequences of attempted mastery:

> The attempt to *master* meaning, which ought to lead to its *unification*, to the *elimination* of its contradictions and its "splits," can reach its goal only at the cost, through the infliction of a new wound, of an added split or distance, of an irreversible "separation." . . . Meaning's *possession* is itself ironically transformed into the radical dispossession of its possessor.[128]

Felman's point, intended to describe the consequences faced both by the governess in her role as detective, and the reader/critic who searches for certainty in James's ambiguous work acquires an almost literal reality in the history of medical circumcision. The circumcision doctors attempted to secure the meaning of their patients' multifarious symptoms in a single diagnosis, and to eliminate the surplus, the behavior that suggested something more than an organic dysfunction. The "new wound" they "inflicted," the "added split" of circumcision, appeared at first as a straightforward medical cure, but as the work on circumcision developed, its initial proponents lost their grip on the narrative, with both the "genital irritation" diagnosis and its associated cures taking on a life of their own, leading to the endless proliferation of the practice.

The psychoanalyst Jean Laplanche has posited that childhood seduction—in the form of an enigmatic knowledge transmitted from adult to child—is a universal trauma constitutive of the development of human sexuality. In the next chapter, we will move away from the specific circumcision cases in order to think about the larger questions this material raises regarding the nature of the human sexuality. What is the relation between sexuality and

[127] James, *Turn of the Screw*, 188.
[128] Felman, "Turning the Screw," 174 (emphasis original).

knowledge? How do our adult caretakers influence our earliest experiences of the erotic? Through an examination of the early history of psychoanalysis we will see how Freud was immersed in the same problems that troubled these circumcision doctors; and how he forged an alternative not by exiting their theoretical paradigm, but by going *through* it, in a form of immanent critique that transformed its internal contradictions. Jean Laplanche's "generalized theory of seduction," which recuperates Freud's early work, will help us understand the threatening nature of sexuality not just for the Victorians, but for the subject as such.

4

The Talking Cure

Psychoanalysis's Answer to Medical Circumcision

In the previous chapter, we saw how nineteenth-century circumcision doctors were eager to treat nervous illness in boys as a physiological problem that could be cured through surgical intervention, while their writing suggested that both the illness and the cure exceeded the realm of the organic. This chapter will bring out the commonalities and fundamental differences between their endeavor and that of Sigmund Freud's.

Freud invented psychoanalysis shortly after the first medical circumcisions for "reflex neuroses" took place. Although these two approaches to nervous illness were never in explicit communication, they had shared concerns and attempted to resolve similar problems.

Freud initially understood manifestations of a split in subjectivity—the lack of conscious control over one's thoughts and behaviors—as contingent, pathological problems. In his earliest work on hysteria, under the influence of his mentor Charcot, he proposed psychological mechanisms for the functioning of the disease and was skeptical of theories that posited a sexual etiology. His subsequent development of the "seduction theory" again treated the unconscious as something pathological and amenable to "cure," yet here he argued that manifestations of unconscious phenomena were the consequence of sexual seductions experienced in childhood, the memory of which was repressed. His description of these seductions shared with reflex theorists a focus on the physiological disturbances allegedly experienced through a premature encounter with sexual sensations.

However, as his work advanced, Freud eventually elaborated a universal theory of infantile sexuality and the unconscious. Whereas reflex theory posited a physiological/sexual "irritant" as the source of nervous illness, psychoanalysis came to understand sexuality as a fundamentally disturbing force encountered from birth onward that produces the unconscious in all of us. I will argue that, effectively, Freud understood the "irritant" the circumcision doctors sought to remove as a central feature of the human condition. While for reflex theory, the symptoms of nervous illness were held to arise from contingent pathologies in the otherwise natural reproductive sexual instinct, psychoanalysis came to understand human sexuality as constitutively denaturalized; symptoms arise as compromises and defenses in relation to the inherently "perverse" and disturbing nature of sexuality.

The psychoanalyst Jean Laplanche has played an important role in helping to articulate the unique status of sexuality for psychoanalysis. Laplanche argues that the child's encounter with the enigma of the adult other is the source of human sexuality's perversion from nature, or what he calls the "vital order."[1] Freud struggled to maintain the most radical aspect of his discoveries on sexuality when he hastily abandoned his seduction theory, Laplanche claims. Laplanche thus helps us understand what it is about the encounter with sexuality, in both theory and practice, that generates defensive maneuvers.

This chapter will work with psychoanalysis in both its historical and theoretical registers, placing Freud's early history and the development of his theories in relation to the reflex theorists. I will show how a psychoanalytic way of thinking, as I conceive of it, not only shines light upon the impetus for the reflex theorists' sexual hypotheses on nervous disorder (leading to the circumcision cure) but also offers a more fruitful alternative. The material in the first half of this chapter is less immediately concerned with circumcision compared to the rest of this book. However, the theoretical insights that I develop underscore the contribution psychoanalysis can make toward a critical evaluation of circumcision, particularly regarding the uncertain boundary between the physiological and the psychical to which circumcision draws our attention. In the conclusion of this chapter, I connect these findings more directly to circumcision via my reading of the Viennese philosopher Otto Weininger.

Laycock and Romberg

Previously, we saw how reflex theory justified genital surgeries by promoting a physiological origin for nervous illness through its claim that invisible irritation in an organ or other local body part could generate manifold bodily and psychic disturbances. The early European proponents of the theory focused on irritations of the ovaries, whereas later, primarily in America, the theory was appropriated by the circumcision doctors and applied to the foreskin. In order to subsume the apparent loss of one's will over one's actions

[1] Laplanche, *Life and Death*.

into a physicalist vocabulary, these theorists needed to generate some account of the mind's capacity to be subject to forces outside of conscious control—the same problem which Freud had to tackle. Let us look more closely at the writings of two early reflex theorists, Thomas Laycock (1812–76) and Moritz Romberg (1795–1893), to appreciate how they attempted this.

Thomas Laycock was an influential English physician and one of the first to develop theories of reflex action that encompassed activity in the brain.[2] He was especially well known for his 1840 *Treatise on the Nervous Diseases of Women*. The book offers a long, metaphysical discussion on the origins of human "will," under the subheading "the brain subject to the laws of reflex action." Essentially, Laycock argued for a conception of the mind as largely continuous with the automatic actions of the nervous system, and therefore subject to influences *from* the nervous system. "Tickling the fancy will excite laughter, as much as tickling the feet," he writes, linking in a literal way the experience of ideas with that of physical actions. "In fact, it may be hypothetically supposed that there is a surface on which sensorial fibers terminate, connected with ideas, and which is analogous to the sensitive fibers on the skin, and on mucous membranes."[3]

Paradigmatic of the nineteenth-century reflex theorists, Laycock sought to prove that the origin of nervous diseases (primarily hysteria) lay in genital pathologies, especially of the ovaries. He justified his focus on the genitals by way of quasi-Darwinian logic: because "the final cause of all vital action is the reproduction of the species," he writes, the "generative organs" must "exert" a special "influence . . . over the whole animal economy" (9). As the symptoms of hysteria were so wide-ranging, manifesting problems throughout the entire span of the body, it stood to reason that these "generative organs" were the biological locus of the disease.

Laycock's ideas about the relation between sexual difference and nervous disorder were in keeping with dominant nineteenth-century professional opinion. The ovaries were exquisitely sensitive organs prone to pathologies that could affect the entire nervous system. Empirical evidence supposedly lay in the "universally acknowledged . . . daily observation" that "hysteric diseases appear only during that period of life in which the reproductive organs perform their functions" (9). Interestingly, he made use of the fact that hysteria "unquestionably occurs in men occasionally" to distinguish his approach from the older uterine-based theories of the disease (82). His

---

[2] Hughlings Jackson, the neurologist mentioned at the beginning of the previous chapter, was one of Laycock's pupils. Jonathan Hutchinson, another English advocate of circumcision, also studied under (and for some time, lived with) Laycock.

[3] Laycock, *Treatise*, 109. Subsequent references are given in text.

updated "nervous" conception allowed for the testicles, as well as the ovaries, to be responsible for hysteria, albeit noting that the former was much rarer. The older doctors were on the right track, Laycock's work suggests, when they linked hysteria to the uterus; but, they lacked the theory of the nerves (and their connection to the genitals) that made his ideas more robust and able to account for the male anomaly.

One quote stands out, for foregrounding not simply the style of nineteenth-century sexism but also the theory of mind that these reflex theorists were implicitly generating: "Without preface it may be stated that by universal consent the nervous system of the human female is allowed to be sooner affected by all stimuli, whether corporeal or mental, than that of the male" (76). By arguing that "mental stimuli" have the capacity to upset the nervous system, Laycock implies that *thoughts* may be equally responsible for hysterical symptoms as physical disturbances. Thus, although he discusses the workings of the mind as something purely physical, his ideas suggest a nascent awareness of the role of the unconscious in nervous illness, which he understands as a primarily feminine problem. Intellectual historian Marcel Gauchet argues that Laycock's "theory of the automatic action of the brain," which influenced William Carpenter's coining of the term "cerebral unconscious" in 1857, paved the way for Freud's psychodynamic unconscious.[4]

Another reflex theorist, the German-Jewish physician Moritz Romberg, was almost universally cited in nineteenth-century works on hysteria, including Freud and Breuer's *Studies on Hysteria*.[5] In 1853, Romberg wrote that hysteria was "a reflex-neurosis dependent upon sexual [i.e., genital] irritation."[6] Similar to Laycock, he explained the behavior of hysterics, including their sexualized performances, as a consequence of the loss of conscious "will" by the hysterical "reflex action," which "dominates over the moral energies of the patient" (89). His description of hysterical attacks yet again incorporates some notion of unconscious psychical forces at play, here referred to as "mental impressions": "The patient yields herself up to, and is overcome by bodily and mental impressions, such as we see in no other disease. . . . The hysterical motto, 'I can't help it,' appropriately expresses this condition" (84). Thus, unconscious aspects of the mind, under the sway of the reflexes, determine the patient's behavior.

---

4   Gauchet, *L'inconscient cérébral*, 46. Salisbury and Shail observe that nineteenth-century neurology "distributed consciousness throughout the nervous system, suggesting . . . the 'invention' of an unconscious mind long before the appearance of psychoanalytic accounts describing a functional entity called 'the unconscious'" (*Neurology and Modernity*, 23).

5   Freud and Breuer, *Studies on Hysteria*, 220.

6   Romberg, *Manual of Nervous Disease*, 99. Subsequent references are given in the text.

Like his predecessors, Romberg argued that male hysteria, while a legitimate illness, was less common and more "transitory" than in women. Whereas male genitals became irritated in a seemingly contingent, external way—"masturbation and other sexual excesses" were the purported cause—female genitals, he argued, naturally existed in a state of constant irritation, leading to much more frequent and often "permanent" hysteria in women (99). An additional disparaging comment on the nature of the female sex suggests that, in Romberg's view, femininity is *itself* a kind of hysteria: "Besides the psychical character which marks the disease, the peculiarities of the sex also come into play, and the natural vanity, coquetry, whimsicality, tendency to exaggeration, and deception, and gossiping communicativeness of the female become more prominent" (84).

In attempting to locate the etiology of hysteria and related disorders in genital irritations that disrupted the nervous system, these nineteenth-century reflex theorists were led to acknowledge the potential for a split between conscious "will" and other mental phenomena (which they believed was connected, via the nerves, to the sex organs). This split was treated as pathological. Ideally, the mind and conscious will transcended the body; in certain cases, due often to the particularity of female physiology, things could go wrong, and unruly or "hysterical" symptoms would ensue.

Freud and Reflex Theory

Over the course of his career, Freud did not wholeheartedly embrace a shift from the physiological to the psychological—which many of his colleagues were happy to do—but struggled quite intensely with negotiating the two, often embracing unfashionable physicalist theories in ways that have puzzled his followers. The most discussed example of this relates to Freud's embrace of the unusual physicalist theories of his friend Wilhelm Fliess. Fliess invented the theory of the "nasal reflex neurosis," which held that nervous disorders often originated in pathologies of the nose. He developed elaborate theories regarding "periodicity" and the nervous system that linked the nose to the genitals and to various biological cycles that he believed governed the functioning of the body. Especially important were his ideas surrounding a supposed link between menstruation and nosebleeds, which enabled him to posit a male form of menstruation that takes place through the nose.[7]

---

[7] See, for example, Sulloway, *Freud*, 147–50.

Fliess advocated nasal surgery in certain cases of what he diagnosed as nasal reflex neurosis. His ideas might therefore be understood as a further abstraction from the theory of genital irritation. The nose was, for Fliess, a substitute for the genitals, due to the alleged nervous links between the two. Freud, in fact, sent his patient Emma Eckstein to Fliess for a nasal surgery which nearly killed her; it has been argued that Freud's regret over this botched operation forms the backdrop to his famous dream of "Irma's Injection."[8] Although Freud eventually rejected Fliess's ideas, culminating in the complete breakdown of their friendship, he was initially one of Fliess's few advocates. In a letter written to Fliess shortly after Freud abandoned work on his "Project for a Scientific Psychology," Freud demonstrated the hope he placed in a physiological way out of the clinical and theoretical problems he encountered:

> I am in a rather gloomy state, and all I can say is I am looking forward to our congress. . . . I have run into some doubts about my repression theory which a suggestion from you . . . may resolve. Anxiety, chemical factors, etc.—perhaps you may supply me with solid ground on which I shall be able to give up explaining things psychologically and start finding a firm basis in physiology![9]

Sander Gilman has offered an influential interpretation of Freud's relationship with Fliess, seeing in the latter's appeal evidence of Freud's struggle with the racist and anti-Semitic medical theories dominant at the time. The "psychological" theories of nervous disorder that contradicted Fliess's physiological "nasal reflex neurosis," Gilman explains, were all based on the popular theory of "degenerationism" (the nineteenth-century precursor to eugenics). No matter how sophisticated, the extant psychological theories of nervous disorder—such as those Freud learned from Charcot—ultimately reduced etiology to "hereditary taint," which, predictably enough, implicated Jews, who were thought to be disproportionately prone to nervous disorders due to "racial" inheritance. "Fliess is not simply a quack," Gilman writes, "his 'quackery' is accepted by Freud since it provides an alternative to the pathological image of the Jew in conventional medicine."[10] Gilman draws a further connection to circumcision, arguing that Fliess's ideas served, in a roundabout way, to redeem the trope of the menstruating male Jew—an image derived from anti-Semitic fantasies about Jewish circumcision—by

8 Schur, "Some 'Additional Day Residues'"; Freud, *Interpretation of Dreams*, 111.
9 Freud, *Origins of Psycho-Analysis*, 169.
10 Gilman, "Struggle of Psychiatry," 304; see also Gilman, *Freud*.

making "male menstruation" a universal, *nasal* phenomenon: "extraordinary caricatures [of Jews] stressed one central aspect of the physiognomy of the Jewish male, his nose, which represented that hidden sign of his sexual difference, his circumcised penis."[11]

Yet, despite his relationship to Fliess's work, Freud's early views on hysteria were heavily influenced by Charcot's more psychological approach. In contrast to the growing professional skepticism surrounding the diagnosis of hysteria, Charcot believed that the complaints of hysterics represented genuine pathological phenomena, and he painstakingly documented the "stages" of hysterical attacks. Freud was impressed with Charcot's approach, particularly with the significance Charcot gave to the role of "ideas" in hysterical symptoms. Charcot argued that hysterics suffered from "split consciousness." Hysterics were predisposed to fall into dissociated mental states, where they became susceptible to the influence of ideas that would dominate their behavior during waking life. In other words, hysterics were suffering from the effects of ideas that were "split off" from their conscious awareness. In his lectures, Charcot put patients under hypnosis to demonstrate that he could both induce and cure hysterical paralyses, thereby proving the psychological nature of hysterical symptoms.[12]

Charcot was opposed to the idea that hysteria had a sexual etiology, and explicitly rejected genital-based theories of the disease. However, despite his psychological discoveries, for Charcot the final determinant of hysteria was, in fact, physiological. The disease, he believed, was the result of an inherited neurological illness—a "dynamic lesion," in his vocabulary—that predisposed the patient to suffer the effects of split consciousness. Hence, he was connected to anti-Semitic theories of degenerationism, which posited hereditary taint as the source of various illnesses that Gilman discusses. Arnold Davidson called Charcot a "bridge or attempted mediation" between psychiatry and pathological anatomy.[13]

Charcot's opposition to a sexual etiology for hysteria occurred at a time when genital surgeries were popular in medicine. Although the Anglo-American enthusiasm for circumcision did not extend to continental Europe, ovariectomy for female reflex neuroses, referred to as "castration" in German medical journals, was frequently practiced and intensely discussed.[14] In 1887, the same year that Freud presented Charcot's psychological theory of hysteria to the medical society of Vienna, and argued, in line with Charcot,

---

[11] Gilman, *Freud*, 301.
[12] See Freud, "Charcot" and "Report on My Studies."
[13] Davidson, "Assault on Freud."
[14] See Bonomi, "Relevance of Castration," 552.

against genital-based theories of the disease, a book by the German doctor Friedrich Merkel cited thirty-five works, from that year alone, on the subject of female castration as a cure for hysteria, naming it "the most discussed topic of the period."[15] Furthermore, in 1896, the surgeon Richard Kromer examined 240 studies on female castration, totaling 300 operations, and claimed that 70 percent of the cases were successful; he said that the number of women who had undergone the operation was "legion."[16] The medical community was at a crossroads, as evidenced in this passage by Friedrich Jolly, a German professor of neurology and psychiatry, in his 1892 article on hysteria:

> In spite of the fact that the theory of hysteria has been, with the passing of time, moving away from Romberg's definition of it as a reflex-neurosis originating from the genitals, and toward a psychic conception of the disease, the contemporary vain sacrifice of a great number of ovaries has once again demonstrated that the latter idea enters practice only very slowly.[17]

Freud's earliest writings demonstrate how he sided with Charcot on this matter in opposition to genital-based theories of the disease. For example, in his 1886 report for the funders of his studies under Charcot in Paris, Freud wrote that hysteria was "under the odium of some very widespread prejudices. Among these are the supposed dependence of hysterical illness upon genital irritation."[18] Additionally, in an 1888 encyclopedia article on hysteria he published while still a close follower of Charcot, he wrote, "Whether changes in the genitals really constitute so often the sources of stimulus for hysterical symptoms is in fact doubtful," and he warned against the practice of "surgeons, whose intervention in [hysterical symptoms] can do nothing but harm."[19]

Although Freud was, like his mentor Charcot, initially skeptical of a "sexual" etiology for hysteria, it is important to note that this skepticism was indistinguishable from his opposition to the theory of genital irritation. At this point, Freud had not yet advanced his enlarged concept of sexuality as the key to the neuroses. Therefore, in his written justification for why a sexual theory of hysteria should be discarded, he tellingly conflates human sexuality

---

[15] Cited in Bonomi, 553.
[16] Cited in Bonomi, 553.
[17] Cited in Bonomi, 554.
[18] Freud, "Report on my Studies," 11.
[19] Freud, "Charcot," 51.

with the mechanical functioning of the genitals in the same manner as the reflex theorists. In the encyclopedia article cited previously, Freud wrote:

> As regards what is often asserted to be the preponderant influence of abnormalities in the sexual sphere upon the development of hysteria, it must be said that its importance is as a rule over-estimated. In the first place, hysteria is found in sexually immature girls and boys, just as, too, the neurosis with all its characteristics also occurs in the male sex, though a great deal more rarely. Furthermore, hysteria has been observed in women with a complete lack of genitalia, and every physician will have seen a number of cases of hysteria in women whose genitals exhibited no anatomical changes at all, just as, on the contrary, the majority of women with diseases of the sexual organs do not suffer from hysteria.[20]

For contemporary eyes, this passage is patently "un-Freudian." He argues that because children and women "without genitalia" can suffer from hysteria, the disease cannot logically be dependent on "abnormalities in the sexual sphere." As the psychoanalyst Carlo Bonomi has observed, such claims make sense only when one equates sexuality with reproductive maturity and the genitals.[21] Freud evidently had not yet conceived of sexuality as a psychical (and infantile) phenomenon, and because he believed in a psychical etiology of hysteria, he could discard the claims of reflex theorists wholesale.

Bonomi has unearthed an impressive amount of evidence suggesting that Freud was, in fact, intimately familiar with the genital irritation reflex theory and the surgeries it spawned. He argues that Freud repudiated the navigation he had to make between the physiological, genital-based theory of hysteria promoted by the reflex theorists, and Charcot's desexualized psychology, when he formulated his own sexual theory of the neuroses.

Bonomi focuses on an often-forgotten aspect of Freud's biography: his training under the pediatrician and prominent reflex theorist Adolf Baginsky, and his subsequent ten years of work in the department of children's nervous disorders at a polyclinic in Vienna. In March 1886, immediately following his study under Charcot in Paris, Freud spent a month training in pediatrics under Baginsky.[22] Baginsky subscribed to reflex theory and, not unlike the circumcision doctors, sought to explain childhood nervous illness by extending the notion of genital irritation into infancy. He became known in the medical community for his *Handbook of School Hygiene*, published in

[20] Freud, 50–1.
[21] Bonomi, "Relevance of Castration," 571–2.
[22] Bonomi, 562–6.

1877, the year when Freud trained with him. In a chapter of this handbook titled "Illnesses of the Nervous System," Baginsky argued that childhood masturbation, which can begin "in the earliest infancy," has disastrous effects on the child's nervous system, stating, "insignificant stimulati coming from the periphery . . . which in the adult pass away without leaving traces . . . [In children] can provoke violent explosions by reflex."[23] He also viewed masturbation as contagious: "certain external stimuli are able to produce the evil and seduction plays . . . a very big role."[24] By this, he meant that the experience of stimulation on the genitals in childhood would lead the child to masturbate. As Bonomi observes, the physicalist framework Baginsky deployed made it "impossible to distinguish between an intentional act of seduction and the physical irritation of the genitals caused by rough clothes or lack of hygiene"; both generated the same consequence, masturbation and the dangerous excitement of the nervous system.[25] While Baginsky raised the issue of childhood seduction—a theme which became very important in Freud's work, as we will examine—he folded it into a theory which ignored its real import: "the meaning of seduction as an action performed on a mind by another mind was ultimately disavowed,"[26] writes Bonomi. He was a typical reflex theorist, subsuming sexuality into a purely physical model that treated nervous disorders as the consequence of genital irritation.

After his training under Baginsky, Freud returned home to Vienna and took up the post at the polyclinic, working three times a week as head of the department of children's nervous disorders. He held this position from 1886 to 1896, during which time the clinic's popularity increased immensely, from 6000 annual patients in 1886 to 17,400 in 1898.[27] "It is patently obvious," Bonomi writes, "that Freud examined hundreds of children each year and that only very few of them were affected by severe neurological diseases; the rest were evidently affected by 'nervous' disorders which would become typical of the psychoanalytic caseload."[28] It would stand to reason that this experience played some role in Freud's development of psychoanalysis. Yet, Freud historians almost universally neglect to analyze Freud's work in pediatrics and mentorship under Baginsky—likely because Freud himself, perhaps symptomatically, rarely discussed it.[29]

---

[23] Cited in Bonomi, 563.
[24] Cited in Bonomi, "Baginsky," 41.
[25] Bonomi, "Relevance of Castration," 565.
[26] Bonomi, 565.
[27] Bonomi, 573.
[28] Bonomi, *The Cut*, 33.
[29] Freud briefly mentions his mentorship under Baginsky in his 1925 "Autobiographical Study," 13.

Bonomi argues that Freud must have faced "a difficult navigation between Scylla and Charybdis, between a sex without mind on the one side, and a mind without sex on the other."[30] Reflex theory, on the one hand, treated "sexuality" as a powerful force that could generate illness outside the patient's conscious control, even in children. Yet, its notion of sexuality was conceptually impoverished, as it equated sex with the hypothesized mechanics and reflexes of the nervous system. Charcot, on the other hand, offered an approach to hysteria that was more directly attuned to psychological phenomena and the power of unconscious ideas. However, Charcot rejected theorizing any connections between sexuality and hysteria, which Freud eventually came to view as unscientific, willful blindness to the evidence at hand. Furthermore, as Gilman argues, Freud was likely repelled by the racist and anti-Semitic theory of degenerationism that underlay Charcot's work. Thus, in his study of hysteria and the neuroses, Freud had to navigate at least two contradictory paradigms: a racist proto-psychology that neglected sexuality and a surgically zealous sexual theory that neglected psychology.

When Freud finally produced a theory of sexuality and the neuroses that overcame these difficulties, which put childhood sexual experiences at the center, he seems to have suspiciously downplayed his familiarity with Baginsky's ideas and his long-standing clinical experience with children. In his 1896 discussion of the role of infantile sexual experiences in hysteria, Freud does not mention his mentorship under Baginsky but says he "learnt from colleagues" of "several publications which stigmatize the frequency of sexual practices by nurses and nurse maids," and he suggests, from the position of an outsider, that the current "evidence" on the existence of infantile sexuality may, in fact, be "scanty."[31] "I had no opportunity of direct observations on children," he writes in his 1914 autobiographical account.[32] Why, Bonomi asks, did Freud not mention his direct work with children and his proximity to the problem of childhood sexuality as it was being theorized by his immediate mentors and colleagues? Why did he create this artificial distance? Bonomi hypothesizes that a severe repudiation of Baginsky and the doctrine of genital irritation, with the concomitant practice of surgical castration, was at work. Consequently, he claims, the specter of genital surgery as a gruesome cure for hysteria haunts psychoanalysis—particularly as the repressed backdrop to Freud's theories on castration and his difficult treatment of Emma Eckstein (the patient he felt he nearly murdered by referring her to Fliess).

[30] Bonomi, "Relevance of Castration," 576.
[31] Freud, "Aetiology of Hysteria," 207.
[32] Freud, "History of the Psycho-Analytic Movement," 18.

Regardless of the degree to which Freud was directly influenced by, or repudiated, the genital irritation reflex theory, when we read his earliest theories on nervous illness we can see how both physicalist and psychological ideas were at play. As Freud formulated his first theory of defense, and then his seduction theory, he began to develop a new, enlarged conception of sexuality and the unconscious. Yet, he never completely discarded the insights provided to him from the biology of the time. Rather, his theories dialectically transformed the contradictions within the extant ideas about the relationship between body and psyche (such as those discussed in the previous section). He managed this, I propose, by focusing on an additional variable that was often neglected: the function of memory, or what Freud called (in quasi-biologistic fashion) "mnemic traces." His attention to the role of memory in psychic suffering necessitated sustained conversation with his patients. A memory, after all, cannot be seen under the microscope or extracted with a knife. The study of his patients' articulated memories, in turn, necessitated thinking about temporality and the role of the other. These crucial ingredients enabled Freud to generate his more radical, universalistic theories on the nature of sexuality and the unconscious. Let us now examine these early theories and their critical treatment and synthesis by Laplanche.

Psychology, Physiology, and Seduction

Freud's theory of defense, first published in the 1894 "Preliminary Communication" of his *Studies on Hysteria* (co-written with Josef Breuer) and then refined in his paper "The Neuro-Psychoses of Defence," is an elegant psychological concept that places emphasis on thoughts and memories rather than bodily processes. Freud argued that certain neurotic symptoms (phobias, obsessions, hallucinations, and hysterical conversions) emerge as a consequence of the patient's attempts to "defend" against a powerful and unpalatable "idea." The patient strives to forget the idea, which often occurs in the context of some disturbing life event, but does not entirely succeed. Instead, the energy or "excitation" attached to the idea either attaches itself to a different but related idea, which the patient obsesses over, or it attaches itself to a part of the body which then behaves symptomatically (becoming paralyzed, or hypersensitive, or painful, etc.). A symptom emerges as a ciphered version of something the neurotic wished to forget. Freud further claimed, without much theoretical elaboration, that in all the cases of defense neuroses he had encountered, the "incompatible ideas" eventually uncovered were of a sexual nature.[33]

---

[33] Freud, "Neuro-Psychoses of Defence," 53.

Consider an example Freud uses in this early formulation of defense. A woman complained of being constantly troubled by the urge to urinate whenever she was in public. She could only manage to go out when she knew there was a toilet close to hand. Yet, the symptom did not occur when she was in the safety of her own home, indicating that the problem was not straightforwardly organic. Over the course of her treatment with Freud, the woman recalled the first time the symptom appeared. She was at a concert hall and was admiring a nearby gentleman. She fantasized about becoming his wife and began to experience erotic sensations in her body, which culminated in "a slight need to urinate," forcing her to leave the hall. This spontaneous eruption of erotic feelings disturbed her otherwise prudish nature, and she tried to forget the incident. The symptom, she realized, emerged after that. It paid tribute to a powerful thought she had tried to suppress, transferring the energy from the idea of marital relations with the gentleman to the need to urinate when in public. The symptom dissolved, Freud reports, after the patient managed to recount the memory and its associated feelings. Through this process of articulation that she underwent, Freud asserts, the trapped "excitation" which had powered her symptom was "discharged."[34]

While Freud's terms "excitation" and "discharge" link neurotic illness to physiological processes and substances in the same spirit as reflex theory, we can see in this theory how problems of memory and memorialization—ignored in physiological theories of nervous illness—are given center stage. It is not just the body that makes us ill, but the ways we *relate* to our bodies, in thoughts, memories, and speech, that govern our states of sickness and health. To account for how this works, Freud invented the theory of repression, which he counterposed to ordinary forgetting. To strive to forget an unpleasant thought is commonplace; but, to *repress* a thought, to make it unconscious, he argued, creates a reservoir of accumulated energy that lacks the means of adequate discharge—a split in the psyche that generates symptoms.[35] In his initial formulation, he treated this process of repression and the consequent creation of this unconscious "reservoir" as a pathological phenomenon which he aimed to help patients undo.

In a subsequent 1896 paper, "Further Remarks on the Neuro-Psychoses of Defense" (where the "seduction theory" made its first published appearance), Freud maintained the position that repression and unconscious ideas were inherently pathological, but acknowledged a stumbling block: Why is it that some people repress certain chance experiences, like an erotic reverie,

---

[34] Freud, 56.
[35] Breuer and Freud, "Preliminary Communication," 10.

while others seem to cope just fine? Everybody pushes away unwelcome thoughts—why do some apparently resort to the more extreme and symptom-generating mechanism of repression? He noted, in a lecture version of this paper, that the repressed memories his neurotic patients uncovered could be "astonishingly trivial": for one "young lady, simply hearing a riddle which suggested an obscene answer had been enough to provoke the first anxiety attack and with it to start the illness."[36] Furthermore, Freud asked, why are *sexual* thoughts always to blame? What makes sexuality so different from other areas of human experience, so potentially traumatic?

Freud wrote that he wished to avoid blaming "heredity" for the neurotic's propensity to fall ill, as his colleagues readily did; this solution, he argued, was too simple and unsophisticated (and we can presume he was wary of its anti-Semitic implications).[37] Instead, he offered a startling claim: It is not the adulthood experience—the forbidden erotic fantasy, in our example—that alone generates repression and makes the patient ill. Rather, for a patient to utilize repression and thus become neurotic, there must be an earlier memory of a "premature" sexual experience from childhood, which had lain dormant. The later experience would reawaken this childhood memory through certain associative links. The reawakening of this memory, after puberty, would produce intense displeasure, attacking the subject like a "foreign body" inside the psyche.[38] The psyche would attempt to defend itself against this attack from within by calling upon the extreme measure of repression, pushing both the childhood memory and the later experience out of consciousness—but the memories would unconsciously persist, generating neurotic symptoms. "'Repression' of the memory of a distressing sexual experience which occurs in maturer years," Freud writes, "is only possible for those in whom that experience can activate the memory-trace of a trauma in childhood."[39] As he introduced this new idea—the experience of seduction in childhood as the original cause of repression and neurotic illness—Freud appeared both very close to, and far from, reflex theory:

> In order to cause hysteria, it is not enough that there should occur at some period of the subject's life an event which touches his sexual existence and becomes pathogenic through the release and suppression of a distressing

[36] Freud, "Aetiology of Hysteria," 200–1.
[37] Freud, 191.
[38] Although this process is described in "Further Remarks" and "Aetiology of Hysteria," the phrase "foreign body" does not appear in these papers but, rather, in the "Preliminary Communication" to *Studies on Hysteria*: "We must presume rather that the psychical trauma—or more precisely the memory of the trauma—acts like a foreign body which long after its entry must continue to be regarded as an agent that is still at work" (6).
[39] Freud, "Further Remarks," 166.

affect. On the contrary, *these sexual traumas must have occurred in early childhood (before puberty), and their content must consist of an actual irritation of the genitals (of processes resembling copulation)*. . . . I have found this specific determinant of hysteria—*sexual passivity during the pre-sexual period*—in every case of hysteria (including two male cases) which I have analysed.[40]

It is worth piecing together Freud's logic on this matter to see how he reaches this surprising thesis. Freud was encountering patients who, in the process of freely associative conversation with him, recalled forgotten memories linked to their neurotic symptoms. He found that behind the more recent memories, those that occurred after puberty, there appeared to lie earlier memories in which the patients experienced some form of "sexual passivity" with an adult (including "actual irritation of the genitals") well before they had reached reproductive maturity. Freud used this unusual evidence not simply to assert that neurotics were abused as children but to form a *theory* about the complicated material at hand. The theory was this: it takes at least two events to make a person neurotic. First, there must be a "determining cause," a sexual violation that took place in childhood. As the child will have been too young to fully appreciate the sexual nature of this violation, the memory of it will lie dormant, quietly awaiting some kind of further stimulus. Then, after sexual maturity, another event must happen, which might seem totally insignificant in itself, but which forms a link to the memory of sexual trauma. Now that the subject is old enough to appreciate the sexual nature of the childhood trauma, she will experience a profound displeasure. The original memory will attack the subject from inside her psyche, generating repression and causing the symptom to emerge in the memory's place. Through the seduction theory, Freud thus moved from a somewhat simplistic theory of defense, which was unable to account for why one memory might be more likely to be repressed than another, to a theory that took into account not just memory but the relation *between* memories—offering a reason, however ultimately unsatisfactory, for repression to operate over seemingly insignificant events.

In a footnote, Freud tried to work out why premature *sexual* experiences, in particular, generated this strange process of repression and symptom formation. It is a dense but interesting passage in which physiology and psychology interact:

It is known that having ideas with a sexual content produces excitatory processes in the genitals which are similar to those produced by the sexual

[40] Freud, 162 (emphasis original).

experience itself. We may assume that this somatic excitation becomes transposed into the psychical sphere. As a rule the effect in question is much stronger in the case of the experience than in the case of the memory. But if the sexual experience occurs during the period of sexual immaturity and the memory of it is around during or after maturity, then the memory will have a far stronger excitatory effect than the experience did at the time it happened; and this is because in the meantime puberty has immensely increased the capacity of the sexual apparatus for reaction. An inverted relation of this sort between real experience and memory seems to contain the psychological precondition for the occurrence of a repression. Sexual life affords—through the retardation of pubertal maturity as compared with the psychical functions—the only possibility that occurs for this inversion of relative effectiveness. *The traumas of childhood operate in a deferred fashion as though they were fresh experiences; but they do so unconsciously.*[41]

Human beings take a uniquely long amount of time to reach physical sexual maturity, while nevertheless achieving highly developed mental functioning beforehand. We are able to mentally register sexual advances long before we have the sexual maturity to physically respond to them. Moreover, Freud reasons, once we have reached sexual maturity, this *memory* of a sexual excitation from childhood will become *more powerful* than the original event because "in the meantime puberty has immensely increased the capacity of the sexual apparatus for reaction." If thinking about sex can sometimes feel like actually having sex, Freud suggests, then *memories* about a premature sexual experience will feel *more* sexually intense, after puberty, than the original event. Something about this imbalance of energy between the original occurrence of a sexual event and the awakening of the postpubertal memory of it is traumatic, he claims, leading to repression and symptom formation.

Let us examine Freud's key example of the seduction theory at work. Emma came to Freud suffering from a phobia of going into shops alone. She related the phobia to an occasion, at twelve years old, when she went into a shop and saw two shop assistants laughing. In reaction to the laughter, she said she experienced a sexual release, and then ran away from the shop in fright, believing that the shop assistants were laughing at her clothes. At this point, we have a somewhat confusing memory which nevertheless links to the phobia of going into stores. After further analysis, Emma recalled two earlier scenes from childhood. In both, she had gone into a sweetshop, and the shopkeeper, an old man, groped her genitals through her clothes. The shop assistants' laughter from the more recent incident, she then reported to Freud, reminded her of the smile on the shopkeeper's face when he assaulted her as a child.[42]

Emma's case played a central role in Freud's theory of seduction, yet as we can see, it involves much more than a fact-finding mission, as Freud's theories are sometimes made out to be. What matters in this case is a peculiar operation of both temporality and memory in relation to the experience of sexuality. When she was a child, there was an assault, yet Emma was too young to appreciate its sexual nature. After puberty, there was no assault—merely some confusing laughter—but she felt a sexual release and a fright. The later event recalled and activated the earlier one, which took on a new, frightening form. Sexuality operated on neither scene alone, but *unconsciously, in the interval between the two,* experienced retrospectively or in a type of temporality Freud called "deferred action."[43]

Emma's childhood experience in the sweetshop may have been confusing and difficult, but the trauma proper began when she witnessed the shop assistants' laughter years later. The laughter awakened and transformed her memory of the original assault, producing a powerful and frightening sexual sensation which generated repression and her phobia. In Freud's formulation of neurosis, there is, indeed, a physiological problem, excessive excitation—or "irritations" of the nerves, in the language of reflex theory—but it is aroused not simply by present circumstances, but by the present's interaction with a metastasized past.

The Seduction Theory versus Reflex Theory

As I have mentioned, Freud's work in this area appears paradoxically both wedded and foreign to the physicalist ideas that undergirded reflex theory. When Freud writes that, in order to become neurotic, a patient must have experienced an "actual irritation of the genitals (of processes resembling copulation)" as a child, and when he discusses neuroses as a consequence of "excitations" that fail to "discharge," he appears to be mobilizing the kind of physicalist description of sexuality and nervous illness that we saw to be highly reductionistic in the case of the circumcision doctors.

[42] Freud, "Project," 353–6.
[43] Freud, "Sexuality in the Aetiology of Neuroses," 281.

It is well known that, however far he went into the realm of psychology, Freud always hoped to "ground" psychoanalysis in biology and believed that his work would not be complete until the natural sciences had advanced far enough that they could account in chemical terms for the mental processes he described. Freud's unpublished "Project for a Scientific Psychology" represents his most sustained attempt at theorizing the action of the psyche within the terms of natural science; as he wrote, his intention was to "represent psychical processes as quantitatively determinate states of specifiable material particles."[44]

Although we have already examined Freud's biographical connections to the reflex theorists, it is worth mentioning a few more examples within Freud's own theories where he appears particularly close to the problematics of reflex theory and the concerns of the circumcision doctors. In his discussion of the seduction theory in the "Project," Freud writes, "Experience teaches us to recognize hysterics as individuals of whom one knows in part that they have become *prematurely* sexually excitable owing to mechanical and emotional stimulation (masturbation)."[45] Here, Freud shares the circumcision doctors' concern with the premature awakening of sexuality via childhood masturbation, and he subsumes both physical and "emotional" sexual experiences into an overarching physiological framework. Additionally, throughout his life's work, Freud maintained a distinction between what he called the "psychoneuroses," those which emerged as a consequence of repression and thus had a psychological component that could be analyzed, and the "actual neuroses," which he believed had a direct bodily cause, the failure to discharge toxic sexual substances.[46] He considered the practice of masturbation to be one of the major causes of the actual neuroses.[47] His work on the actual neuroses included a critical reworking of neurasthenia, a diagnosis popularized by the nineteenth-century American doctor George Beard and based explicitly on reflex theory.[48] Finally, in the *Interpretation of Dreams*, Freud writes, "the psychical apparatus must be constructed like a reflex apparatus. Reflex processes remain the model of every psychical function."[49] In this case, psychoanalysis appears as if it could be a mere

---

[44] Freud, "Project," 295.
[45] Freud, 357 (emphasis original.)
[46] See Freud, "Further Remarks," 167–8.
[47] Freud, "Sexuality in the Aetiology of Neuroses," 268; see also Freud, "Contributions to a Discussion." For an interesting Lacanian revision and contemporary clinical application of the "actual neuroses," see Verhaeghe, Vanheule, and De Rick, "Actual Neurosis."
[48] See Freud, "On the Grounds," 90; and "Sexuality in the Aetiology of Neuroses," 279.
[49] Freud, *Interpretation of Dreams*, 538.

supplement to reflex theory, in which the psyche functions as an additional variable.

In summary, both Freud and the reflex theorists shared in common the view that "irritations" (in the vocabulary of reflex theory) or "excitations" (in Freudian vocabulary), originating in the sexual sphere, have the capacity to severely disturb the healthy functioning of both mind and body through mechanical or "reflex" processes outside the conscious command of the subject. For the reflex theorists, the irritations needed to be removed, and for Freud, the excitations needed to be discharged. However, there is a crucial difference: Freud was concerned not simply with the physical presence of excitations, but with the complicated process of repression he theorized in which such excitations were linked to memory and temporality, and thus to the life history of a subject as articulated in speech.

Moreover, in the texts we've just examined, Freud produces a major shift in how a split in consciousness can be understood. For the reflex theorists, bodily dysfunction alone was responsible for interfering with conscious intention. The sufferers of nervous illness were those whose minds had fallen prey to the pathological effects of irritated organs (for earlier reflex theorists, the ovaries, and for the circumcision doctors, the penis via the foreskin). Behaviors that occurred outside the conscious command of the subject were therefore biological problems that could be overcome through physical, medical intervention. In contrast, the unconscious, in Freud's seduction theory, is the *psychical* consequence of an imbalanced relation between the mind and the body: the overdeveloped mind "holds onto" a sexual experience that occurred on the underdeveloped body, with retroactive consequences after puberty. The unconscious is thus the traumatic psychical residue of a *disjunction* between mind and body, rather than standing for one or the other of those polarities.

This is a radical idea. However, in the seduction theory, Freud located the source of the neuroses in prepubertal sexual experiences that could, in theory, be prevented. "The unconscious"—understood by Freud at the time as the reservoir of undischarged excitation—was the pathological consequence of a contingent violation, an unfortunate deviation from a normal state of health and self-integration, rather than a universal human phenomenon. Only those who were subjected to a sexual assault as children resorted to the mechanism of repression, thereby developing a split in consciousness and suffering its effects throughout their lives. The theory therefore shares with the reflex theorists the idea that the determining cause of nervous illness was a chance problem that could be prevented or possibly reversed.

This implicitly preserved an ideal version of sexuality—one unaffected by repression and the unconscious—as attainable. In the seduction theory, sexuality is strange and traumatic only for those who have been traumatized by it. It will take a few more steps for Freud to discover that sexuality is inherently this way—or, in Laplanche's formulation, that everyone has been traumatized by sexuality, "prematurely" seduced.

The Generalized Theory of Seduction

In his 1925 "Autobiographical Study," Freud wrote that he was demoralized and embarrassed when he realized that the "scenes of seductions" his patients reported "had never taken place, and that they were only phantasies which my patients had made up or which I myself had perhaps forced on them."[50] Elsewhere, he describes his abandoned seduction theory as a "mistaken idea . . . which might have been almost fatal" for his "young science,"[51] and goes on to discuss his twin discoveries of psychical reality and infantile sexuality as the fruitful consequence of his heightened scrutiny toward hysterical fantasies of seduction.

Freud's abandonment of the seduction theory has been a lightning rod of controversy for admirers and critics alike. In a polemical book that became a centerpiece of the "Freud Wars," J. M. Masson argued that Freud suppressed the seduction theory and evidence of his patients' experiences of childhood sexual abuse due to a "failure of courage."[52] Masson quotes Freud selectively, neglecting to include instances in which Freud categorically stated the reality, prevalence, and etiological significance of seduction even after he abandoned the theory.[53] As Theresa Brennan explains, "What Freud abandoned was the idea that the sole cause of a psychoneurosis was an actual seduction. . . . The significance of the discovery of psychical reality was less that it discounted . . . accounts [of seduction] as 'real events,' more that it emphasized that phantasies of seduction had similar effects to real events."[54] Thus, many others

---

50 Freud, "Autobiographical Study," 34.
51 Freud, "History of the Psycho-Analytic Movement," 17.
52 Masson, *Assault on Truth*, 10–11.
53 For example, in the *Three Essays*, Freud writes that he "cannot admit that in my paper on 'The Aetiology of Hysteria' I exaggerated the frequency or importance of [seduction]" as the most prominent "accidental *external* contingency" in the production of neuroses (190, emphasis original).
54 Brennan, *Interpretation of the Flesh*, 29. See also Rose's feminist critique: "[Masson's] polemic states more clearly than any other that the concept of an internal psychic dynamic is detrimental to politics—in this case explicitly feminism—since it denies to women an unequivocal accusation of the real. There must be no internal conflict, no desire and no dialogue; conflict must be external, the event must be wholly outside, if women are to have a legitimate voice" (*Sexuality*, 12).

have praised Freud's abandonment of the seduction theory as the beginning of psychoanalysis proper.

French psychoanalyst Jean Laplanche, a one-time disciple of Lacan, takes a different view. Although he agrees Freud was correct to shift the focus to unconscious fantasy, he argues that Freud's abandonment of the seduction theory threw the baby out with the bathwater. In giving up the theory, Laplanche argues, Freud constructed an overly "endogamous" theory of sexuality and the unconscious that lost the traumatic, "exogamous" aspect of transmission from adult to child. Rather than viewing seduction as limited to a physical sexual violation from childhood, Laplanche proposes an alternate interpretation, the "generalized theory of seduction," in which *every* child is "prematurely" seduced by the enigmatic sexuality that adults unconsciously transmit. As Laplanche writes, seduction is "a fundamental situation in which an adult professes to a child verbal, non-verbal, and even behavioral signifiers which are pregnant with unconscious sexual significations."[55] Adult caretakers unconsciously transmit enigmatic sexual signifiers that children endlessly attempt to translate or "bind"; this process constitutes the traumatic origins of infantile sexuality, repression, and unconscious fantasy. Laplanche's influential theory universalizes both the process of repression and the formation of the unconscious that Freud identified in his hysterical patients. By maintaining the focus on the alterity—the enigmatic otherness—constitutive of human sexuality, it also helps us understand why sexuality is so often experienced as strange and threatening (for the circumcision doctors among others).

The conditions for generalized seduction arise out of the human child's premature birth and delayed onset of sexual maturity, Laplanche argues.[56] In my view, the theory can be understood as a helpful elaboration of the installation of lack in Lacanian castration and its relation to the genesis and felt experience of sexuality.[57] As children, we are in a fundamentally passive

---

[55] Laplanche, *New Foundations*, 126.

[56] Laplanche, *Life and Death*, 43–4.

[57] The term "enigmatic signifier" is originally Lacan's ("Direction of the Treatment," 518). The relationship between Lacan and Laplanche is famously contentious: Laplanche was an analysand and disciple of Lacan, but cut his therapy short and helped found, with fellow ex-Lacanians, the *Association Psychanalytique de France,* recognized by the International Psychoanalytic Association in contradistinction to Lacan's *École Freudienne de Paris* (see Roudinesco, *Lacan & Co.,* 357). The source of the initial theoretical division between Lacan and Laplanche lies in a metapsychological paper co-written by Serge Leclaire and Laplanche, "The Unconscious: A Psychoanalytical Study" (see Roudinesco, 307–18). Lacan summed up the difference between Laplanche's view of the unconscious and his own in a discussion with his student Anika Lemaire: "To state, as does Laplanche, that 'the unconscious is the condition of language' is, [Lacan] says, to go directly against the very point on which [Lacan's] own statements leave absolutely no possible doubt, namely that, on the contrary, language is the condition of the unconscious" (Lemaire, *Lacan*, 249).

position, dependent on and vulnerable to the adult other for a prolonged period of time. Consequently, the adult other gets into our skin: it suckles us, caresses us, wipes us clean, and so on. Such moments of passive penetration leave behind enigmatic deposits, of something "more" than the simple provision of our biological needs. We are drawn into this surplus, striving to figure out, or translate, what it means. "Translation," writes John Fletcher in his introduction to Laplanche, "describes the child's attempts from infancy to transpose and bind the stimulating and intrusive intimacies of the other. These are attempts to translate into representations, fantasies, 'infantile sexual theories,' the enigma of the other's desire and designs on the child. What does he or she want with me?"[58] These attempts at translation and mastery are always incomplete, especially after the acquisition of language; something remains enigmatic about the other's signifiers, and this "something," we realize, has been put inside us. These enigmatic messages, the residue of our attempts at translation, become hypercathected, empty places in the order of meaning. Unconscious fantasy forms as a screen in the place of these enigmas, an imperfect attempt to bind an excess which otherwise threatens to overwhelm the psyche. Recall Freud's comments about the "inverted relation" between a childhood experience of sexual assault and the postpubertal memory of it, which "seems to contain the psychological precondition for the occurrence of a repression." For Laplanche, the fundamental human condition *is* this "inverted relation," the temporal disjunction, in which, due to the process of translation, encounters with the other perpetually take on new and sometimes traumatic significance *after* they originally occur.

Freud, in fact, hinted at this universality of seduction and its consequences. As we saw, in the seduction theory, Freud argued that sexual experiences have the unique propensity to cause neurosis because of the human being's uniquely delayed onset of sexual maturity alongside its receptiveness to sexual advances and impressions. Although Freud thought it was only in

---

Zupančič has offered a related Lacanian critique of Laplanche: "The expression 'enigmatic message' seems to suggest that the original/traumatic thrust is caused by some mystery of meaning. . . . [However,] an enigma can only emerge together with the presupposition of meaning. . . . It is not enough that the subject encounters something that comes from the Other and is enigmatic in itself . . . before trying to figure out what it means, there must be a subjective positing of the fact that 'it means'" (*Why Psychoanalysis?*, 30). I take her point to be an implicit critique of the dyadic tendency in Laplanche's theory of seduction: for Laplanche, there is the caregiver with her enigmatic messages and the child, whereas for Lacan, there is also the big Other—the presupposed locus of meaning wherein the subject places his fundamental fantasy. While I agree that Laplanche neglects the necessity of the "subjective positing" of meaning (and thus the crucial function of the big Other), I find his work helpful as a means of grappling with the genesis of sexuality and the unconscious in a subject.

[58] In Laplanche, *Essays on Otherness*, 16.

cases of actual sexual violation that this state of affairs could lead to neurosis, he nevertheless ventured a broader claim: "Every adolescent individual has memory-traces which can only be understood with the emergence of sexual feelings of his own," he wrote, "and accordingly *every adolescent must carry the germ of hysteria within him.*"[59] All children are witnesses to events that do not immediately make sense to them, that become "memory-traces" demanding some kind of sexual knowledge not yet possessed. These enigmatic memories, Freud suggests, constitute the "germs of hysteria" within us all. Laplanche's move is therefore less a supplementation than an excavation and reconstruction of an important but forgotten insight of Freud's.

However, whereas Freud assumed it was the eventual *presence* of knowledge about sexuality that retroactively made the memory traumatic, Laplanche puts the emphasis on an irreducible *lack* of knowledge. The repressed proper, he maintains, is not the memory itself but that aspect of the encounter that remains enigmatic *after* everything else has been translated—after the subject has submitted her past to all the knowledge and understanding she has presently acquired. The essence of sexuality is the unknown and unknowable in the encounter with the other. "The primacy of sexuality," he writes, "opens directly onto the question of the other, and in the case of the child, onto the adult other in his or her alien-ness."[60]

It is helpful to revisit Freud's patient Emma in Laplanchean terms. Emma's childhood experiences in the sweetshop involved an initial "inscription" (the assault of the shopkeeper) which underwent a postpubertal "translation" triggered by the later scene in the clothing shop. According to Freud, her memory became a malignant entity, an internal assailant necessitating harsh measures of defense. However, from a Laplanchean perspective, it is not the memory as such that constituted the trauma, but something that must have escaped the process of translation, *after* Emma "made sense" of the childhood assault. In fact, Freud writes that the "associative link" between the two scenes was an element which remains enigmatic in both: "the laughter of the shop-assistants," Emma told Freud, "had reminded her of the grin with which the shopkeeper had accompanied his assault."[61] Both the obscure laughter and the grin exemplify that nightmarish aspect of a traumatic experience that can never be adequately understood or translated, an image that forces one to ask, "What does the other want of me? What mysterious satisfaction is he obtaining at my expense?"

While Emma's case is one of sexual violence, Laplanche's argument requires us to map its coordinates onto everyday experience; the generalized

---

[59] Freud, "Project," 356 (emphasis mine).
[60] Laplanche, "Theory of Seduction," 658.
[61] Freud, "Project," 354.

seduction theory helps us understand how sexuality is experienced as something foreign and threatening universally, not just in particular cases. In the most ordinary conditions of child-rearing, we are left with enigmatic deposits, obscure traces of the other's desire, that generate symptomatic responses, desperate attempts at binding that which is ultimately boundless; we construct fantasies to screen ourselves from and pacify these gaping mysteries. This is the level where, according to Laplanche, psychoanalysis must locate its "enlarged" concept of sexuality: neither in the genitals, nor even the thoughts that make one consciously aroused, but in the dialectic between fantasies (conscious and unconscious) and the mysterious, insatiable bodily pressures that feel simultaneously "foreign" yet intimate. Laplanche calls these pressures the "source-objects of the drive": "foreign bodies that cannot be jettisoned, constant sources of excitation which will be reactivated and intensified by all the other inter human exchanges of the same order."[62]

These "constant sources of excitations," I propose, are the psychoanalytic version of what the reflex theorists called "irritations." However, to grasp the difference between the reflex theorists' physiological conception of sexuality and this enlarged psychoanalytic sexuality, we must combine Laplanche's insights on sexuality's alterity with Freud's work on autoerotic infantile sexuality and the polymorphously perverse body.

Sexuality and the Body

Freud wrote that by abandoning the seduction theory, he was led to appreciate the "auto-erotic activity of the first years of childhood."[63] Although he treats the seduction theory and infantile autoerotism as opposed, his study of the emergence of bodily erotic pleasure in infancy offers a space through which the relationship between infantile sexuality, seduction, and the body can be theorized—providing a way for us to understand sexuality as both "foreign" yet intimately related to one's own body. Freud's evocative description of the autoerotic nature of thumb-sucking, in the *Three Essays on the Theory of Sexuality*, is a useful starting point:

> It is clear that the behaviour of a child who indulges in thumb-sucking is determined by a search for some pleasure which has already been experienced and is now remembered. In the simplest case he proceeds

[62] Scarfone, "Introduction," 555.
[63] Freud, "History of the Psycho-Analytic Movement," 18.

to find this satisfaction by sucking rhythmically at some part of the skin or mucous membrane. It is also easy to guess the occasions on which the child had his first experiences of the pleasure which he is now striving to renew. It was the child's first and most vital activity, his sucking at his mother's breast, or at substitutes for it, that must have familiarized him with this pleasure. The child's lips, in our view, behave like an erotogenic zone, and no doubt stimulation by the warm flow of milk is the cause of the pleasurable sensation. The satisfaction of the erotogenic zone is associated, in the first instance, with the satisfaction of the need for nourishment. To begin with, sexual activity attaches itself to one of the functions serving the purpose of self-preservation and does not become independent of them until later. . . . The need for repeating the sexual satisfaction now becomes detached from the need for taking nourishment.[64]

There are two important insights for our purposes here. First, that our earliest libidinal pleasures emerge out of the attempt to retrieve a satisfaction no longer present. We discover substitutes to make up for lost pleasures, particularly for the "first and most vital" enjoyment of being sated by milk. Second and relatedly, the libido "attaches itself to" the bodily endeavor to obtain necessary nourishment, the "function . . . of self-preservation." Freud suggests here that the genesis of sexual pleasure occurs in a small deviation from intersubjective acts of biological survival, the taking in of nourishment from the other. The infant wants milk, and when milk is not available, it forms a substitute, deriving pleasure from its thumb as the closest available substitution for the experience of receiving milk from the mother's breast. This process of substitution marks a primordial disjunction between the fulfillment of a biological *need*, and the emergence of something "extra," a pleasure *beyond* the preservation of the soma. Laplanche and Pontalis theorize it as follows:

The "origin" of auto-erotism is thus considered to be that moment— recurring constantly rather than fixed at a certain point in development— when sexuality draws away from its natural object, finds itself delivered over to phantasy and in this very process is constituted qua sexuality.[65]

Sexuality, Laplanche and Pontalis argue here, is constituted at the moment of transition from a natural object of instinctual need (such as milk) to its

[64] Freud, *Three Essays*, 181–2.
[65] Laplanche and Pontalis, "Auto-Erotism," 46.

fantasmatic substitutes. An inchoate sense of dissatisfaction propels the child into a search for what it feels to be missing, and this search leads to pleasures of a qualitatively different kind, as it involves the process of fantasy: the construction of a chain of associations connecting the absent object to its representative or substitute. Through this emergence of sexuality the natural body is thus submitted to the "unnaturalness" of fantasy. "Sexuality," writes Laplanche, "at first entirely grounded in the [vital] function, is simultaneously entirely *in the movement which dissociates it* from the vital function."[66]

This theory of infantile sexuality, while closely tied to physiology, radically undermines any conception of "natural" sexuality based on heterosexual reproduction. Whereas most nineteenth-century thinkers (including especially the reflex theorists) understood nonreproductive sexual acts, such as masturbation, as pathological perversions of an otherwise reproduction-oriented sexual instinct, in Freud's schema, we *begin* as "polymorphously perverse": our first sexual pleasures involve diverse forms of bodily enjoyment tied to fantasy and ignorant of reproductive aims.[67] Freud's reasoning thus inverts the temporality of the ordinary understanding of sexuality: "No one who has seen a baby sinking back satiated from the breast and falling asleep with flushed cheeks and a blissful smile can escape the reflection that this picture persists as a prototype of the expression of sexual satisfaction in later life," he writes.[68] It is not that the sexually active adult eroticizes nonsexual activities like sucking; rather, these activities are always-already eroticized and form the building blocks of adult sexuality. "Foreplay" is not only "before" the sexual act but contains its basic ingredients; genital reproductive sex is only an eventual and tenuous (if not entirely forsaken) attempt to bring these infantile pleasures into a normative order. As Freud writes, "The detaching of sexuality from the genitals has the advantage of allowing us to bring the sexual activities of children and of perverts into the same scope as those of normal adults."[69] In "detaching sexuality from the genitals," Freud definitively gives up the approach toward sexuality, the "fantasy physiology,"[70] that characterized the circumcision doctors.

How does our study of seduction in the previous section intersect with this autoerotic emergence of sexuality in the body? Some interesting comments Freud made while he still held onto his seduction theory, and had not yet discovered the infant's polymorphous perversity, point the way. Freud

[66] Laplanche, *Life and Death*, 18.
[67] See Davidson, *Emergence of Sexuality*, chp. 3.
[68] Freud, *Three Essays*, 182.
[69] Freud, "Autobiographical Study," 38.
[70] Marcus, *The Other Victorians*, 23.

argued that the physical symptoms of hysterics displayed evidence of their repressed scenes of seduction. They did so, he argued, because the parts of the body involved in hysterical symptoms behaved as "substitutions" for the reproductive organs. The "exceedingly common hysterical phenomena— painful need to urinate, the sensation accompanying defaecation, intestinal disturbances, choking and vomiting, indigestion and disgust at food," Freud writes, were all "shown in [his] analyses" to derive from exposure to premature sexual acts in which the mouth and the anus were exploited by the adult seducer as substitutes for the child's undeveloped reproductive organs.[71] In other words, Freud viewed the eroticization of these body parts made manifest in hysterical symptoms as marks of sexual violation and of a disordered sexuality. "People who have no hesitation in satisfying their sexual desires upon children," Freud writes,

> cannot be expected to jib at finer shades in the methods of obtaining that satisfaction; and the sexual impotence which is inherent in children inevitably forces them into the same substitutive actions as those to which adults descend if they become impotent.[72]

Consequently,

> these grotesque and yet tragic incongruities [the use of the mouth and anus for sexual satisfaction] reveal themselves as stamped upon the later development of the individual and of his neurosis, in countless permanent effects which deserve to be traced in the greatest detail.[73]

Freud is arguing that when the functions of ingestion and excretion play a role in hysterical symptoms, it is because their corresponding organs were unnaturally eroticized during (repressed) scenes of seduction, by those who, Freud supposes, needed to utilize substitutes for the genitals in order to obtain sexual satisfaction. It is a theory in which nongenital sexuality is a pathology that belies a childhood violation rather than part of ordinary sexual activity. Freud does not synthesize these ideas with his later theories on polymorphous perversity, which posit the eroticization of the mouth and anus as primary and universal. Instead, the seduction theory and the theory of infantile sexuality appear here at loggerheads: in the former, the nonsexual child has her sexuality prematurely awakened and perverted by the adult; in

[71] Freud, "Aetiology of Hysteria," 214.
[72] Freud, 214–15.
[73] Freud, 215.

the latter, the child is inherently sexual and draws erotic satisfaction from her caretaker's provision of her vital needs.

However, using Laplanche's generalized seduction theory, we can find something insightful in Freud's seemingly anachronistic remarks, and resolve the contradiction between a nongenital sexuality caused by the adult other's seduction and one that emerges autonomously in the infant. Polymorphously perverse infantile sexuality relies on unconscious transmission from the adult, Laplanche asserts. The child's radical dependence on the adult other generates this "grotesque" and "tragic" reconfiguration of human sexuality from natural and reproductive to unnatural, non- or extra-genital, and fantasmatic. The child's nonreproductive vital functions become "perversely" eroticized because they involve those sites of the body where parental care is most focused and, therefore, where unconscious parental fantasies and enigmatic messages are absorbed. This process generates the "erotogenic zone":

> a kind of breaking or turning point within the bodily envelope, since what is in question is above all sphincteral orifices: mouth, anus, etc. It is also a zone of exchange, since the principal biological exchanges are borne by it . . .

> These zones *focalize parental fantasies* and above all *maternal fantasies*, so that we may say, in what is barely a metaphor, that they are the points through which is *introduced into the child that alien internal entity* which is, properly speaking, *the sexual excitation*.[74]

Thus, the emergence of polymorphous perversity involves both infantile sexuality *and* seduction: the eroticization of the vital functions in infancy (which leads to fantasmatic substitutive pleasures), and the introduction of alterity, an enigmatic otherness that enters the skin like a "stowaway passenger on the carrier wave of the relation of attachment."[75] The sexual drive is fundamentally "autoerotic," indifferent to questions of personhood and reproduction; yet at the same time, it is "foreign," coming into being as a consequence of the seduction by the adult other.[76]

---

74 Laplanche, *Life and Death*, 23.
75 Scarfone, "Introduction," 550.
76 Critically adopting Laplanche's view on seduction, Van Haute and Geyskens have thrown doubt on whether sexuality is truly primary for psychoanalysis. They write: "Although Laplanche succeeds in confirming the structural character of the trauma [of seduction] and the essential asymmetry between the child and adult, he does not succeed in providing a basis for its essential sexual character. It thus may not be the

This revised and synthesized Freudian theory of sexuality we have developed via Laplanche both undermines the work of the reflex theorists and sheds light on their motivations. Whereas reflex theory posited that nervous illness was the result of a sexual-physiological irritation that might be eliminated through surgical intervention, psychoanalysis places such "irritations" at the heart of subject formation. Through seduction, the child becomes subject to an ineradicable, "alien internal entity" that will lead to endless processes of translation, binding, and defense—attempts to contain and manage an enigmatic otherness that constantly threatens the narcissistic enclosure of the self. Because seduction involves the eroticization of the body and its vital functions, human sexuality has a parasitic relationship to what we consider natural bodily processes. Sexuality both magnifies the importance of biology for the human and subverts biology's reproductive aims. It both tears us away from "nature" and sets up the conditions in which we may fantasize about a return to it—the wish for a harmonious relationship between libido and the reproductive body, excised of "foreign" contamination. It is this wish that generated the self-defeating struggle which the circumcision doctors waged.

Otto Weininger

As we saw earlier, the reflex theorists did not only strive to understand sexuality in purely physiological terms; they also portrayed the experience of a split in consciousness as caused by the interference of the sexual body (typically female) with the conscious will. The philosophical underpinnings of this medical theory are given their fullest expression by nineteenth-century Viennese philosopher Otto Weininger. Weininger wrote one book in his short lifetime, *Sex and Character*, published in 1903. He was twenty-three years old when the book was published, and he committed suicide a few months later. Glowing with the intrigue of Weininger's spectacular death (he chose to kill himself in the same room where Beethoven died), the book became an instant bestseller. Nearly all the intellectuals of the era had something to say about the book (usually a mixture of criticism and admiration), while

---

primacy of sexuality, but rather the essential asymmetric relation between the child and adult—that is, the structural and constitutive confusion of tongues between the two—that is the *shibboleth* of psychoanalysis" (*Confusion of Tongues*, 143). I think they reach this conclusion only by neglecting to fully appreciate the interrelation between seduction and bodily autoerotism we have just analyzed. When these two factors are considered together, seduction and sexuality are, in my view, co-constitutive and equally primary.

many angst-ridden adolescents found their inner struggles reflected and made meaningful in Weininger's misogynistic and anti-Semitic portrait of humankind.[77]

Interestingly, the only extended remarks Freud published on Weininger occur in his famous "circumcision footnote" in Little Hans. There, after Freud links anti-Semitism and misogyny to castration anxiety (evoked by the Jew's circumcised penis and the woman's lack of a penis, respectively), he adds:

> Weininger (the young philosopher who, highly gifted but sexually deranged . . .) . . . treated Jews and women with equal hostility and overwhelmed them with the same insults. Being a neurotic, Weininger was completely under the sway of his infantile complexes; and from that standpoint what is common to Jews and women is their relation to the castration complex.[78]

Circumcision, psychoanalysis, and sexual difference thus make an important intersection at the figure of Otto Weininger. In this concluding section, I wish to extend our understanding of the libidinal dynamics of the circumcision cure and reflex theory, and of psychoanalysis's dialectical transformation of that approach, through a critical examination of Weininger's views on sexual difference, Jewishness, and the psyche. Weininger's work refines the views of the reflex theorists, revealing, through the articulation of his wish for men to transcend "femininity," the links that the reflex theorists implicitly established between womanhood, the body, and psychic division. His philosophically distilled, symptomatic defense against castration allows us to see through contrast how psychoanalytic theory "feminizes" and "Judaizes" subjectivity, offering a radically alternative approach that takes on the problem of castration rather than constructing a defensive escape.

The central argument of *Sex and Character* concerns the metaphysical status of the distinction between the sexes. Weininger brackets out empirical men and women from what he considers the ideals of masculinity and femininity. The ideal man, in his view, is the embodiment of the Kantian

<hr />

[77] Recent reviews of Weininger's book on Amazon testify to his continued appeal: "An old book I definitely recommend, comparing to those crap everyone can reed from Waterstone's:) Homoxeuality, feminism, etc. it explains everything about this world controlled by feminized world that we are" (unedited 2013 Amazon.com review of *Sex and Character*). His work also resonates with the contemporary "incel" and "Men Going Their Own Way" movements. A page is dedicated to him on IncelWiki, see https://incels .wiki/w/Otto_Weininger.

[78] Freud, "Analysis of a Phobia," 36 n.1. The first part of this quote was discussed in was discussed in Chapter One.

transcendental subject. He is an autonomous, pure individual, endowed with the capacity to abstract himself from his empirical surroundings and thereby pursue truth. He is in full, conscious possession of will, immune from all "pathological" traces of external influence. The highest form of man, what Weininger designates the "genius," strives for total mastery over the symbolic universe, banishing all remainders of the unknown, which is "why *he*, of all, suffers most from anything that even in him is still unconscious, still chaos, still fate."[79]

Woman, on the other hand, represents everything that undermines man's individuality, coherence, and powers of logic and abstraction. Woman stands for fusion, for impressionability, and, ultimately, for nothingness as such: "Woman knows no *boundaries* to her self, which could be penetrated and which she would need to guard" (259). She "has no relationship with the idea, which she neither affirms nor denies . . . no share in ontological reality . . . no relationship with the thing-in-itself . . . with the absolute . . . or with God" (258). Consequently, "*Women have no existence and no essence, they are not and they are nothing*" (258). Man's "deepest fear" is "the *fear of woman,* that is, the *fear of meaninglessness,* the fear *of the tempting abyss of nothingness*" (268). In Weininger's articulation, woman, castration, and the unconscious appear as one and the same terrifying thing.

In a move that brings us in close proximity to the psychoanalytic theory of sexuality, Weininger aligns this ontological "nothingness" of Woman with sexuality:

> Woman is exclusively and entirely sexual, and because this sexuality covers her whole body. . . . What is commonly described as sexual intercourse is only a *special case* of the utmost intensity. . . . The urogenital tract is not the only, but merely the most effective, *route* to having sexual intercourse with a woman, who may feel *possessed* through a mere *glance* or *word*. A being that has *sexual intercourse* everywhere and with everything can also be impregnated everywhere and by everything. (205–6)

Women are represented here as embodying "sexuality" in its most total form. The statement is not only a description of femininity but a theory of sexuality itself. Sexuality is understood not as a set of particular genital acts but in the expanded sense we encountered previously. It takes place not only via

---

[79] Weininger, *Sex and Character*, 151. Subsequent references are given in the text. Unless otherwise noted, the emphases are Weininger's.

the reproductive organs but at the level of signification: glances or words. Moreover, sexuality indicates a radical openness and pregnability toward anything and everything, akin to the psychoanalytic view of the unconscious. Yet, whereas psychoanalysis generalizes Weininger's view, treating sexuality and the unconscious as the foundation of the human subject, Weininger, like the reflex theorists, *naturalizes* these phenomena and *localizes* them onto the woman, thereby freeing men to transcend them.

Weininger's discussion of hysteria makes this clear. He read and wrote approvingly of Freud and Breuer's *Studies on Hysteria* but took their early ideas in a different direction. Recall that Freud's early formulations of neurosis held unconscious or "split off" ideas to constitute, in themselves, something pathological; through catharsis the subject would overcome repression, bringing all her unconscious ideas into consciousness and ideally ridding herself of her illness-generating psychic split. While this position would need revision, it nevertheless treated hysteria as emerging from conflicts *within* the subject: things the hysteric both wished for and defended against. In Weininger's view, female hysteria occurs not as the result of the woman's own conflicting wishes, but from a struggle between masculine ideas she has artificially imposed on herself and her true sexual "nature," striving to break free:

> A woman has had a sexual observation or idea, which she *understood*, either at the time or in retrospect, as relating to herself. Under the influence of a male judgement, which has been forced on her and totally adopted by her, which has become *part of her*, and which exclusively dominates her *waking consciousness*, she *indignantly and unhappily rejects* that observation or idea *as a whole, but, given her nature as Woman, at the same time affirms, desires, and attributes a positive value to it in her deepest unconscious.* The conflict festers and ferments in her, until it bursts out from time to time in a fit. Such a woman shows the more or less typical picture of hysteria, and that is why she feels as if the sexual act, which she *believes* she abhors, but which something in her—her original nature—actually *desires*, were "a foreign body in her consciousness." (240)

Woman, infinitely receptive to the ideas of others, adopts the mask of masculine morality, but underneath it lies her "original," sexual "nature," seeking expression. In Laplanche's explication, the "foreign bodies" in the psyche that Weininger mentions are the enigmatic deposits of the other. In Weininger's version, these "foreign bodies" are "*in reality Woman's very own female nature.*" Sexuality is not traumatically "other" to Woman, but the positive substance of her being. It is everything else—the "masculine" world of ideas and judgments—that women are traumatized by.

From a psychoanalytic perspective, Weininger's interpretation thus amounts to a defense against the subject's fundamental relation to alterity. A subject, in Weininger's view, is not one who comes into being through constitutive dependence on, and fundamental openness to, the other. Rather, Man is a self-positing, nonporous subject, whereas Woman is the name for a dangerous opening, a void that takes human form, threatening to engulf Man in the "tempting abyss of nothingness." The split subject of psychoanalysis is repaired by the transmutation of this split onto sexual difference. Man's struggle is to transcend otherness and obtain total self-mastery. The impediment to his autonomy, to his overcoming of lack, is not internal to his subjectivity, but the external threat of femininity. The original reflex theorists offered a similar view, albeit treating "femininity" as a biological rather than metaphysical entity.

Weininger's parents were assimilated Viennese Jews, and he eventually converted to Protestantism. In keeping with the fin de siècle cultural imaginary, Weininger drew a direct link between his observations on femininity and Jewishness. If Woman is the physical manifestation of nonbeing, Jewishness, he proposed, is the "cast of mind" through which an entire community—men and women—might identify with all the negative attributes of womankind. "The Jews . . . do not live as free, autonomous individuals who choose between virtue and vice, as do the Aryans. The Aryans are automatically pictured by everybody as an *assembly of individual men*, the Jews as a coherent plasmodium spread over a wide idea" (280). This was not a racial theory of Jewishness but a thoroughly metaphysical one, "*a* possibility *for* all *human beings*" (274). The Jew's psychic constitution is characterized, above all, by division, a duplicitous split in place of a simple unity. "Anything undivided, anything whole, is alien to [the Jew]. *Inner ambiguity . . . is absolutely Jewish, simplicity is absolutely un-Jewish*" (293). The image of the Jew's circumcision, the split imposed from without that constitutes the male Jew's communal identity, here comes to mind. Weininger does not mention circumcision explicitly, but as Freud's footnote on him suggests, the fantasmatic significance of the rite suffuses the text.

Unlike Woman, constitutionally confined to her condition, the male Jew is capable of overcoming Jewishness, but it involves an ethical struggle:

> [The Jew] must stop trying to achieve the impossible, that is, to esteem himself as a *Jew* . . . and strive to gain the right to honor himself as a *human being*. He will long to achieve the *inner* baptism by the spirit,

which may only then be followed by the symbolic external baptism of the body. (282)

This division between the inner spirit and symbolic external body evokes the Pauline distinction between circumcision of the spirit and of the flesh. In order to be recognized as a member of universal humanity, the Jew must shed the particular identity through which he has unsuccessfully sought recognition. Doing so involves not external acts but internal transformation. Weininger's philosophy places a high value on the realm of the invisible absolute, of the pure transcendence of all fleshly particulars (the same view that Daniel Boyarin criticized in Chapter 2 on St. Paul). "Belief is everything," he writes, designating Jesus Christ as the most sublime example of heroism.

Although Weininger's thought displays the obsessional hallmark of isolating and exteriorizing the obstacle to goodness and purity—figured in his work as the Woman and the Jew—it would be mistaken to characterize his philosophy as advocating fascistic violence toward the other to achieve a longed-for unity. Rather, Weininger offers a thoroughly self-centered vision of transcendence that forces the subject to endlessly confront, and hold *himself* responsible for, his failure to achieve his ideals. Thus, throughout the text, he consistently demands no curtailment of the rights of women or Jews, no display of cruelty or hatred toward those considered inferior. In a passage nearly indistinguishable from the writings of Freud, he maintains that anti-Semitism is a form of projection:

> Whoever hates the Jewish character hates it first in himself. By persecuting it in the other, he is only trying to separate himself from it, and by trying to localize it entirely in his fellow-human, in order to dissociate himself from it, he can momentarily feel free of it. Hatred, like love, is the result of projection: we only hate those who remind us unpleasantly of ourselves. (275)

Hatred is the projection of the hated part of the self onto the other; love is the attempt to realize one's ego ideal in the fantasied perfection of the other.[80]

---

[80] Weininger's equally Freudian commentary on male romantic love could easily be taken for a radical feminist rallying cry: "Love of a woman is possible if this love, instead of taking any notice of her real qualities and considering her own wishes and interests . . . exercises no restraint in *substituting a completely different* reality for the psychic reality of the loved one. A man's attempt to find himself in a woman . . . necessarily presupposes a neglect of her empirical person. Such an attempt, therefore, is extremely *cruel* to the woman" (223).

Consequently, man's biggest problem is his own personal failure. "Woman is . . . the objectivization of male sexuality, *the embodiment of sexuality, Man's guilt made flesh,*" he concludes (270). Woman exists only because empirical man has failed to live up to the masculine ideal. The advancement of humanity is contingent upon man overcoming sexuality in all its manifold forms, in spirit as well as deed. Weininger's "final solution" is therefore not murder but asceticism; for men to achieve ultimate transcendence they must renounce sexuality. Woman will be eliminated without recourse to violence because, with the end of man's participation in sexual reproduction, the human race itself will cease to exist. It is hard to avoid the conclusion that Weininger's impossibly heroic and superegoic imperative was the source of his untimely demise.

At first glance, the circumcision doctors' professed commitment to empirical science may not seem to have much in common with Weininger's grandiose metaphysics and virulent anti-positivism (he dismissed as "fools" those who reduced madness, which he considered a spiritual struggle, to the "effects . . . of . . . spinal degeneration" [159]). However, if Weininger's project could be said to constitute a suicidal battle of the intellect against the undefeatable trauma of sexuality, I propose that the circumcision doctors' project was merely a more pragmatic—if equally failed—version of the same fight.

By localizing sexuality to a piece of the genitals that could be excised, the circumcision doctors believed they could eliminate manifestations of the unconscious, and restore subjective unity, through surgical intervention. Although they framed their ideas in physiological vocabulary, they were ultimately concerned with how infantile sexual activity appeared to exceed physiology: linking their patients' puzzling and compulsive behaviors to foreskin-induced "genital irritation" was an attempt to reduce sexuality to something reassuringly physical. If the children's symptoms seemed to express something gone haywire in the order of the sexual, better to attribute this to an organic disturbance that medical science could correct, than to the manifestation of a universal condition. Thus, whereas Weininger defensively attributed the alterity of sexuality to Woman, the circumcision doctors attributed it to the foreskin.

While Weininger demanded the absolute overcoming of the "Jewish character" within, the circumcision doctors' scientific discourse inverted the signified of the quintessential Jewish signifier from castrating to reparative. That is, they took a ritual associated in the Victorian mind with degeneration and femininity and transformed it into a modern medical miracle. Under the technical mastery of the surgeon, circumcision was not the perverse blood sacrifice of a degenerate race but an eminently sanitary and sanitizing medical intervention capable of curing the very neuroses often considered the province of the Jews themselves.

Yet, as we saw in the previous chapter, the doctors' attempt to reinvent and gain phallic mastery over the symbolic import of circumcision—figured, in their writings, as a kind of medical rescue from sexual contaminants—was accompanied by a fantasmatic, castrative underside. Were the doctors saving the boys from the premature and therefore dangerous awakening of their sexuality? Or was the attempt to *reverse* the onslaught of prepubertal sexuality, to restore the patients' innocence and wholeness, *itself* a kind of "seduction"? Following Laplanche, it would seem that the enthusiasm for circumcision as a "cure" for sexuality was, in fact, an unconscious reenactment of the primordial trauma, the genesis of sexuality as the effect of the seduction into the enigmatic signifiers of the adult other. Through circumcision, the doctors attempted to master the unmasterable: to translate the enigma of (their own) seduction into the knowledge of its undoing. Like all defensive attempts to master trauma, the practice of circumcision was not a form of "working through," but that of repetition compulsion.

Weininger lamented what he saw as the Jewishness and effeminacy of his time:

> Our age is not only the most Jewish, but also the most effeminate of all ages . . . an age without the appreciation of the state and law . . . an age for which history, life, science, everything, has become nothing but economics and technology; an age that has declared genius to be a form of madness, but which no longer has one great artist or great philosopher. (299)

Lacan argued that the turn of the twentieth-century was marked by the decline of the figure of the master, of the symbolic authorities previously felt to incarnate the law and guarantee the social pact.[81] For Weininger, this decline of traditional authority seems to have prompted his vicious condemnation of all representations of lack and fragmentation and his heroic vision of renunciatory transcendence. A radical solidity was needed, purified of all particularities, capable of responding to the chaos of the times. The circumcision doctors offered a less radical solution, working to usher in a new *kind* of authority: not the priest but the doctor, not the master but the expert. Dangerous eruptions of sexuality—metonymic for the disorder of the times—could be brought under control with surgical precision. Authority

---

[81] See Lacan, *XVII*.

was reasserted not as naked power or the Weiningerian Absolute but as technical expertise, the ability to manipulate the extant symbolic machinery.

Both Weininger and the circumcision doctors generated defensive responses to the void in the social structure—the absence of the Lawmaker—made manifest by modernity. Weininger's project ended in suicide; the circumcision doctors, in unconsciously re-inscribing the very lack they wanted to repair. Laplanche's emphasis on enigma can be thought of as a way to describe the sexuality that this void generates and track its genesis in a subject. What is ultimately traumatic about the enigmatic signifiers of the other is that there exists no final authority capable of determining their meaning. We know the other wants something of us, but nobody can finally pronounce what that something is. Instead, we are faced with the struggle of endlessly translating the particular way that the enigma of the other has impressed itself on us. The absence of an ultimate authority, of a final guarantor of meaning, is thus not just a modern social phenomenon, but the condition of the psychoanalytic subject—the "lack in the Other" is another name for Lacanian castration. The circumcision doctors constructed a symptom, a compromise enabling them to both relive and disavow castration and the trauma of seduction. Weininger refused this easier path, determined to locate and repair the fault in meaning to its fatal conclusion.

In this analysis of Weininger, I have not focused on Freud's own complicated relationship with Jewishness and femininity. As we examined in Chapter 1, scholars have done significant work in this arena. With different emphases, they have revealed the multifarious and occluded ways that Freud's ideas were bound up in the surrounding climate of anti-Semitism and misogyny, and symbolic associations with circumcision. To varying degrees, these scholars have treated psychoanalysis as the product of Freud's attempted repudiation of the feminine, Jewish, and otherwise "queer" aspects of himself that were so denigrated by Viennese popular and scientific culture. While I consider this literature interesting and important, I have intended this psychoanalytic examination of sexuality and the medicalization of circumcision to offer a different perspective.

Certainly, Freud, like Weininger and others, developed his ideas in reaction to the Enlightenment misogyny and anti-Semitism in which he found himself implicated. But while Weininger's philosophy advocated an impossible escape from femininity, and the circumcision doctors developed a procedure to defend against sexuality (profoundly linked to the problem of femininity), Freudian theory, I argue, constitutes a kind of *universalization* of femininity, Jewishness, and sexuality. The prejudices and fears of the fin de siècle, visible in the circumcision doctors' work and in Weininger's philosophy, can be understood as giving particular, historically situated forms to a universal problem: the subject's constitutive and traumatic relation to alterity—to that which renders one, in Lacan's polyvalent phrasing, a "subject of the unconscious." In the Enlightenment imagination, to be a Jew or to be a woman is to represent, in varying ways and degrees, sexuality and the unconscious—that which threatens the imagined integrity of the Enlightenment subject. We owe it to Weininger to have made this linkage absolutely explicit. What makes Freud's thought stand out is how it treats sexuality and the unconscious as the very *condition* of subjectivity. For psychoanalysis, both the "irritant" that the reflex theorists sought to excise and the brokenness that Weininger sought to overcome become the central feature of the human condition. If the circumcision doctors' "circumcision of the flesh" involved the unconscious undercurrent of feminizing, Judaizing, and sexualizing the patient, Freud "circumcised the spirit": he universalized this phenomenon, the pollution of subjectivity with its own excess.

5

The First Cut Is the Deepest

Contemporary Struggles over the Penile Cut

In 2018, former Harvard University employee Eric Clopper put on a one-man show entitled *Sex and Circumcision: An American Love Story* in Harvard's Sanders Theatre. Over the course of two and a half hours, through a mixture of monologue, PowerPoint slides, performance art, and lecture, Clopper delivered a passionate, if factually questionable, case against male circumcision, accusing his Jewish faith of being a "genital mutilation cult" that has "raped essential elements of men's humanity" and "sexuality," and has had a "demonstrably evil influence" on America. The evening culminated in Clopper appearing fully nude on stage, dancing to Britney Spears's "Toxic" while simulating intercourse with an inflatable sex doll. Clopper was fired from his job immediately after the performance and faced an investigation for making anti-Semitic comments during the show. His Gofundme page, set up to cover "living expenses and legal fees," has raised over $25,000 from small donations.[1] One donor commented, "Your passion is commensurate to the enormity of the crime being committed daily against our children. Thank you for defending the defenseless victims of this barbaric practice."

In the previous two chapters, we saw how nineteenth-century advocates for medical circumcision indexed sexuality to the foreskin. Their views on circumcision exceeded the terrain of anatomical science, evincing a fantasy that the removal of the foreskin might also excise the traumatic nature of sexuality. However, if justifications *for* circumcision are laden with fantasy, it does not mean arguments *against* the practice are any less so. In this chapter, we will examine the libidinal undercurrents of contemporary stances for and against male circumcision at both the individual level and as a larger sociopolitical phenomenon (in the case of legal attempts to ban or regulate the practice). In so doing, we will see how seemingly opposed wishes for the presence or the absence of the foreskin can be understood as equally

---

[1] Clopper, "Eric Clopper's Defense Fund"; see also Wang, "Federal Judge Dismisses Former Harvard Employee Lawsuit."

symptomatic responses to problems of identity and enjoyment plaguing modern subjectivity. Here, it will not be possible to provide an exhaustive survey of the contemporary debate on circumcision; instead, I have selected some key examples from the ever-evolving archive on the subject. Readers who wish to delve further into the subject should consult my bibliography.

Who Are Intactivists?

Over the past forty years, a movement has developed of activists opposed to the routine or religious circumcision of infants and young boys, which unites under the signifier "intactivist." This portmanteau of "intact" and "activist"—activist for intactness—is polemical and evocative. It is intended to communicate the notion that a circumcised penis is mutilated, disfigured, or otherwise not whole. Because an intactivist is primarily concerned with male circumcision over other putatively disfiguring practices, it also suggests a certain primacy to the penis as the site upon which one's physical and psychic integrity is measured. To "be intact" in this community is shorthand for possessing a penis with foreskin (the term "uncircumcised" is opposed because it supposedly perpetuates the idea that circumcision is the norm). The question of one's "being" is thus linked to the state of one's penis and whether it has been subjected to a surgical cut. The term invites men to share powerful sentiments surrounding their sense of incompleteness or lack (and the wish to overcome this) through specific phallic parameters. For example:

> The shock and surprise of my life came when I was in junior high school, and I was in the showers after gym. . . . I wondered what was wrong with those penises that looked different than mine. . . . I soon realized I had part of me removed. I felt incomplete and very frustrated when I realized that I could never be like I was when I was born—intact. That frustration is with me to this day. Throughout life I have regretted my circumcision. Daily I wish I were whole.[2]

Circumcision here represents an irrecoverable loss in the form of a brutal separation from nature. It is not that he can remember the pleasures the foreskin once conferred—he would have been too young to appreciate them—but, rather, he experiences a painful, unbridgeable gap between what

---

[2]   Boyle et al., "Male Circumcision," 336.

is and what, he imagines, could have been. For him, this is a loss that could, and ought to, be prevented. One wonders whether the fantasy of undoing this loss, and the ability to blame concrete perpetrators, serve a defensive function, providing an alibi for suffering, and shielding him from an encounter with a more fundamental and unsettling loss. This, indeed, is the psychoanalytic position: the prelapsarian wish to restore wholeness, which can appear in any number of guises, is a major defensive fantasy against the subject's foundational fracture. Behind every measurable, material loss lies the one which we can never account for, undo, or mitigate, in the face of which we must construct some kind of compromise to go on living. In the case of intactivists, these phallic problematics play themselves out directly on the penis. As a commenter on the subreddit r/Foregen wrote, in support of a project to regenerate foreskin using stem cells:

> I just wanted to thank the Foregen team for everything they've been working towards. Whenever I'm angry at what was done to me and feel like breaking a window, I come to this sub to remind myself that there is still some hope. Remember that the mutilation and abuse that was forced upon us. Is only temporary. Our scars will heal, both literally and figuratively. At least, that's what I like to tell myself.[3]

The style of intactivism, as evidenced in these quotes, often involves intensely personal testimonials of victimization, echoing the language of identity politics. "Circumcised men," writes Eric Silverman,

> express, in the uniquely modern American practice of public confession, their intimate experiences with sexual dysfunction, poor relationships, and feelings of parental betrayal, violation, victimization, powerlessness, distrust, shame, abuse, deformity, and alienation.[4]

Though intactivists primarily focus on the pain and alleged loss of sexual pleasure that circumcision entails, they have attributed nearly all the major physical, psychological, and social ills of our era to the procedure, including ADHD, autism, sexually transmitted disease, sudden infant death syndrome, PTSD, anxiety, depression, low self-esteem, and (why not?) Islamic terrorism.[5]

---

[3] lord_autist, "Foregen."
[4] Silverman, "Anthropology and Circumcision," 435.
[5] The Circumcision Complex, "Circumcision to Terrorism." On autism, see Frisch and Simonson, "Ritual Circumcision"; cf. Morris and Wiswall, "'Circumcision Pain' Unlikely to Cause Autism." A good place to begin exploring intactivist testimonials online is reddit.com/r/Intactivists/.

Moreover, although the majority of circumcised men rarely complain about their lack of foreskin, intactivists generally consider the unenlightened to be suffering false consciousness or repressed trauma that returns in various forms of psychological disorder or violence (hence Islamic terrorism). One sympathetic intactivist writes:

> I do think we need to be a little careful with cut guys that are in denial. I consider how terrible circumcision makes me feel—I feel I have been sexually assaulted. I feel violated, and I feel damaged. I truly wish that this sort of abuse would be made illegal. I truly wish that people recognized how heinous this abuse is. However, I really don't wish for anyone to *feel* the way I do. If people are comfortable in their bodies, I wouldn't want to convince them to feel differently.[6]

A popular refrain among intactivists is that sex without foreskin is "like viewing a Renoir color-blind."[7] This is a particularly interesting claim given that many of them have never experienced sex *with* foreskin—although an entire community and cottage industry exists around "foreskin restoration" using skin-tugging devices, as well as hope placed in the abovementioned Foregen research project. As Amanda Kennedy notes in her study of foreskin restorers, "the sex which they imagine will follow restoration is deeply connected to cultural imagery and masculine norms."[8] Here is a testimonial from one restorer, who expresses resentment at the lack of recognition he receives for his pursuit of phallic restitution: "People who have lost legs or [undergone] a mastectomy, everyone rallies behind them when they are pursuing self-image changes. But when it comes to men regaining what they lost, men who have been altered, where's their support to do this?"[9]

Intactivists fill online discussions of circumcision (such as the comments page of relevant articles) with their views, often angry and aggressive.[10] Some set automatic key word searches, enabling them to respond first and set the parameters of the discussion. Responding to intactivist discourse, a Jewish a'capella group produced a tongue-in-cheek, pro-circumcision YouTube video, in which they sing, to the tune of the 2013 pop hit *Royals*, "Cause

---

6   waraukaeru, "Got Banned from r/sex."
7   NORM, "Why Should I Restore?"
8   Kennedy, "Masculinity and Embodiment," 45. On gender and foreskin restoration, see Osserman, "Is the Phallus Uncut?"
9   Swanson, "Uncut," n.p.
10 See Stern, "How Intactivists Broke the Internet."

we're gonna be Mohels/We're not afraid of a little blood/Your man-made law just ain't for us/We serve a different kind of boss."[11] In the comments section below the video, an intactivist writes, "YOU FUCKING SCUM! YOU FUCKING RAPE APOLOGIST!"

As this appropriation of anti-rape sloganeering suggests, intactivists have a vexed relationship with feminism. A 1965 anti-circumcision article entitled "The Rape of the Phallus," published in the Journal of the American Medical Association, is a kind of ur-text for the movement. The author contends, "Perhaps not least of the reasons why American mothers seem to endorse the operation with such enthusiasm is the fact that it is one way an intensely matriarchal society can permanently influence the physical characteristics of its males."[12] Many intactivists argue that mainstream feminist opposition to "female genital mutilation" has overshadowed recognition of the plight of circumcised men, referring to circumcision as male genital mutilation, or "MGM."[13] Thus, while intactivists would say that they are anti-FGM, "intactivism" does not connote a gender-neutral stance to the issue of genital cutting; more often, intactivists instrumentalize the anti-FGM cause to point to a supposed double standard, appropriating the language of feminism to express male victimhood. Underscoring how the movement generates a form of bonding through shared testimony of suffering, trauma, and rage, one intactivist writes to another:

I feel you brother. What helps me best in terms of controlling my foreskin aggression is Risperdal :) My mutilation is an example of costly signalling that one day I hope I can take back. One love <3[14]

This side of intactivism has close links with the "men's rights movement," a network of men who believe themselves to be victims of feminism. Popular men's rights websites, such as Avoiceformen.com, regularly feature anti-circumcision content. In recent years, men's rights have morphed into a component of the "alt-right" and the so-called "manosphere," those areas of the Internet covering "everything from progressive men's issues activists dealing with real neglect of male health, suicide and unequal social services to the nastier corners of the Internet, filled with involuntary celibacy-obsessed, hate-filled, resentment-fueled cultures of quite chilling levels of

---

[11] Kol Ish, *Mohels*.
[12] Morgan, "Rape of the Phallus," 124.
[13] See, for example, Inaction, "Female Genital Cutting."
[14] talierch, "Foregen."

misogyny."[15] Indeed, intactivists' discourse on the absent foreskin as the cause of their social and sexual deficiency closely mirrors the language and meme-culture of "incels," who obsess over small differences in facial bone structure, believing "guys with weak chins and slight overbites are doomed to lives of solitude."[16] Cementing the link between intactivism and the far-right is an image that appeared in news reports of a protester at the 2021 storming of the US Capitol, alongside Q-anon believers and other conspiracy theorists, holding placards that read, "Make America's penis great again, with a foreskin! No foreskin, no peace!"[17]

Kennedy argues, "Male circumcision has been actively politicized by the Men's Rights Movement (MRM). . . . Circumcision can be a feminist issue, but not the way [men's rights activists] talk about it."[18] Her point is well taken. As we have seen throughout this book, circumcision has often functioned as a patriarchal attempt to consolidate phallic mastery. Intactivists argue that the physical and psychological harm allegedly caused by male circumcision renders it manifestly "anti-man," yet as Kennedy observes, "what [intactivists] are missing is that harm [caused by circumcision] has historically and symbolically been in service of men's power."[19]

Equally noteworthy are the implicit ways intactivist discourse mobilizes unconscious hostility toward femininity to generate sympathy for the cause. For example, members of the intactivist group "Bloodstained Men" hold demonstrations wearing all white clothes with a red circle painted around the crotch of their trousers (somewhat reminiscent of anti-abortion signage displaying graphic images of fetuses).[20] The images of trousers stained with genital blood conveyed by these costumes is, of course, intended to elicit horror and disgust, feelings which the protesters want their audiences to associate with the practice of circumcision. Yet, if intactivists assume the phenomenon of genital bleeding is inherently disgusting, what does that imply about the regular genital bleeding experienced by those with female reproductive organs? The sympathy that Bloodstained Men protesters wish to induce for men "mutilated" by circumcision trades on a form of castration anxiety linked to the misogynist aversion to menstruation. If Bruno Bettelheim believes men undergo circumcision because they

---

[15] Nagle, *Kill All Normies*, 86.
[16] Salecl, *Passion for Ignorance*, 118.
[17] Bromley, "Thank You"; Riminton, "America."
[18] Kennedy, "Circumcision Is a Feminist Issue," n.p.
[19] Kennedy. For additional feminist criticism of intactivism, see also Kennedy and Sardi, "Male Anti-Circumcision Movement"; Filipovic, "How Intactivists Are Ruining the Debate"; and Valeii, "Men's Rights Activists."
[20] Bloodstained Men, "Homepage."

unconsciously treat menstruation as something women possess that they have been denied (discussed in Chapter 1), for intactivists the problem is the inverse: masculine lack/dispossession, their discourse suggests, is the consequence of the proximity to menstruation and femininity generated through circumcision. Circumcision, in other words, emasculates men.[21] There are female intactivists (two members of Bloodstained Men's board of directors are women). Nevertheless, the pathos of victimization expressed by intactivists is bound up with questions of sexual difference and the attempt to overcome castration. Like circumcision more generally, intactivism provides a literal outlet through which phallic (dis)possession can be negotiated.

Although these polemical aspects of intactivism lend themselves most readily to psychoanalytic interpretation, the movement also has its soberer members. Academic books, scholarly articles, and other interventions by ethicists and medical practitioners have made a number of convincing arguments against the practice, such as the following:

- The foreskin is a unique piece of tissue that performs various functions for the penis, including lubricating and protecting the glans, and responding to touch.[22]
- Studies that claim circumcision confers hygienic benefits or protects against STDs (including a controversial 2014 Centre for Disease Control report, which endorsed circumcision) have multiple methodological weaknesses and argumentative flaws. Even if these studies were accurate, they do not justify the surgical removal of healthy tissue—just as doctors do not routinely amputate breasts to prevent breast cancer, for example.[23]
- While circumcision advocates assume that the procedure was made routine in service of the health benefits now associated with it, opponents demonstrate (as discussed in the Chapter 3) that the original justifications, such as the prevention of masturbation, would not hold water under today's medical standards—suggesting that the procedure is a repressive Victorian hangover crudely repackaged by contemporary medicine.[24]

[21] We might also speculate that erotic preferences for (un)circumcised penises among gay men are related to interpretations of sexual difference attached to circumcision status. On gay male sexuality and foreskin preference, see Allan, "The Lost Inches" and "The Foreskin Aesthetic."
[22] See, for example, Svoboda, Adler, and Van Howe, "Circumcision is Unethical"; Bronselaer et al., "Male Circumcision"; Earp, "Infant Circumcision and Adult Penile Sensitivity"; cf. Morris and Krieger, "Contrasting Evidence."
[23] See Earp, "Male or Female Genital Cutting."
[24] See Darby, *Surgical Temptation*; Gollaher, *Circumcision*.

- Complications arising from circumcision may be rare, but when they occur, they can be very serious.[25]
- Even when genuine medical problems occur with the foreskin, such as phimosis, many doctors circumcise before exploring nonsurgical options. (In circumcision-happy America, intactivists argue, doctors often misdiagnose as phimosis what is actually the normal childhood state of the foreskin, which loosens as the boy's body matures.)[26]
- The medically unnecessary circumcision of infants and young children, whether practiced in a secular or religious context, appears to contradict modern values of consent, individual rights, and bodily integrity.[27]

The parallels between female and male genital cutting have also been addressed with more sophistication by some circumcision opponents. Bioethicist Brian Earp and political scientist Rebecca Steinfeld outline "the overlapping harms to which female, male, and intersex children may be exposed as a result of having their genitals cut." They argue that the civilized/ savage distinction often made between male and female genital cutting is untenable, given that the symbolic significance and physical invasiveness of the two practices vary across cultures and locations. They propose a "gender-neutral" approach to evaluating "non-therapeutic genital alteration." Although they make their opposition to circumcision clear, they suggest milder alternatives to criminalization, such as "community engagement and education," admitting that "strict legal prohibitions prior to cultural readiness can backfire, creating intense resistance among those who are dedicated to the practice, often driving it underground."[28]

In 2014, the Jewish Museum of Berlin held a special exhibit on circumcision, inspired by the controversy on the issue that occurred in Germany (discussed later). The exhibit displayed various ritual objects,

[25] For example, a freedom of information request submitted to the Birmingham Children's Hospital revealed that twenty-four children were treated for life-threatening hemorrhage, shock, or sepsis following circumcision since 2002. FOI Lead, "Birmingham Children's Hospital." The tragic case of David Reimer involved a man raised as a girl on the advice of sexologist John Money, following a botched infant circumcision that severely damaged his penis. Reimer eventually learned the circumstances of his childhood and declared himself male, but his life ended in suicide. See Colapinto, *As Nature Made Him*; and Osserman, "Is the Phallus Uncut?"
[26] See Circumcision Reference Library, "Conservative Treatment of Phimosis."
[27] See, for example, Svoboda, "Promoting Genital Autonomy"; Fox and Thomson, "Short changed?"; Earp, "Ethics of Infant Male Circumcision."
[28] Earp and Steinfeld, "Gender and Genital Cutting," n.p. In 2020, Earp was nominated for the prestigious John Maddox Prize, linked to the journal *Nature*, for his work on the ethics of genital cutting.

works of art, and films related to the practice in Jewish, Muslim, and Christian contexts. The carefully curated exhibit appeared as proof that it was possible to think about circumcision with an open mind and without rush to judgment.[29] Yet, my discussion with the exhibit's curator revealed a darker side. In her many years at the museum, she told me, this was the first time she felt threatened by her work on an exhibit. Some intactivists thought that the museum's nonjudgmental portrayal of the topic was tantamount to endorsement or complicity, and they circulated her personal information on intactivist web forums. There was also, the curator told me, a certain, easily identifiable style of writing which appeared in some of the emails she received and the exhibit's guestbook entries: an angry, repetitive recitation of the harms and moral wrongs of circumcision, with no reflection on the actual material displayed and the complexity of the issues it raised.

Even in the more reasoned anti-circumcision literature, there is something peculiar. A quick Google search reveals that those who write against circumcision do not do so merely once or twice; their social media profiles are usually dedicated to the cause, as if their whole lives circulate around it. There's a certain "I've seen the light" attitude apparent in even the most thoughtful and respectful anti-circumcision activists that necessitates pause. Although a much smaller presence, those who *defend* circumcision against intactivists seem similarly invested in the cause, as suggested by the work of Professor Brian Morris, who runs a webpage dedicated to debunking intactivist claims and has published over sixty articles advocating circumcision, often replete with self-citations.[30] As anthropologist James Boon writes, "In recent and venerable sources alike, whether pro-, con-, analytically 'neutral,' or interpretively empathetic—words about (un) circumcision tend to be hypertrophied: either oddly laconic and allusive or overwrought and effusive. This ritual *topos* keeps calling forth the textual marks and prose registers of obsession."[31] Why is this the case?

Circumcision's Enigmas

We live in statistical times, yet the effects of circumcision are inherently impossible to measure. To what degree does circumcision reduce (or

---

[29] See Berlin Jewish Museum, "Snip It! Stances on Ritual Circumcision."
[30] See Earp and Darby, "Does Science Support Circumcision?" Examples of pro-circumcision forums include circinfo.net (run by Morris); circumcisionchoice.com; and r/DebunkingIntactivism.
[31] Boon, *Verging on Extra-Vagance*, 67. Of course, the same can be said about my decision to write a book on the topic.

enhance) a man's capacity for sexual pleasure? Does the pain that a baby boy experiences during circumcision leave a lasting psychological trauma? These are questions that touch on the most deeply personal, idiosyncratic, subjective phenomena involved in being human: memory and sexuality. No study can answer these questions satisfactorily because how a person experiences his sexuality, and whether he suffers from a traumatic memory, depend not only on the external things that happen to him but on the particular way he generates meaning out of them.[32]

As an anti-circumcision article readily admits, "men do not experience sex as embodied statistical averages."[33] While some have attempted to quantify the number of nerve endings in the foreskin and measure variances in penile skin sensitivity among circumcised and uncircumcised men, one does not need Freud to appreciate that sexual enjoyment concerns something more than the physiological capacity to appreciate friction on the genitals (what one scholar critical of intactivism has termed "genital determinism").[34] It is clear that both circumcised and uncircumcised men are capable of having sex and achieving orgasm. Beyond that, it is impossible to definitively determine where the (un)circumcised body ends and the mind begins. Complaints by men circumcised as adults are rare, which would suggest that the sexual effects are at least not hugely deleterious (although these are usually done for therapeutic reasons, providing relief from penile suffering).[35] Obviously, the problem is much more difficult to study for those circumcised at birth. Unsurprisingly, the medical studies that have attempted to resolve this via statistical analysis are inconsistent, some finding vast differences in reported sexual sensation between circumcised and uncircumcised men, others none at all.[36]

What if, as a hypothetical, scientists had somehow proven that infant circumcision was neither particularly medically advantageous nor harmful— like piercing a baby's ears? How then, within the parameters of modern ethical values, might we decide on its permissibility?

One paper that tries to answer this question, Joseph Mazor's "The Child's Interests and the Case for the Permissibility of Male Circumcision," is particularly interesting for the way its rigorous application of analytical thought falls into a temporal paradox.[37] Mazor constructs the hypothetical

---

[32] See Fonagy, *Attachment Theory and Psychoanalysis.*
[33] Earp and Darby, "Circumcision," n.p.
[34] See Johnsdotter, "Discourses on Sexual Pleasure."
[35] See Tian et al., "Effects of Circumcision."
[36] Bronselaer et al., "Male Circumcision"; cf. Morris and Krieger, "Contrasting Evidence."
[37] See also Benatar and Benatar, "Between Prophylaxis and Child Abuse."

case of orthodox Jewish parents who want to circumcise their newborn son. He argues that they are ethically justified in doing so because they are acting in their child's "best interests," including primarily his ability to identify with and feel a sense of belonging to his surrounding religious community. Mazor compares the issue to the case of a child born with a nonmedically threatening cleft lip. We would readily consider parents to be acting in their child's best interests were they to have their child's cleft lip surgically repaired; though medically unnecessary and physically painful, it would spare the child much social alienation. When considering a boy born into an observant Jewish family, we should understand circumcision in the same way.

Yet, Mazor admits a problem: if the parents *do not* end up circumcising their boy, it is possible that the boy would choose to remain uncircumcised his entire life. If the adult version of this child would not necessarily elect to undergo circumcision, how can we claim that the parents are acting in their son's best interests by circumcising him at birth? This is where fantasy, masquerading as reason and probability, appears. Mazor claims that if this hypothetical boy chose to remain uncircumcised as an adult, it would likely be due to his fear of the pain and complications associated with the procedure, which increase in adulthood. Mazor argues that he would likely *wish* that his parents had circumcised him when he was a baby, so that he would have been spared the difficulties of undergoing it as an adult. Orthodox Jewish parents who circumcise are acting in their sons' best interests, even *if* the sons would not undergo circumcision as adults, because they know what their sons *will have wanted*, given what they are to become.

I borrow the wording of this phrase from Lacan, who writes that the process of psychoanalysis involves a change in the analysand's relationship to the "future anterior": "what I will have been, given what I am in the process of becoming."[38]

Circumcision is concerned with this unusual temporality, which helps to explain why it is so resistant to rational calculus, and therefore so potentially troubling to the modern subject. The procedure involves the physical imprinting of the wishes of an Other—one's parents and their religion/ culture, or, for secular Americans, the medical establishment—onto the most "private" part of the self. It suggests that what we are to become is marked

---

[38] Lacan, "Function and Field," 247. A 2020 UK High Court judgment that prohibited trans and gender questioning youth under the age of sixteen from accessing puberty suppressants also exemplifies this temporality. The judges believed that young people did not have the capacity to consent to the treatment, because they would not be able to fully understand the implications of the medical transition that purportedly awaited them. The possibility of regret was too great for young people to be deemed able to consent to an unknowable future (High Court, "Bell v Tavistock").

in advance by this Other, or, in Mazor's take, what we will want is shaped by what the Other wants of us (a neat example of Lacan's dictum, "Desire is desire of the Other"). When undergone in infancy, it concerns a period of time we don't remember, a period when we were absolutely vulnerable and dependent on others. As IntactAmerica.org writes on their homepage, "Every man who has been circumcised has two stories: the one he can't remember, and the one he can't forget." It is disturbing to think of this state of total defenselessness, of a person I cannot remember being, but who I am told is an earlier me. What was done to me in this mysterious time? Why should I have to bear its traces?

It is a foundational, anxiety-provoking mystery—the obscurity of our past and the uncertain impact that others have made on us—that circumcision puts in brutal relief. This has always been the case, yet under late capitalism, with its relentless promotion of voluntarist self-fashioning (a particularly taxing iteration of phallic mastery), circumcision can appear particularly threatening. What is more foreign and mysterious than the exigencies of my desire? What does it mean to confront the fact that my sexuality is not wholly mine? Mazor tries to domesticate these questions, but, like intactivists, his reasoning only draws our attention to more fundamental unknowns.

Confronting us with an enigma, on the porous border zone between self and other, circumcision provokes a wish for certainty that intactivists—like conspiracy theorists—try to answer. Frederic Jameson argues that a key feature of late capitalism involves the difficulty of producing a "cognitive mapping" of the totality of social and economic relations. The efflorescence of paranoia and conspiracy theories, he argues, is "the poor person's cognitive mapping in the postmodern age . . . [the] degraded figure of the total logic of late capital, a desperate attempt to represent the latter's system."[39] What Q'Anon adherents and intactivists share in common—why their slogans appeared side by side in the storming of the Capitol—is a frantic attempt to make sense of structures of power that are deeply obscured. While Q'Anon believers grasp toward an understanding of how the elite dominate society (mired in paranoid delusion rather than an analysis of the profit motive), intactivists search for an answer to the problem of subjectivity itself, against a system that places impossible demands on what the individual ought to be and achieve. The excessive passion of intactivists, that extra bit of zeal which makes even their most scholarly arguments seem polemical, derives not from the things that they know about circumcision but from the attempt to resolve the anxiety of what cannot be known about it.

---

[39] Jameson, "Cognitive Mapping," 286.

Drawing on Lacan, Eric Santner writes that the modern experience of anxiety is "not of absence and loss but of over proximity, loss of distance to some obscene and malevolent presence."[40] While it seems as though intactivists are complaining about the former, portraying the absent foreskin as the source of all misery, their rage toward those who practice circumcision expresses something else—a sense of intrusion, of the dissolution of boundaries, of the violation of body and mind. Behind their articulation of lack, their prelapsarian wish for the return of the lost object, lies the fear of an overbearing presence, an evil entity that violates the defenseless child and leaves an irreversible, protean trauma.

A "Dear Abby" advice column published in 2016 exemplifies this combination of lack and violation, along with the traumatic temporality foregrounded by circumcision. "Cut Short in California" writes,

> When I was in grade school, I was sexually assaulted by an older classmate, but I feel much more violated from [my] circumcision because it took a part of me that I can never get back. I am filled with hate and anger toward my parents, even though I know it is unfair to them because they believed they were making the right choice at the time.[41]

In the face of the anxiety occasioned by the enigmatic and traumatic influence of the Other, circumcision appears as a seductive culprit, a concrete place in which one can find the relief, or enjoyment, of laying blame.

The German Case

Contemporary circumcision controversies must be analyzed differently in the European context, where it is understood as a minority religious practice for Jews and Muslims. Despite WHO's endorsement of circumcision for HIV/AIDS prevention, most European medical and bioethical associations dispute its purported advantages, and many have come out strongly against it.[42] European skepticism, and opposition, toward nontherapeutic circumcision is mainstream and has taken on a particular character in a time of heightened racialized oppression of Muslims and other minorities. Although no government has yet banned the practice, several have considered or come

---

[40] Santner, *My Own Private Germany*, xii.
[41] Van Buren, "Dear Abby: College Man Still Mad."
[42] See WHO, "Neonatal Male Circumcision"; Doctors Opposing Circumcision, "Medical Organization Statements."

close to doing so, including Iceland, Denmark, Norway, Sweden, Finland, the Netherlands, and the Council of Europe.[43] Support for a circumcision ban among the public is often high; for example, a 2018 poll found 83 percent of Danish people supported prohibiting male circumcision under the age of eighteen.[44] Of all attempted bans, the Germany case has received the most international publicity, and the debate around it is exemplary in highlighting the complexities and contradictions involved.

In 2011, an appellate court in Cologne ruled that nontherapeutic male circumcision violates "the right of the child to bodily integrity and self-determination."[45] The case concerned a four-year-old Muslim boy who was brought to the hospital by his mother due to secondary bleeding following his circumcision. The boy was treated and recovered, but the hospital staff believed his mother, who did not speak German well, had not consented to the circumcision, and that the procedure was not performed according to medical standards. They reported the case to the police. An investigation found that both parents had consented to the circumcision and that the doctor was qualified, but the doctor was nevertheless suspected of malpractice and charged with aggravated criminal battery.

In the trial court, a urologist testified that the circumcision was performed in a "medically unimpeachable manner."[46] However, the court did not restrict its concern to the doctor's technique but turned its attention to the larger question of the permissibility of male circumcision. The court took as its task to "weigh" what it understood to be competing rights claims: the right to bodily integrity (which it believed circumcision violated) against the parents' rights to religious freedom and autonomy in the care and upbringing of their child. It concluded that the circumcision did not constitute criminal battery because the parents had the "best interests" of the child in mind when they consented to the procedure; in other words, they had reasonably exercised their right to raise their child as they saw fit. The court considered the fact that the ritual marked the child as belonging to the Muslim community, and prevented the threat of stigmatization from that community, as evidence that the parents were acting in the child's best interests (similar reasoning to Mazor's hypothetical case discussed earlier). They also considered that the medical benefits of circumcision mitigated the possible violation of bodily

---

[43] See Wikipedia, "Circumcision and Law."
[44] Sorensen, "Denmark Talks (Reluctantly)."
[45] For a translation of the judgment, see District Court of Cologne, "Amtsgericht Cologne Judgement." For a summary of the German circumcision controversy, I rely on Munzer's "Secularization."
[46] Quoted in Munzer, "Secularization," 513.

integrity. The doctor was therefore acquitted. However, the use of a weighing test that treated circumcision as a potential violation of basic rights opened the door for an alternate interpretation. The prosecution appealed to the Cologne regional appellate court. There, the judges applied the same test and reached the opposite conclusion: "the circumcision of a boy unable to consent to the operation," they argued, "is not in accordance with the best interests of the child even for the purposes of avoiding a possible exclusion from their religious community and the parental right of education."[47]

When the Cologne decision became news, "all hell broke loose."[48] Thrown into legal uncertainty, hospitals across Germany stopped performing circumcisions. Jewish and Muslim organizations denounced the ruling and international press coverage ensued. "Germany has been talking about penises for weeks now. It's become customary to discuss the pros and cons of life without a foreskin over lunch," wrote *Der Spiegel* in July 2012.[49] Conscious of the "public relations disaster" that the decision had caused, German chancellor Angela Merkel sped through an emergency resolution in the Bundestag affirming parents' rights to have their children circumcised, declaring that she didn't want Germany to be the "only country in the world where Jews and Muslims couldn't practice their rituals."[50] Subsequently, a full parliamentary debate on the matter was held and a bill passed codifying parents' right to have their children circumcised under certain constraints: that the procedure be done by a trained professional, and that the child's own wishes, if he is old enough to express them, are taken into account. Although the controversy was legally settled, popular and professional opinion was divided. Many had supported the Cologne decision; hundreds of German medical professionals, academics, and lawyers signed a letter urging Merkel to uphold the court's ruling. A public opinion survey conducted at the time found that 48 percent disapproved of Merkel's resolution, while 40 percent approved and 12 percent were undecided.[51]

The judges' interpretation of religious freedom is particularly revealing of the ideology at play. Rather than understanding religious freedom as encompassing the right of a community to practice its rituals on its members, they argued that, because "circumcision changes the child's body permanently and irreparably," it "runs contrary to the interests of the child in deciding

[47] District Court of Cologne, "Amtsgericht Cologne Judgement," 2.
[48] Munzer, "Secularization," 520.
[49] Quoted in Munzer, 521.
[50] Munzer, 528; Gareth Jones, "Circumcision Ban."
[51] Cited in Munzer, "Secularization," 522.

his religious affiliation later in life."[52] In other words, they interpreted the meaning of "religious freedom" as the freedom to choose one's religion at an appropriate age, unencumbered by filial baggage. If Mazor emphasized the probability that a young child will eventually identify with the religion of his parents and therefore ought to be subjected to that religion's defining rituals in order to prevent communal exclusion (the reasoning of the first court), the Cologne judges, instead, prioritized the child as an eventual free agent who should not be burdened by communal ties.

The intactivist scholar Robert Darby provides the philosophical underpinnings of this view in an article connecting circumcision to the principle, first proposed by the liberal legal philosopher Joel Feinberg, of the "child's right to an open future."[53] The principle is concerned with maximizing the future adult's options to determine its identity and the shape of its life: "Every child is a potential adult, and it is precisely that future adult whose autonomy and capacity for later choice must be protected now," writes Darby.[54] Another way of putting this might be that parents and caregivers ought to *minimize* their influence on the child. Darby suggests such an interpretation: "Whenever a child is too young to express preferences, the imperative is to refrain from actions that unnecessarily and irreversibly close off options."[55] In addition to the wish to eliminate the traumatic influence of the Other, it is difficult not to hear the ideology of neoliberal capitalism here, with the consumer-friendly language of "preferences" and "options." This produces an impoverished conception of religion as one among many "lifestyle choices." Indeed, in Darby's vision, the future of circumcision sounds something like a visit to the hairdresser:

> If, for any reason, an adult male prefers to have a circumcised penis, the open future principle ensures that he is free to make this decision for himself, and also that he will be able to select his own surgeon, style of cut, degree of pain control and postoperative care and so on, thus maximizing the likelihood that he will be happy with the outcome, and reducing the likelihood of regrets.[56]

Absent from this hypervoluntarist depiction of circumcision is the acknowledgment of worldviews in which religious rites are undergone

52 District Court of Cologne, "Amtsgericht Cologne Judgement," 3.
53 Darby, "Open Future"; see Feinberg, "Open Future."
54 Darby, "Open Future" 464.
55 Darby, 466.
56 Darby, 467.

(or performed on one's kin) not in the service of "happiness," but as a fulfillment of religious law. Although the Cologne judges portrayed their decision as compatible with religious pluralism—as did most mainstream voices in support of the decision—they avoided acknowledging how their reasoning compels religion to remold itself to liberal, secular norms. Many intactivists happily denounce religiously ordained circumcision, "religious tolerance" be damned. (Richard Dawkins once tweeted, "If circumcision has any justification AT ALL, it should be medical only. Parents' religion is the worst of all reasons—pure child abuse."[57]) They at least cannot be accused of disingenuousness. By contrast, the more mainstream opposition to circumcision at play in the German controversy pursues a more insidious form of secularization.

By "secularization," I do not mean simply areligious, but rather, as Saba Mahmood puts it, a "regulation and reformation of religious beliefs, doctrines, and practices to yield a particular normative conception of religion (that is largely Protestant Christian in its contours)."[58] Secularism, in her critical analysis of the term, is a form of governmentality that molds religious practices and beliefs into a Western, liberal framework deriving ultimately from a Protestant worldview. We can see a key example of this Christian dimension of secularism in anti-circumcision debates, in the emphasis on bodily imprinting as necessarily more problematic than other forms of parental influence or indoctrination. Darby cites approvingly the Royal Dutch Medical Association's position against circumcision:

> The right to physical integrity and the right to religious freedom of the child imply that religiously motivated, irreversible interventions to the body of the child should be avoided. This leaves the child the freedom to make up its own mind whether and in what form he/she wishes to relate to a particular religious community. Baptising children, for example, leaves no irreversible marks on the body, and as such is not a curtailment of the child's religious freedom, whereas irreversible non-therapeutic circumcision is.[59]

Here, the Pauline distinction of circumcision of the spirit (via Christian baptism) versus of the flesh is reformulated into a secular ideal. Baptism paves the way for—or is at least not incompatible with—"free choice,"

---

[57] Dawkins, "Circumcision."
[58] In Asad et al., *Is Critique Secular?*, 87.
[59] Cited in Darby, "Open Future," 466.

whereas circumcision places unacceptable limitations on the individual's capacity for self-fashioning.

What appears to be at stake in such opposition to the practice is not protection from grievous harm but from a form of parental influence deemed unacceptable: a religiously motived physical intervention that foregrounds questions of sexuality and its imbrication in the Other. It is particularly suspect that those who decry that such minority religious practices curtail individual freedom rarely question the unfreedom produced by neoliberal capitalism's hyperexploitation, enforced precarity, and environmental devastation.

Circumcision's Liberal Defenders

Žižek argues that under late capitalist modernity, "the two most basic rights are freedom of choice, and the right to dedicate one's life to the pursuit of pleasure (rather than to sacrifice it for some higher ideological cause)."[60] This is one way to read European anti-circumcision discourse, with its willingness to criminalize religious practices precisely in order to safeguard these rights. Yet, while Germany's opponents of religious circumcision displayed an ideological commitment to (neo)liberal secularism that contradicted their self-understanding as "tolerant" of religious difference, those who argued in *favor* of the legal permissibility of the practice were closer to their adversaries than may be assumed. The defenders of circumcision generally portrayed the practice as perfectly compatible with Western secularism—a minor cultural variation posing no threat to freedom of choice and the pursuit of pleasure.

For example, after the Cologne decision, the German Council of Jews released a dossier on circumcision, arguing the practice is fundamental to Jewish identity both secular and observant, and that its criminalization would amount to an attack on Jewish life in the country.[61] They were careful to emphasize how the procedure is compatible with modern sensibilities, listing the putative health benefits associated with it and the permissibility of the use of local anesthetic to minimize pain. Although it provided the scriptural basis for the requirement that circumcision be performed when the child is eight days old (thus making a law that would require postponing the rite until the child is old enough to consent incompatible with the religious prescription), it also cited the World Health Organization's argument that the procedure is less painful and less likely to result in complications when

[60] Žižek, "Against Human Rights," 115.
[61] Discussed in Munzer, "Secularization," 523–9.

performed in infancy—quelling fears of religious irrationality with secular scientific wisdom. Indeed, the minimization of pain (a corollary to Žižek's notion of the untrammeled pursuit of pleasure) serves as a guiding principle for both circumcision's liberal advocates and opponents. Mazor's paper in favor of circumcision similarly emphasized the fact that the procedure is less painful in infancy. And in a broader sense, we can see this logic at work in the argument that circumcision prevents religious exclusion: the rite must be permitted not so people can obey the commandments of their God but to prevent the pain of social alienation.

The conservative Jewish studies scholar Jon Levenson, in a critique of intactivism, offers a pro-circumcision Jewish perspective that eschews apologetics about circumcision's compatibility with liberal ideals and acknowledges the ideological conflict between religious observance and modern secularism:

> Classical Judaism takes its place unmistakably on one side of the struggle over the long-term effects of contemporary liberal culture. Where that culture speaks in terms of human rights and the supremacy of personal choice, the ancient sources of Judaism speak powerfully of human duties (and of more duties for Jews than for Gentiles). Where it tends to endorse the voluntary character of identity, classical Judaism speaks of an inherited membership in a people from whom the individual is not free to resign. Where many today celebrate being whole ("intact"), classical Judaism pursues holiness, and always prefers the moral to the aesthetic.... Where much of contemporary American culture now places the value on pleasure, especially sexual pleasure, and on the avoidance of any sort of pain, the classical Jewish texts value the willingness to suffer for a worthy cause, speak of the sanctity of marriage, and elevate self-control over self-expression.[62]

However reactionary such remarks may appear, they make the problem explicit: there is an antagonism between contemporary liberalism and certain forms of religious observance. We might also consider philosopher Carl Schmitt's attack on liberal proceduralism, which speaks to prolonged parliamentary debates that avoid the real ideological conflict at stake:

> The essence of liberalism is negotiation, a cautious half measure, in the hope that the definitive dispute, the decisive bloody battle, can be

---

[62] Levenson, "New Enemies," 36.

transformed into a parliamentary debate and permit the decision to be suspended forever in everlasting discussion.[63]

Although we need not endorse Schmitt's apocalyptic vision of society, his comments on the avoidance of the "decisive bloody battle" seem apposite to liberal squeamishness on circumcision. The Belgian Advisory Committee on Bioethics's report on circumcision, while recommending that minorities "strive for a symbolic practice, in which physical integrity would be respected," epitomize Schmitt's depiction in their concluding words: "The Committee unanimously proposes reflection on how to transcend the controversies."[64]

The return of the repressed "bloodiness" of circumcision emerges, however, in popular discussions of FGM. Just as intactivists link male circumcision to FGM to generate sympathy for their cause, liberal *defenders* of circumcision sharply contrast the two in order to place male circumcision within the scope of Western modernity. Indeed, it might be argued that Germany's relegalization of circumcision relied on this construction of a civilized/savage divide between male and female genital cutting. Shortly after the bill legalizing the practice was passed, a new law was added to the German penal code setting higher penalties for anyone found guilty of mutilating the genitals of a girl or woman.[65] A speech delivered in the Bundestag by Gunther Kring, a member of Merkel's Christian Democratic Union, in defense of the new male circumcision law, is exemplary:

> Circumcision . . . similar to a Christian baptism does not prescribe a life-long commitment to one faith or community. . . . All points of the draft legislation's content can clearly be seen to define exact boundaries. . . . Firstly, [the circumcision must be] a professional procedure according to medical expertise. This expertise includes educating parents about the procedure and its risks, efficient pain management, [ensuring] a gentle procedure, and anesthetization adopted to the individual case. Second, parents can only decide for children who can't do so themselves yet. . . . *This draft legislation also contains a clear rejection of the barbaric practice of genital mutilation of girls.* . . . [FGM] does not constitute inclusion in a religious community, it signifies the degradation of women, which is why we in the German Parliament categorically reject it. [*applause*] Genital mutilation remains a serious criminal offense in Germany, and

---

[63] Schmitt, *Political Theology*, 63.
[64] Belgian Advisory Committee on Bioethics, "On the Ethical Aspects of Nonmedical Circumcision," 32.
[65] See Munzer, "Secularization," 559–62.

I personally believe that we should counteract it more rigorously, even outside our borders.[66]

Kring's speech accepts wholesale the ideology of those opposed to circumcision, arguing only for a different interpretation of the practice, in which it is fully compatible with the consumer-friendly, "open future" approach to religious affiliation. Male circumcision signifies here all the pain-free, positive forms of communal belonging that liberal multiculturalism idealizes, while female circumcision stands for the barbarism of the Other.[67] For those who might fear that sanctioning male circumcision constitutes a form of minority appeasement signifying the weakness of the state, Kring reassures his audience that he wishes Germany to engage in an even more muscular battle, "even outside our borders," against the true threat of FGM.

This same strategy was repeated in a pro-circumcision video released by the Council of European Rabbis in response to the German controversy. The video offers a summary of the liberal legal reasoning advanced by those in favor of the practice, invoking FGM as the limit point to religious freedom through which male circumcision may be justified. After a lengthy discussion of the legal and ethical permissibility of circumcision, the narrator says, "Naturally, religious freedom cannot be unlimited," as shaky footage of African women engaged in some kind of tribal dance appears on the screen, suggesting that a female circumcision ritual is about to take place. "We would never argue that procedures posing a clear and direct danger to a person could be defended on the grounds of religious freedom. Indeed, Jewish law forbids circumcision in cases where such danger might exist," the narrator concludes.[68] Here, a form of respectability is sought at the expense of a less tolerated Other.

Žižek's analysis of the contradictions of liberal tolerance helps us understand the function of this genital cutting dichotomy:

Liberal "tolerance" condones the folklorist Other deprived of its substance—like the multitude of "ethnic cuisines" in a contemporary megalopolis; however, any "real" Other is instantly denounced for its "fundamentalism" . . . the "real Other" is by definition "patriarchal," "violent," never the Other of ethereal wisdom and charming customs.[69]

[66] Quoted from Berlin Jewish Museum, "Debate in the German Parliament" (emphasis mine).
[67] Many Jewish ritual circumcisers claim that the traditional procedure, done quickly without anesthesia, is less painful than one undergone in hospital. Whatever the accuracy of this claim, it makes a clear appeal to modern secular sensibilities.
[68] See Conference of European rabbis, *Circumcision - Pro and Contra*.
[69] Žižek, "Multiculturalism," 37.

Debates on circumcision hinge upon the degree to which the practice evokes the specter of this "fundamentalist" Other. Are religiously circumcised penises harmless indicators of cosmopolitanism, or do they signify the threatening presence of the Other? Practices like FGM are condemned with such passionate fervor in part because they serve as stand-ins for that aspect of Otherness that is truly Other; the threat of something fundamentally inassimilable, "violent," or excessive. This is why German politicians stressed how the new law would also *regulate* circumcisions. Beyond "legitimate" concerns about sanitation and pain reduction lay the wish to eliminate anything that might evoke libidinal excess.

This distinction between the "folklorist" and the "fundamentalist" Other often plays itself out via Islamophobia. While Jewish circumcision may be defended as a safe and sanitary form of cultural difference, when practiced by Muslims—especially on women—it is much more readily viewed with suspicion, reflecting the (uneven and precarious) tolerance of Jews in the Western world, against widespread hatred of Muslims. Whereas concerns about the hygiene of Jewish ritual circumcisers once served as a smokescreen through which Europeans expressed anti-Semitism, today this has partly shifted to Islamophobia. For example, an article in the Guardian describes as "utterly obscene" a Manchester clinic that offers circumcisions "quite literally in a backstreet above a kebab shop."[70] We may detect here a metonymic link between the doner kebab slicer and circumcision, which replicates an older fantasmatic tie between mohels and kosher butchers.[71] Indeed, many of the countries that have sought to ban circumcision have also pursued bans on Kosher and Halal ritual slaughter.[72]

Despite the fact that the Cologne case concerned the circumcision of a Muslim boy, coverage of the incident was dominated by discussions of anti-Semitism in post-Holocaust Germany. That a circumcision ban would affect the Muslim community as well was treated largely as an afterthought. Many Muslims felt that had the practice applied exclusively to Islam and not to Judaism, there would be no similar parliamentary effort to overturn the ban.[73] (Danish prime minister Mette Frederiksten expressed her opposition to a legislative ban on circumcision by saying, "Denmark has a special obligation

---

[70] Fogg, "Male Circumcision." Attempted bans on circumcision may have reignited anti-Semitic discourse, however. One observer wrote during the German debate, "Hardly a week goes by without a talk show commentary or newspaper article directly or indirectly charging Jews and Muslims with torturing, disfiguring or traumatising their children" (Leicht, "German Left").

[71] See Judd, *Contested Rituals*.

[72] See Law Library of Congress, "Legal Restrictions on Religious Slaughter in Europe."

[73] See Munzer, "Secularization," 509.

to protect Jews after Second World War," excluding mention of Muslims entirely.[74]) Indeed, Germany has shown much less concern about religious tolerance regarding another "hot-button" debate in multiculturalism, the wearing of the burqa: in April 2017 the German Parliament passed draft legislation banning the burqa in selected professions, and Angela Merkel has expressed support for an even wider-reaching ban.[75] Moreover, the contrast between male circumcision as a legitimate religious rite versus FGM as a "barbaric practice" that "does not constitute inclusion in a religious community," as Kring put it, ignores the fact that, for some Muslims, female and male circumcision are valued equally.[76] (This fact was also elided in the report on circumcision in Islam released by the Central Council of Muslims in Germany in response to the Cologne decision, which focused only on male circumcision, likely in an attempt to garner mainstream sympathy.[77])

As I noted in the book's introduction, there are a wide range of female genital cutting practices, some of which are less physically invasive than male circumcision. An instructive example is known as the "Seattle case," which took place in 1996.[78] In the Harborview Medical Center in Seattle, which aims to be culturally sensitive to the large immigrant community it serves, doctors struggled to respond to Somalian mothers who routinely requested circumcision not only for their sons but for their daughters as well. After a series of consultations between the mothers, hospital staff, and other experts, a compromise was reached, based on some mothers' own suggestion: the hospital would agree to perform a symbolic genital nick on girls "old enough to understand the procedure and give consent," drawing a small amount of blood under local anesthesia and without removing any tissue.[79] This was seen by the hospital as preferable to the possible alternative: that mothers would take their daughters to local midwives or ritual circumcisers in Somalia, where they would undergo more severe and possibly unhygienic cutting. The hospital hoped that, with this compromise in place, future generations would eventually abandon the procedure, as more established Somalian Americans had. They were forced to backtrack following a massive public outcry— including multiple death threats directed at the hospital staff—spearheaded

[74] Quoted in European Commission, "Denmark."
[75] Dearden, "German Parliament." In the era of Covid-19, where facial coverings are mandatory, legal and popular support for such bans have faced new contradictions and uncertainties. See Stoppard, "Will Mandatory Face Masks End the Burqa Bans?"
[76] On the theological and cultural differences among Muslims on this, see Coleman, "Seattle Compromise," 725–38.
[77] Cited in Munzer, 526.
[78] I rely on Coleman, "Seattle Compromise," for an overview of the case.
[79] Hospital spokesperson quoted in Coleman, 744.

by anti-FGM campaigners.[80] The idea that this symbolic cut could in any way be compared to male circumcision was seen as beyond the pale (many opponents also appeared not to understand what the proposed procedure entailed, referring to it as "female circumcision.") The example makes clear that at stake in liberal views on the matter is not an evaluation of relative harm involved in different religious practices, but an ideological division between what is deemed compatible with secular multiculturalism and what appears threateningly Other.

Metzizah b'peh

While Judaism, and Jewish ritual practices, are generally viewed as within the range of acceptable forms of cultural difference or Otherness today (contemporary anti-Semitism notwithstanding), a notable exception exists surrounding the practice of *metzizah b'peh* (MBP). The procedure involves the mohel using his mouth to suction blood from the newly circumcised penis as the final component of a bris. Although rarely practiced by mainstream Jews, MBP is commonplace among those belonging to *Haredi* ("ultra-Orthodox") communities.[81] Every so often, MBP attracts media attention and public scrutiny, often focused on the risk of transmitting disease from the mohel to the infant. Today, the greatest danger from MBP is the herpes virus, a common infection among adults (many are unaware that they are carriers of the virus) but potentially life-threatening when acquired in infancy.

In New York City, home to one the largest communities of Haredi Jews, the practice has become embroiled in city politics. The NYC Department of Health has reported twenty-two cases of neonatal herpes linked to MBP since 2006, with two infants having died from the disease and two more suffering from brain damage.[82] In 2012, responding to these reports from the health department, then-mayor Michael Bloomberg passed a law requiring mohels to inform parents of the risks of MBP and obtain written permission before performing the ritual.[83] Although many Jews and non-Jews supported the move—or felt it didn't go far enough—it caused a significant outcry in the Haredi

[80] A similar dynamic played itself out with the American Academy of Pediatrics, which initially endorsed the option of a ritual nick then retracted it following public outcry. See Louden, "AAP Retracts Controversial Policy."
[81] In the UK, because many mohels are Haredi, it is not uncommon for mainstream Jewish parents to hire a Haredi mohel and inadvertently subject their son to MBP (personal communication, Stephen Frosh).
[82] Daskalakis and Schillinger, "2020 Alert #2"
[83] Shire, "Why Ultra-Orthodox Jewish Babies Keep Getting Herpes."

community. Many Haredi mohels openly flouted the law, denying the health risks involved and refusing to provide parental consent forms, and a variety of Orthodox groups sued the city, asserting that the law violated their religious freedom. Subsequently, in his successful 2013 bid for city mayor, Bill de Blasio courted the substantial vote of the Haredi community in part by suggesting that he would rescind the parental consent law. He repealed the law in 2015 in exchange for an agreement from Haredi leaders that they would help the health department identify mohels responsible for transmitting herpes infections. Following subsequent cases of herpes transmission, De Blasio promised to "do a much more intensive effort to educate parents, particularly mothers, as to the dangers of this practice," while continuing to assert that parents ultimately have the "religious freedom" to allow their sons to undergo MBP.[84]

The New York controversy is different from the German circumcision ban in many important respects. Religious freedom is sacrosanct in American law and culture in a way that exceeds that of most other Western countries; religious bans of any kind, with the notable exception of FGM, are rare. New York legislators thus had to tread carefully in dealing with the matter out of a need to prevent religious freedom challenges, to avoid perceptions of anti-Semitism (particularly in a city so strongly identified with Jewish culture), and in order not to alienate a powerful voting base. (Tight-knit Haredi communities constitute one of the few remaining voting blocks where members follow the decision of community leaders.) All of this meant that an outright ban on MBP was never proposed, and a ban on circumcision itself, such as occurred in Germany, would be unthinkable.

While legislators and public health authorities may be genuinely concerned about disease transmission, the fantasmatic dimensions of MBP are impossible to ignore. A florid description of the rite in the New York Times makes this clear:

> The mohel lifted the infant's clothing to expose his tiny penis. With a rapid flick of a sharp two-sided scalpel, the mohel sliced off the foreskin and held it between his fingers. Then he took a sip of red wine from a cup and bent his head. He placed his lips below the cut, around the base of the baby's penis, for a split second, creating suction, then let the wine spill from his mouth out over the wound.[85]

If ordinary Americans think of circumcision in terms of hygiene and modern medicine, MBP returns to the practice the jouissance of ritual bloodshed

[84] Gartland and Campanile, "De Blasio."
[85] Otterman, "Regulation of Circumcision."

and taboo sexual practices. At the level of fantasy, MBP is not the same as FGM, but they belong to the same series: FGM standing for the foreign Other (of tribal Africa), MBP for a more local Other. Moreover, Haredi communities themselves, with their strict and highly regulated gender division, dietary restrictions, and so on, represent the Jewish version of Žižek's "fundamentalist" Other, in contrast to the contemporary "culturally Jewish," "folklorist" Other. The fundamentalist Other, as a source of mystery, fear, and intrigue, inspires all sorts of libidinally charged reactions. Hence the popular and often sensationalized accounts of escape from Haredi life, as well as salacious tabloid stories: "This Hasidic couple's kinky open marriage could get them 'shunned forever'" and "I left the Hasidic community to become a nude model" are two NY Post headlines.[86] The Post referred to the Haredi community's refusal to engage with the health department's investigation into MBP as part of a "code of silence," evoking the image of a secretive and conspiratorial sect.[87]

It is likely that the German circumcision law, requiring that the practice be done according to the "rules of medical practice," would render MBP illegal. Yet, so far, German authorities have made no public pronouncements on the matter and apparently little effort to determine whether MBP occurs in the country. Not long after the law was passed, Rabbi Yehuda Teichtal, head of Chabad-Lubavitch in Berlin, organized a bris for his son with over 400 people in attendance.[88] A well-known mohel, Menachem Fleischmann, flew in from Israel to perform the rite. The German newspaper *Der Tagesspiegel* published a story on its website about the event, including a video of the occasion. Shortly afterward, an anti-circumcision child rights organization filed a complaint against the rabbi for criminal battery, alleging that the rabbi's son underwent MBP. The prosecutor's office declined to take up a prosecution. Contrary to the claims of the complainants, the video did not include any footage of the circumcision actually being performed, and therefore it could not be discerned whether MBP occurred.[89] Yet, while the prosecutor questioned the journalist who reported on the circumcision, it is intriguing

---

[86] Melkorka, "Hasidic Couple's Kinky Open Marriage"; Klausner, "I Left the Hasidic Community." The Netflix miniseries *Unorthodox*, loosely based on Deborah Feldman's autobiography of escape from her ultra-orthodox community in Brooklyn, quickly became a global hit, garnering eight Primetime Emmy nominations. For a more nuanced portrayal of this phenomenon, see Cappell and Lang, *Off the Derech.*

[87] Campanile, "'Code of Silence.'"

[88] See Munzer, "Secularization," 556–9.

[89] McGowan's Lacanian observations on the nature of enjoyment are apposite: "Considering the enjoyment of the other, we never know if it is there or not. If we experience it, we do so through the lens of our own fantasy" (*Enjoying What We Don't Have*, 118).

that he apparently did not interview any of the 400 people in attendance, which would have likely provided a clearer indication of whether the bris included MBP. "So far as one can tell the prosecutor's investigation reveals little enthusiasm for getting to the bottom of what actually happened," writes Munzer in his summary of the case.[90] It seems likely that the prosecutor's office wanted to avoid reigniting the country's circumcision debate by bringing into public discourse the specter of ritual oral-penile suction. For the threatening jouissance of the "fundamentalist Other," it appears that different solutions exist: in the case of FGM, public outcry (bolstered by Islamophobia); in the case of MBP, disavowal. Both responses enabled Germany to uphold male circumcision and thereby position itself as embracing multiculturalism while avoiding a confrontation with the limits of liberal tolerance.

Metzizah b'peh within the Community

To appreciate the fantasmatic significance of MBP and its role in circumcision debates, we must also consider the perspective of its practitioners. Why, and in what ways, have today's ultra-Orthodox Jews defended the practice when other observant Jews have renounced it? While advocates and opponents of controversial religious practices often see themselves on either side of a dichotomy between ancient religious tradition and secular modernity, the reality is more complex. MBP became an official part of the Jewish circumcision ceremony in approximately 200 CE via its codification in the Mishna (the first major work of rabbinical literature) and was subsequently reaffirmed in the Talmud in approximately 700 CE.[91] In both cases, the procedure was apparently prescribed not for spiritual but health reasons, likely in keeping with the Galenic theory of bloodletting: the Talmud law reads, "Any mohel who does not suction [the circumcision wound] creates a danger to life, and we therefore remove him from his post."[92] In 1837, Rabbi Horovitz of Vienna wrote to his teacher, the esteemed Rabbi Chasam Sofer, reporting that MBP appeared to be causing a deadly outbreak of sores among Jewish children in the city and asking whether it was permissible to perform the suction with a sponge or "some other means."[93] Chasam Sofer responded with concern for the outbreak of disease and definitive permission to modify the practice:

[90] Munzer, "Secularization," 557.
[91] See Rosenberg, "The History of Metzizah B'Peh."
[92] B.T. Shabbat 133b.
[93] MacDowell, "The Chasam Sofer's Ruling," n.p.

We do not find the metzitzah [suction] is specifically with the mouth, save for the position of the Kabbalists who say that [the process] enacts a neutralization of strict judgment through the lips and the mouth. We are not engaged in mysteries when there is some concern for physical danger.[94]

He goes on to say that the entire portion of the rite involving suction "is not an integral part of the circumcision, but only adjoined because of a health measure," and therefore if it is causing disease, it can be changed "to another method which accomplishes the same thing"—by which he means the putative healing benefits of bloodletting—"so long as we heed qualified physicians."[95]

Chasam Sofer's enlightened position on the matter was gradually accepted by the majority of rabbis, who either banned the practice or replaced oral suction with the use of a sponge or sterile tube. However, this change coincided with the rise of Jewish assimilation, secularization, and the Reform movement, which "spurned the practice as anachronistic, repugnant, and unhygienic," hoping that "a modernized version of circumcision would finally cut the Jew into European society," Silverman explains.[96] Consequently, those rabbis who were invested in actively resisting assimilation and secularization—the most radical of which would eventually comprise the Haredi movement—rejected the ban because "it could be viewed as a deviation from the traditional Judaism they claimed to uphold."[97] While non-Haredi observant Jews reiterate the permissibility of alternatives to MBP every time the controversy flares up, Haredi leaders have not only dug their heels in but transformed the rite into a symbol of Jewish resistance. A petition circulated throughout Haredi communities after Bloomberg's parental consent law claimed that the NYC health department "spread lies . . . mischaracterizations and exaggerations of instances of illness after Brit Milah, in order to justify their evil decree."[98] It went on to portray the matter as a form of holy war:

It should be known that this is only the beginning of their decrees, for their plan and desire is to undo the foundations of Bris Mila in its entirety, may the merciful one save us.

---

[94] MacDowell.
[95] MacDowell.
[96] Silverman, *Abraham to America*, 136; 178. On the relation between the reform movement and hygiene, see Schlich, "Medicalization and Secularization."
[97] Rosenberg, "Why Do Haredim Do Metzitzah B'Peh?"
[98] See Rosenberg, "Hundreds of Haredi Rabbis."

Therefore, we are declaring in the gates of the public—not to be deaf or be silent, until their thoughts to remove us from our holy Torah are completely negated, and we are obligated to battle with all our might and with all our strength, for the fulfillment of Torah and Mitzvos in all its detail and Halacha.[99]

A soberer perspective might find that the NYC health department's relatively meek attempt to intervene in MBP hardly threatened the continued existence of Haredi Judaism. (A similar dynamic has also occurred with regard to some Haredi Jews engaging in COVID-19 denialism and defying rules on social distancing, despite extremely high levels of transmission and death within these communities.[100]) What is at stake here—as with the earlier refusal to follow Chasam Sofer's counsel—seems less about Jewish observance than the jouissance of embattlement as a thoroughly modern response to secular life.

The Injunction to "Enjoy!"

The nineteenth-century advocates for circumcision, today's intactivists, and Haredi defenders of MBP share in common the fact that their discourse is legibly permeated with libidinal excess or jouissance. Given this, how might we put these different causes into relation with one another?

Developing Lacan's claim that the ultimate imperative of the superego is "Enjoy!" (*Jouir!*), Žižek argues that there has been a cultural shift from the dominance of the "traditional authoritarian" superego associated with Freud to today's "postmodern" superego.[101] Previously, the superego was the name for the paternalistic psychic agency that obtained a perverse pleasure through relentlessly seeking out and punishing illicit thoughts and wishes. Nineteenth-century circumcision advocates exemplified this relation to the traditional superego in their drive to eliminate masturbation and infantile sexuality (which constantly threatened to reemerge) via circumcision. In his 1891 book, Charles Remondino, one of the most fervent advocates for circumcision (discussed in Chapter 3), demonstrated the multitudinous ways in which, under the spell of the superego, the foreskin was made to stand

99 Rosenberg.
100 Halbfinger, "Virus Soars Among Ultra-Orthodox." Gaskell et al. produced data on COVID-19 seroprevalence in an ultra-Orthodox community in London, emphasizing several other factors responsible for the high rate of transmission, including socioeconomic deprivation and crowded living conditions ("SARS-CoV-2 Seroprevalence").
101 Lacan, *XX*, 3; Žižek, "'You May!'"

in for a threatening jouissance, an ultimate sinfulness, that needed to be excised:

> The prepuce seems to exercise a malign influence in the most distant and apparently unconnected manner; where, like some of the evil genii or sprites in the Arabian tales, it can reach from afar the object of its malignity [. . .] affect him with all kinds of physical distortions and ailments, nocturnal pollutions, and other conditions calculated to weaken him physically, mentally, and morally; to land him, perchance, in jail or even in a lunatic asylum. Man's whole life is subject to the capricious dispensations and whims of this Job's-comforts-dispensing enemy of man.[102]

Remondino's comments are not dissimilar to those of Isaac ben Yedaiah, a thirteenth-century follower of Maimonides, who, unlike other rabbis, viewed the rite as part of an ascetic program. Ben Yedaiah makes the libidinal economy of superego—the sadistic enjoyment derived through the attempt to enforce prohibitive law—even more explicit:

> [An attractive woman] will court the man who is uncircumcised in the flesh and lie against his breast with great passion, for he thrusts inside her a long time because of the foreskin, which is a barrier against ejaculation in intercourse. . . . When an uncircumcised man sleeps with her and then resolves to return to his home, she brazenly grasps him, holding on to his genitals, and says to him, "Come back, make love to me." This is because of the pleasure that she finds in intercourse with him, from the sinews of his testicles—sinew of iron—and from his ejaculation—that of a horse— which he shoots like an arrow into her womb. They are united without separating, and he makes love twice and three times in one night, yet the appetite is not filled.

> And so he acts with her night after night. The sexual activity emaciates him of his bodily fat, and afflicts his flesh, and he devotes his brain entirely to women, an evil thing. His heart dies within him; between her legs he sinks and falls. He is unable to see the light of the King's face, because the eyes of his intellect are plastered over by women so that they cannot now see light.[103]

---

[102] Remondino, *History of Circumcision*, 255.
[103] Quoted in Glick, *Marked in Your Flesh*, 67–8.

Failing to appreciate the fantasmatic nature of the entire circumcision enterprise (and his own implication within it), the intactivist scholar Leonard Glick takes ben Yedaiah's comments literally, seeing them as evidence that the rabbi "understood that the foreskin is a highly sensitive source of sexual pleasure" that circumcision curtails.[104]

With just a few adjustments in style, both Remondino's and ben Yedaiah's feverish treatises sound nearly identical to a contemporary intactivist Twitter page. Nearly all of the problems blamed on the *presence* of the foreskin are the same as those that intactivists attribute to the *loss* of it. If chastity were previously a cultural ideal, with circumcision advocates occasionally representing this ideal's superegoic underside, today's intactivists represent the victims of the cultural ideal of maximum enjoyment. As Foregen.org writes in their advertising for donations, "Regain the full sexual experience. How does circumcision affect you?"[105]

Rather than facing a prohibition on sexual pleasure, today we are subject to unceasing imperatives to partake in it, explains Žižek. We should sleep with our partners every night to keep the oxytocin flowing, masturbate regularly to fight depression, and for a healthy prostate, we should try anal beads. No longer overtly punitive, today's authorities, in the guise of scientific experts and their pop culture spokespeople, induce us to maximize our enjoyment—for our own as well as society's good. That is why, for those public health authorities that promote it, circumcision is not about preventing masturbation but about preventing AIDS and urinary tract infections, optimizing our sexual health.

Intactivists are fully on board with this "sex positive" ideology; however, like incels, they represent a symptomatic response to its superegoic underside. Contrary to those who would think that our era's sexual permissiveness is unproblematically liberatory, Žižek argues that our "freedom" to enjoy comes at a price, the constant questioning of whether we are enjoying *enough*, and whether others might be enjoying *more*—or whether they have *stolen* our enjoyment.[106] We accept the pro-pleasure ethos of our times only to find

---

[104] Glick, 68.

[105] Internet forums where men exchange techniques and advice on foreskin restoration are full of visual progress reports and penis comparsions. The inventor of one foreskin restoration device did not stop after he achieved a "natural" foreskin length but documented his continued growth beyond the maximum "coverage index" (the name restorers have given for the degree to which the foreskin covers the head of the penis) (Kennedy, "Masculinity and Embodiment"). Perhaps this points toward the unsatisfiability of the desire that underwrites the pursuit of restoration.

[106] See Dean, *Žižek's Politics*, chp. 1.

ourselves faced with a relentless pressure that no amount of sex, consumption, or social media activity seems to discharge.

Importantly, the superego does not simply represent an ideal; rather, it is an agency that relentlessly makes felt one's distance *from* an ideal. The difference between the "traditional" and "postmodern" superego is thus not at the level of the functioning of the agency, which remains the same, but only in the changed cultural ideals through which it punishes the ego. The superego has always been a force of enjoyment; previously, it enjoyed prohibiting enjoyment, whereas today it enjoys making one feel that one does not enjoy enough (or in the right way)—structurally the same thing.

Intactivists are those who have chosen to articulate the failure to enjoy sufficiently in terms of the loss of the foreskin. For the intactivist, circumcision steals sexual pleasure from one who will thereafter literally not know what he is missing. To quote an intactivist, "I don't know anything other than the sex life I've had, yet I can't help but wonder what my sex life could be like had I been allowed to keep the body nature designed."[107] It is as if, in an encapsulation of superegoic logic, there is an "x-factor" of intensity lost from each orgasm, a loss that guarantees that any orgasm is a shadow of what it should be. One fails repeatedly by an unknown degree, and part of the suffering (and perverse enjoyment) of the superego is the inability to measure or know precisely just how far one has fallen short of one's ideal.[108]

Žižek argues that manifestations of religious fundamentalism today are merely the flipside response to this superegoic pressure:

> Caught in the vicious cycle of the imperative of jouissance, the temptation is to opt for what appears its "natural" opposite, the violent renunciation of jouissance. This is perhaps the underlying motif of all so-called fundamentalisms—the endeavour to contain (what they perceive as) the excessive "narcissistic hedonism" of contemporary secular culture with a call to reintroduce the spirit of sacrifice. A psychoanalytic perspective immediately enables us to see why such an endeavour goes wrong. The very gesture of casting away enjoyment—"Enough of decadent self indulgence! Renounce and purify!"—produces a surplus-enjoyment of its own. Do not all "totalitarian" universes which demand of their subjects a violent (self-)sacrifice to the cause exude the bad smell of a fascination with a lethal-obscene jouissance?[109]

---

[107] Gualtieri, "Our Bodies."
[108] I thank Evan Malater for suggesting this interpretation.
[109] Žižek, "Against Human Rights," 120.

We can situate today's MBP controversy within this analysis. The spirit of sacrifice that the Haredim invoked in their letter protesting the "evil decrees" of the NYC health department imbue the cause of religious purity with surplus enjoyment. Consider, for example, the defense of MBP articulated by Rabbi Adam Epstein, a New York Haredi mohel:

> A person who grows up in a pornographic country is going to have trouble understanding these purity customs. Of course it sounds archaic and disgusting to a pornographic mind. I can't defend my view to the general public that has been exposed to different ideas.[110]

In attempting to turn the accusation of MBP's perversity back onto its accusers, who suffer from a "pornographic mind," Rabbi Epstein "protests too much"; his condemnation of secular Americans (like ben Yedaiah's condemnation of the uncircumcised man's excessive sexual performance) "exudes the bad smell of a fascination with jouissance." At the level of fantasy, the sexualized images underlying MBP perhaps play as much a role in the Haredi defense of the rite as they do in mainstream opposition to it; that is, the passionate defense of MBP is powered in part by the repression of its libidinal undertow.[111] As Todd McGowan writes, contrary to its self-understanding, "contemporary fundamentalism derives its energy not from the idea of restricting enjoyment but from the idea of unleashing it."[112] Far from offering a solution to the problem of enjoyment in the form of traditional religious observance, Haredi defenders of MBP appear as ensconced in the jouissance-laden dynamics of the superego as their apparent ideological opposites, intactivists.

Cuts in the Body

Many Jews and Muslims who are otherwise nonobservant nevertheless continue to circumcise their children or experience conflictual feelings over the issue—in the case of interfaith relationships, sometimes igniting serious marital discord. A German public television documentary on this subject, *Baptism or Circumcision*, depicts a previously happy Muslim-Catholic couple nearly driven to divorce when the Muslim husband demanded that their son be circumcised, despite being largely areligious himself and content to let

[110] Quoted in Shire, "Why Ultra-Orthodox Jewish Babies Keep Getting Herpes."
[111] For an analysis of the homoerotic and incestuous elements of MBP, see Malev, "Jewish Orthodox Circumcision"; and Silverman, *Abraham to America*, 135–9.
[112] McGowan, *Enjoying What We Don't Have*, 115.

his wife raise their children as Catholics.[113] The determination of one parent to circumcise is not an uncommon feature of custody battles; in 2015, a Florida mother was thrown in jail when she refused to obey a judge's orders to circumcise her son, according to the father's wishes.[114] Upon hearing about the subject of this book, many Jews have confessed to me that they find the question of whether to circumcise—even if purely hypothetical, in the case of having a son in the future—very difficult. Often, they feel ambivalent about their Jewish identification and uncomfortable about both the symbolic implications and physical consequences of the rite, while nevertheless experiencing some inner compulsion to carry on the tradition (or guilt at the idea of failing to do so), despite having no similar concern over observing any other Jewish laws or holidays. As Sherwin Wine, the founder of secular humanistic Judaism, writes, "To announce to your fellow-Jews that you intend to remain a ham-eating atheist is far less traumatic than to declare that you intend to leave your son uncircumcised."[115] (Unsurprisingly, doubt about circumcision is significantly alleviated for those who accept the American medical view on prophylactic circumcision, and can therefore "have it both ways"—practicing the rite without the fear of causing harm.)

Why does this rite exert such a powerful hold on people who are happy to do away with practically every other aspect of their religion? Many things must be taken into account. Circumcision is considered within Jewish law the most important religious obligation of all, the founding covenant. Additionally, as circumcision is closely linked to the long history of anti-Semitic persecution, including the Holocaust, the decision *not* to circumcise feels to many Jews like a betrayal or failure to commemorate historical trauma. For Muslims in the West, similar issues arise surrounding the need to signify one's communal, minority belonging in the face of social hostility and oppression. There are the complex psychic resonances we have examined surrounding castration and sexed subjectivity, which make the practice enigmatically threatening and alluring. Here, I wish to propose an additional perspective, resonant with the question of jouissance we have just examined, and particularly applicable to our postmodern times: namely, at stake in the wish to practice ritual circumcision today is an attempt to mobilize the apparent "real" of the body as an anchor within a symbolic universe that is often described as fragmented, unmoored, desubstantialized, "post-truth," and so on.

---

[113] Kolano, *Gott Und Die Welt*; see also Greenberg, "When Jewish Parents Decide Not to Circumcise."
[114] Associated Press, "Florida Woman."
[115] Wine, "Circumcision," 4.

Renata Salecl has argued along similar lines in her juxtaposition of the practice of female genital cutting among contemporary African immigrants with the work of body modification performance artists such as Orlan. Salecl argues that these two phenomena (FGC versus postmodern body art) should not be seen as belonging to different symbolic/temporal spaces.[116] She posits a difference in the way we should theorize bodily initiation practices such as male and female circumcision when they occurred in pre-modernity compared to today. Such initiatory practices initially functioned to impose a paternalistic law and secure a subject's place within the social: the "mark on the body [was] . . . the answer of the big Other," the guarantee that one was a member of a symbolic universe with a social location and sexed identity (146). With the collapse of traditional societies and the rise of the patriarchal nuclear family, physical markers and initiation ceremonies were often replaced, in the West, by symbolic substitutes. "Circumcision of the spirit" functioned sufficiently well to impose law; however, without such "ritual[s] of initiation," she argues, the modern subject became "an individual who has to find and establish his or her place in the community again and again," opening up greater space for rejecting one's community (144). Under postmodernity, the "guarantee" of the big Other has become its weakest: "The postmodern subject no longer accepts the power of institutions or society's power to fashion his or her identity" (151). With this apparently greater degree of freedom comes also the "subject's anger and disappointment in regard to the very authority of the big Other," and the desperate search for an "anchor" (151). Within this context, Salecl suggests, both the practice of "traditional" rites like female circumcision by immigrants to Western countries, *and* body modification art, should be interpreted as ways that "contemporary subjects deal with the deadlocks in a highly individual society":

> The symbolic structure today seems more and more often to have been replaced by imaginary simulacra with which a subject identifies. Life is like a computer game in which the subject can play with his or her identity, can randomly follow fashion rituals, have no strong national or religious beliefs, etc. But the fact that life appears as a screen on which everything is changeable has resulted in a desperate search for the real behind the fiction. The cut in the body thus appears as an escape from the imaginary simulacra that dominate our society. (160)

In female circumcision and postmodern body art, we witness a unity of opposites. In the former, there is a "desperate endeavour to identify with

---

[116] Salecl, *(Per)versions*, 141–68. Subsequent references given in the text.

some symbolic law that would guarantee the subject's identity" (155). The latter appears to embrace fluidity and changeability; Orlan, for example, undergoes live-streamed facial plastic surgeries to emphasize the malleability of identity. Yet, such art anxiously raises the question, "If [the body] is just a playground for various identities, what is real here?" (162):

> The paradox of contemporary cuts in the body is that they seem, at the same time, to be a realisation of these theoretical beliefs [surrounding performativity and the deconstruction of identities] and a reaction against them. Making a cut in the body does not mean a subject is merely playing with his or her identity; by irreversibly marking the body, the subject also protests against the ideology that makes everything changeable. The body thus appears as the ultimate point of the subject's identity. Since the subject does not want to simply play with the imaginary simulacra presented by the dominant fashion ideologies, he or she tries to find in the body the site of the real. (160)

Contrary to those who would see extreme bodily modification as a liberated embrace of postmodernity against the retreat into traditional life represented by female circumcision, both practices look to the body for a source of permanence and "reality" in response to today's absence of a symbolic guarantee of identity.[117] Put differently, we might say that today's female circumcision practitioners are just as "postmodern" and "performative" as Orlan.

Salecl's analysis equally applies to the anxieties of secular Jews and Muslims vis-à-vis circumcision. One answer to the question, "Why does this rite matter so much to you (when you have gladly forsaken all the others)?" is that the penile cut appears as the last promise of some kind of stability, the last set of coordinates—however threadbare—through which a subject may feel a sense of rootedness. Both to be circumcised and to circumcise one's offspring, in today's world, can provide the sense of something "real" behind all the fiction and ephemera. Although circumcision is arguably the discursive rite par excellence, it is tempting to believe that such a cut is "pre-discursive," that by virtue of its fleshiness and permanence it escapes the indeterminacy and fluidity of meaning that so troubles us today. No wonder

---

[117] These questions also appear at stake in contemporary debates within trans studies and activism, especially in the tension between trans as embracing gender fluidity versus as securing one's place in sexual difference (see Rose, "Who Do You Think You Are?"). This is not to dismiss trans as a "postmodern phenomenon," but, rather, to suggest that the questions that trans people negotiate reflect a more general contemporary impasse regarding identity.

that those who otherwise embrace secular ideals are often conflicted over whether to perform the rite.

This analysis also illuminates the MBP controversy. We have seen how the rite has been reconstructed by Haredim from an ancient health precaution into a guarantee and sign of one's "traditional" Jewish status, in opposition to the rootlessness of secular culture. "Public support for all kinds of religious fundamentalism in contemporary society can also be understood as an attempt to find a coherent big Other," writes Salecl (155). The New York Times's story about the rite focuses on a non-Haredi, mainstream Jew who specifically sought out a mohel who would perform MBP on his firstborn. "'I don't want a 99 percent job, I want a 100 percent job," the father said. "I want [my son] . . . to be fully Jewish."[118] For this father, circumcision required all the trimmings, as it were, for the promise of identity to hold.

* * *

We have examined a variety of contemporary stances toward circumcision: from virulent anti-circumcision activists to liberal defenders of the rite, to fundamentalist proponents of metzizah b'peh. Throughout this study, a few major themes have emerged: circumcision's disturbing challenge to the ideology of voluntarist self-fashioning, the division of the "folklorist" from the "fundamentalist" Other in the liberal regulation of libidinal excess, the superegoic injunction to enjoy, and the postmodern disintegration of the big Other. In all of these diverse cases, we can observe a central problematic: circumcision is a kind of phallic "stage" upon which the deadlocks of symbolic identity and enjoyment can be rehearsed with utmost intensity.

When I spoke with Joseph Mazor, who argued in favor of the ethics of circumcision, he asked me whether I thought that the trauma expressed by intactivists was "real." It's a difficult question to answer. I do not doubt that they truly feel the pain, anger, and sense of urgency that they express to others. However, as we have seen, stances on circumcision, be they personal or political, cannot be examined in a vacuum. Discourse on circumcision today is permeated by the fantasies and anxieties that arise in relation to the particular configuration of authority and social-symbolic life experienced under late capitalism, played out in phallic parameters. To quote a skeptical urologist, intactivists "are fighting much larger demons." The real question is whether any of us, intactivist or not, wants to face them.

[118] Quoted in Otterman, "Regulation of Circumcision."

Conclusion
"The Damn Thing Never Goes Unregistered"

At the end of Philip Roth's novel, *The Counterlife*, protagonist Nathan Zuckerman imagines how his relationship with his new, Gentile, English wife Maria may end. Within the context of a larger conflict surrounding Zuckerman's Jewish identity and readiness to perceive anti-Semitism where it might not actually exist, he imagines battling with Maria over whether to circumcise their yet-to-be-born son. The fight takes the form of an epistolary exchange. Both of them, he argues in his letter to her, have harbored dreams of "the pastoral." "We all create imagined worlds, often green and breastlike, where we may finally be 'ourselves,'" he writes. Maria idealizes the "mists and meadows of Constable's England"; he, on the other hand, and despite his hard-nosed New York Jewish cynicism, has treated their child-to-be as his "little redeemer . . . the most innocent (and comical) vision of fatherhood with the imagined child as the therapeutic pastoral of the middle-aged man." These and countless other dreams represent the "idyllic scenario of redemption through the recovery of a sanitized, confusionless life." Now, he declares, "that's over. The pastoral stops here and it stops with circumcision":

> That delicate surgery should be performed upon the penis of a brand-new boy seems to you the very cornerstone of Jewish irrationality, and maybe it is. . . . But why not look at it another way? I know that touting circumcision is entirely . . . [against] the thinking these days that wants to debrutalize birth and culminates in delivering the child in water in order not even to startle him. Circumcision is startling, all right . . . but maybe that's what the Jews had in mind and what makes the act seem quintessentially Jewish and the mark of their reality. Circumcision makes it as clear as can be that you are here and not there, that you are out and not in—also that you're mine and not theirs. There is no way around it: you enter history through my history and me. Circumcision is everything the pastoral is not and, to my mind, reinforces what the world is about, which isn't strifeless unity. Quite convincingly, circumcision gives the lie to the womb-dream of life in the beautiful state of innocent prehistory, the appealing idyll of living "naturally," unencumbered by man-made ritual. To be born is to lose all that.[1]

---

[1] Roth, *Counterlife*, 326–7.

Zuckerman's philosophical sermon suggests that circumcision subverts any of the easy comforts one may take in identity. While he acknowledges that the practice is intended to make you "mine and not theirs," in no way does this anti-pastoral act par excellence seem to promise a harmonious existence among a unified national race. If circumcision grants you an identity as a Jew, it is only insofar as this identity stands for a foundational trauma rather than some kind of fulfillment. Yet, a few moments later, his argument makes a subtle shift:

> Aided by your sister, your mother, and even by you, I find myself in a situation that has reactivated the strong sense of difference that had all but atrophied in New York. . . . Circumcision confirms that there is an us, and an us that isn't solely him and me. England's made a Jew of me in only eight weeks. . . . A Jew without Jews, without Judaism, without Zionism, without Jewishness, without a temple or an army or even a pistol, a Jew clearly without a home, just the object itself, like a glass or an apple.[2]

In this line of reasoning, Zuckerman suggests that he has given up hope in the pastoral, that he has finally "drained the domestic idyll of its few remaining drops of fantasy."[3] Yet, much as he appears now, in his diasporic condition in London, to take up a strident defense of difference, what could express better the hope for a transcendent, "strifeless unity," than his claim, "Circumcision confirms that there is an us, and an us that isn't solely him and me"? Zuckerman is willing to give up his beautiful Gentile wife and many other "breastlike" hopes and dreams besides—but have his reflections on circumcision truly enabled him to relinquish his desire for the pastoral? Or have they merely offered him the most powerful iteration of it, emptied of all particularities ("Zionism," "Jewishness," "army," and so on), and steeped in the most seductive fantasy of all, an identity (the "Jew") as pure, Platonic essence, both uniting and transcending father and son?

In an exchange published in the *New Yorker* between Philip Roth and the Gentile writer Mary McCarthy—which, oddly enough, mirrors Zuckerman's exchange with Maria so closely I had to double-check it wasn't an elaborate satire—McCarthy diagnoses Roth with "a severe case of anti-anti-Semitism," and asks him why, in *The Counterlife*, he gets so caught up in "all that circumcision business." Roth replies with yet another interesting take on the import of the rite:

> I think you fail to see how serious this circumcision business is to Jews. I am still hypnotized by uncircumcised men when I see them at my

2   Roth, 328.
3   Roth, 328.

swimming pool locker room. The damn thing never goes unregistered. Most Jewish men I know have similar reactions, and when I was writing my book, I asked several of my equally secular Jewish male friends if they could have an uncircumcised son, and they all said no, sometimes without having to think about it and sometimes after the nice long pause that any rationalist takes before opting for the irrational.[4]

Here, the significance of circumcision hinges on the "hypnotic" effect that the sight of an uncircumcised penis has on the Jew. The cut penis acquires its importance against the backdrop of the uncut. Something about this encounter with difference, with what one does not have or has lost, is so captivating, so powerful, that it cannot be forsaken: the enigmatic experience must be transmitted, inflicted through circumcision, from one generation to the next.

In my discussion on "the cut" of circumcision in the first chapter of this book, I explored a series of interrelated issues—concerning the entry into the symbolic order, communal constitution, and the emergence of desire—that the practice of circumcision makes manifest. Because it is an initiation rite staged on the penis, circumcision, I argued, attempts to "naturalize" a man's entry into the symbolic order, presenting us with the idea that cultural systems are well-ordered and harmonious extensions of our basic reproductive endowments; yet also, due to its inherently discursive character, circumcision shows up the very artificiality of this process—the way symbolization "cuts" us away from our "natural" bodies. Additionally, circumcision rites function both to constitute *particular* communities, marking the boundary of one symbolic network from others, and also to reference the process of communal constitution as such—the "wound" which, as Derrida said, "is universal."[5] Finally, circumcision represents both the individual subject's interpellation by the symbolic order, and his failure to ever be identical with this order— the gap, which emerges retroactively, between the subject and the symbolic system through which he is constituted. This concerns, as Lacan put it, the "intimate relationship between desire and the mark"; desire involves the specific way in which one both *takes on* one's symbolic "mark" and *refuses* to be fully "marked," interpellated, by the symbolic.[6] All of these issues, I argued, circulate around the question of the phallus and phallic mastery: circumcision imaginarily represents man's subjection to a constitutive incompleteness and dispossession that, in a second instance, provides the illusory promise

[4] McCarthy and Roth, "An Exchange."
[5] Cixous and Derrida, "Language."
[6] Lacan, *V*, 290–1.

of an eventual restitution, phallic wholeness/possession. Through the penile cut, the possibility of prelapsarian wholeness is both suggested and denied. Circumcision, this book has argued, is an inherently ambivalent procedure that enables multitudinous and contradictory responses to the constitutive encounter with lack to be played out on the site of the penis.

In this regard, Zuckerman's apparent wavering over the significance of circumcision—does it tear one away from pastoral unity, or might it finally restore an ultimate masculine Oneness?—is entirely appropriate. It is also fitting, I would argue, that *The Counterlife* (like much of Roth's work) is ultimately a story about phallic potency: in the opening pages, we are presented the tragicomedy of how Nathan Zuckerman's brother Henry died on the operating table, pursuing an unnecessary heart surgery that, if successful, would have allowed him to discontinue taking the medicine that eliminated his ability to achieve an erection. Henry Zuckerman's desperate attempt to regain a fantasied phallic fulfillment—he wished to resume an extramarital affair that, his brother observed, was probably never that exciting while it actually took place—came at a lethal price.

This book's subsequent chapters have explored how this question of phallic mastery is at the heart of stances and controversies surrounding circumcision throughout Western history. In the second chapter, circumcision functioned, for Alain Badiou, as a "form of branding,"[7] a way of constituting an identitarian (phallic) order: St. Paul needed to express his "indifference" to Jewish circumcision in order to "cut" through communitarian Jew/Pagan differences and offer a universal form of belonging situated in the void of being. For Daniel Boyarin, circumcision represented the very inverse of this, a mark of one's subjection to symbolic castration that resisted sublation into phallic Christian transcendence and that held out the promise for a more genuinely open and embodied relation to otherness. Although they offered divergent interpretations of Paul, and Paul on circumcision, both authors, I argued, took a stance in opposition to phallic mastery, which I identified as closely related to the "feminine" side of Lacan's formulas of sexuation. The fact that they offered such opposing readings on circumcision could be explained, I concluded, by the inherent ambivalence of the practice itself. In Chapters 3 and 4, we saw how nineteenth-century doctors attempted to domesticate the "otherness" of circumcision—its problematic status as a residue of Jewish difference—by transforming it into a signifier of civilized morality, a professional, surgical cut that promised to overcome infantile sexuality and subjective division (and the femininity associated

---

[7] Badiou, *Saint Paul*, 19.

with it). Their writings testified, against their own wishes, to the inherent impossibility of this phallic enterprise, and psychoanalysis emerged as a useful alternative to their paradigm, which faced the problem of subjective division head-on, universalizing the castrative otherness of circumcision rather than promising a medico-physiological escape. In the final chapter, we saw the castrative side of medical circumcision make a "return of the repressed" via intactivist discourse, which portrays circumcision as the cause of man's phallic incompleteness and his separation from pastoral, sexual harmony. We also saw how contemporary, liberal defenders of circumcision maintain a domesticated view of the rite by displacing its castrative side onto what they consider more "barbaric" manifestations of the practice (FGM and metzizah b'peh), while "fundamentalist" practitioners embrace these popularly rejected forms of circumcision as a jouissance-laden attempt to secure the big Other in opposition to postmodern social fragmentation. Finally, we noted how the desire among secular Jews and Muslims to continue practicing circumcision today is also tied to the wish to achieve some sense of belonging—some shred of phallic consistency—in an otherwise unmoored world. If Roth emphasized the mystery of seeing a penis different from one's own as a reason to continue circumcising, I suggested that this installation of difference transmits not only an enigma but also the comfort of a sense of belonging.

In his study of Jewish circumcision, Eric Silverman writes, "debates over circumcision only marginally concern the penis and focus instead on clashing worldviews concerning ethics, personhood, and the politics of identity."[8] Although I agree, I think this statement moves a little too fast. Indeed, as we have observed, debates on circumcision always concern issues far beyond the biological penis. Yet, our psychoanalytic approach to the issue pauses to ask: How does the penis become the material site upon which these larger debates turn? It is because circumcision is one of the ways that the penis is imaginarily rendered into the symbolic phallus—with all of the uncertainties involved therein—that the organ can serve as the image upon which fundamental questions of subjectivity may be posed. We saw, in Chapter 1, a few explanations for why the anatomical peculiarity of the penis lends itself to phallic symbolization—why, therefore, male circumcision occurs as often and cross-culturally as it does. However, it is not my intention to promote the penis as the "natural" and sole representative of phallic (dis)possession. Rather, through the focus on controversies surrounding circumcision that have occurred *in history*, I have tried to situate the *particular, varying ways*

---

[8] Silverman, *Abraham to America*, 203.

that the penis has been mobilized, *via* circumcision, to explore the problems of symbolic castration. At the same time, my use of psychoanalytic theory has refused a purely "historicist" approach: circumcision is not "just" a "cultural construction"—as popular academic discourse may have it—with a significance that can be distilled into a series of historical accidents. It is also, and more fundamentally, a particular (and particularly compelling) way to give form to the subjectivizing encounter with lack that, Lacanian psychoanalysis maintains, is the universal feature of the human condition. The approach taken therefore both offers an account of the complex relationship between anatomy and sexed subjectivity and, I hope, leaves open the space for alternate forms of this relationship to be imagined and enacted.

This research can be carried forward in a number of directions. Although I have offered explanations for why female genital cutting, as well as Muslim and pagan circumcision practices, were given short shrift, it would be fruitful to explore these within the psychoanalytic framework established here. Throughout this book, I have highlighted feminist concerns. Nevertheless, subsequent research on circumcision might move from the phallic parameters of the practice into the possible relationship (or antagonism) between circumcision and that aspect of subjectivity Lacan designated as "beyond the phallus."[9] Such a project would, I imagine, draw on the work of thinkers such as Bracha Ettinger, Hélène Cixous, Luce Irigaray, and Julia Kristeva to explore the alternatives to phallic modes of representation, inscription, and enjoyment, which circumcision may either open up or shut down.[10] Bice Benvenuto points out the challenge involved in such an approach when she writes, "The problem is that to speak is already a phallic function";[11] but, as circumcision sits at the intersection of representation and the body, it may at least helpfully clarify the paradoxes at stake. Of course, Lacanian psychoanalysis itself has a notoriously complicated relationship with feminism, even in the critical and revisionist forms that "French feminists" have constructed. In my study of circumcision, I think it has been valuable to focus on the great theoretician of the phallus, given what I have discerned as the inherently phallic nature of the practice. Nevertheless, non-Lacanian psychoanalytic approaches to circumcision would also be possible.

Finally, there is a relevant area of Lacanian theory that I have not had the opportunity to develop. If circumcision marks both the universal entry into the symbolic and the singularity of the subject's desire (that which is an

[9] Lacan, *XX*, 74.
[10] See, for example, Cixous, "Sorties"; Ettinger, *Matrixial*; Irigaray, *Irigaray Reader*; and Kristeva, *Revolution in Poetic Language*.
[11] Benvenuto, *Concerning the Rites*, 75.

effect of, but refuses to coincide with, the symbolic), how are we to appreciate the nature of the relationship between these two things? Here, I think, we enter into Lacan's theory of the object *a*, what Nobus calls "the object, or that aspect of the object which occupies the place of what is no longer present, and therefore proves that what, at one point in time, may have been available is no longer accessible."[12]

In Seminar Ten, Lacan elaborates on the concept of the object *a* alongside extensive discussion of circumcision. Subsequently, in a dramatic session that Lacan intended to be the introduction to his eleventh seminar (the seminar was canceled and later redesigned, owing to Lacan's "excommunication" from the IPA), he makes the link between circumcision and the object *a* explicit. He states:

> The Hebrew hates the metaphysico-sexual rites which unite in celebration the community to God's erotic bliss. He accords special value to the gap separating desire and fulfillment. The symbol of that gap we find in the same context of El Shadday's relation to Abraham, in which, primordially, is born the law of circumcision, which gives as a sign of the covenant between the people and the desire of he who has chosen them . . . that little piece of flesh sliced off. It is with that petit a . . . that I shall leave you. (Lacan, "Introduction," 94)[13]

The foreskin, in circumcision, may thus be considered one example of the object *a*; once removed, it comes to stand for all that "is no longer accessible" to the subject, which therefore "elicits the subject's desire to return to the original [fantasied] state of full satisfaction."[14] However, if the foreskin is a kind of socially designated object *a*, the exact nature of the loss it refers to— the precise "thing" that the subject imagines, due to the spectral presence of the object *a*, it might retrieve—is, according to the theory, singular to each individual subject. The object *a* is therefore the "objective" ground of the individual subject itself: "the object *a* is not objectified by the subject. . . . Matters are, rather, the other way round, the divided subject [is] . . . objectified

---

[12] Nobus, "Obscure Object," 177.
[13] Additionally, in the (actually delivered) Seminar Eleven, Lacan invents the strange myth of what he calls the "lamella": "libido, qua pure life instinct . . . what is subtracted from the living being by virtue of the fact that it is subject to the cycle of sexed reproduction . . . of [which] all forms of the *objet a* that can be enumerated are the representatives" (*XI*, 198). In English, "lamellae" is "the anatomical term given to the precursors of the prepuce (the foreskin in men, or protective tissue around the clitoris in women) during the development of the reproductive organs" (Harris, *Lacan's Return*, 75).
[14] Nobus, "Obscure Object," 182.

by the object . . . re-caused, re-divided by the desire that the object *a* elicits in it."[15]

If there is anything to criticize Philip Roth for, it is neither his obsession with circumcision (far be it for me to make that case) nor his "anti-anti-Semitism," but, rather, his apparent resignation in the face of the phallic dilemma. Rather than stating circumcision as *his desire*—as something he wants, however conflictually, to inflict—he presents the rite as something that a Jew can only acquiesce to, a truth before which he stands helpless. This preserves the "pastoral" fantasy that an Other holds the final answers (however cruel they may be). To be subjected to circumcision is to be confronted with one's inconsistent inscription in the symbolic order; to *subjectify* one's circumcision is to claim this inconsistency as one's own. It is only through this latter act that one can encounter one's circumcised, desiring subjectivity as "just the object itself, like a glass or an apple."

---

[15] Nobus, 183.

Acknowledgments

Mairéad Hanrahan and Stephen Frosh were invaluable sources of knowledge and support when this project first began. Dany Nobus has provided vital feedback and mentorship.

My postdoctoral work on the *Waiting Times* project, funded by the Wellcome Trust, has allowed me to see this book through to completion. The team have been delightful collaborators: thanks Laura Salisbury, Michael Flexer, Martin Moore, Jocelyn Catty, Kelechi Anucha, Stephanie Davies, Martin O'Brien, and especially Lisa Baraitser, who has been a generous friend and mentor.

Several institutions and organizations fostered and refined my thinking, including the Psychoanalytic Thought, History, and Political Life forum; Stephen's work-in-progress group; CFAR; the Site for Contemporary Psychoanalysis; the Freud Museum; Das Unbehagen; the Centre for Multidisciplinary and Intercultural Inquiry at UCL; and the Department of Psychosocial Studies at Birkbeck. I relied on the British Library not only for its collection but also as a working space and intellectual hub that facilitated the circulation of morale-sustaining gossip.

Lawrence Kritzman's class "Psychoanalysis and Literature" opened my eyes to the world of Freud. Michael Bronski introduced me to Jewish studies in "Jews and Hollywood" and has shared innumerable intellectual and political insights in the years since; he is a brilliant teacher and a dear friend.

During the Covid-19 lockdown, when this book was finalized, a new horizon of political struggle opened up. Thanks to fellow travelers of #CoronaContract, Somerford Grove Renters, and Socialist Alternative. No thanks to John Christodoulou.

A circle of comrades and confidantes, haphazardly united under the banner of the "Lacanian Phrontisterion," provided intellectual and emotional nourishment: Foivos Dousos, Daniel Mapp, Aimée Lê, Rob Price, Jaice Sara Titus, Greg Shreeve, Natasha Silver, Marcella Bruno, and Graham Smith. Thank you.

Thanks to Roger Litten for patiently listening and showing me how to do it too.

Rahul Rao welcomed me into his home when I first arrived in the UK and has been a vital companion ever since. Although some things have changed, my love and gratitude remain constant.

Marc Sutton is the hand that reached back when I went to grab the pretty flower. He has given me joy I didn't know I could have.

Keeping my best interests at heart, my mother and father ensured that the *mohel* was not only religiously but also medically trained. For that, and much more, I am grateful.

Bibliography

Action for Stammering Children. "When Does It Begin?" n.d. http://www.stam meringcentre.org/when-does-it-begin.

Ahmadu, Fuambai. "Ain't I a Woman Too? Challenging Myths of Sexual Dysfunction in Circumcised Women." In *Transcultural Bodies: Female Genital Cutting in Global Context*, edited by Ylva Hernlund and Bettina Shell-Duncan, 278–310. New Brunswick, NJ: Rutgers University Press, 2007.

Alanis, Mark C., and Richard S. Lucidi. "Neonatal Circumcision: A Review of the World's Oldest and Most Controversial Operation." *Obstetrical & Gynecological Survey* 59, no. 5 (May 2004): 379–95.

Allan, Jonathan A. "Is the Foreskin a Grave?" In *Raw: PrEp, Pedagogy, and the Politics of Barebacking*, edited by Ricky Varghese, 3–26. Regina: University of Regina Press, 2019.

Allan, Jonathan A. "The Foreskin Aesthetic or Ugliness Reconsidered." *Men and Masculinities* 23, no. 3–4 (August 1, 2020): 558–78.

Allan, Jonathan A. "The Lost Inches: Circumcision Debates in Gay Men's Magazines." *Porn Studies* 6, no. 4 (October 2, 2019): 377–90.

American Academy of Pediatrics. "Cultural Bias and Circumcision: The AAP Task Force on Circumcision Responds." *Pediatrics* 131, no. 4 (April 1, 2013): 801–4.

American Academy of Pediatrics, Task Force on Circumcision. "Circumcision Policy Statement." *Pediatrics* 130, no. 3 (August 31, 2012): 585.

Androus, Zachary T. "Critiquing Circumcision: In Search of a New Paradigm for Conceptualizing Genital Modification." *Global Discourse* 3, no. 2 (June 1, 2013): 266–80.

Angel, Katherine. *Tomorrow Sex Will Be Good Again: Women and Desire in the Age of Consent*. London: Verso Books, 2021.

Angulo, Javier C., and Marcos García-Díez. "Male Genital Representation in Paleolithic Art: Erection and Circumcision Before History." *Urology* 74, no. 1 (July 2009): 10–14.

Anonymous. "Circumcision in the Neuroses." *Chicago Medical Review* III, no. 12 (June 20, 1881): 270.

Anonymous. *Onania: Or, the Heinous Sin of Self-Pollution and All Its Frightful Consequences (in Both Sexes) Considered with Spiritual and Physical Advice to Those Who Have Already Injured Themselves by This Abominable Practice . . .* Accessed March 12, 2015. http://wellcomelibrary.org/player/b20442348.

Anonymous. "R/MensRights - Conference: The Fragile Phallus (Warning: Postmodern Trash)." *reddit*. Accessed March 18, 2021. https://www.reddit.c om/r/MensRights/comments/8q7x0d/conference_the_fragile_phallus_wa rning_postmodern/.

Arnaud, Sabine. *On Hysteria: The Invention of a Medical Category Between 1670 and 1820*. Chicago. IL: University of Chicago Press, 2015.

Asad, Talal, Wendy Brown, Judith Butler, and Saba Mahmood. *Is Critique Secular?: Blasphemy, Injury, and Free Speech*. New York: Fordham University Press, 2013.

Associated Press. "Florida Woman Who Tried to Block Son's Circumcision Freed from Jail." *The Guardian*, May 24, 2015, sec. Society. http://www.theg uardian.com/society/2015/may/24/florida-woman-son-circumcision-freed -jail.

Auchter, Jessica. "Forced Male Circumcision: Gender-Based Violence in Kenya." *International Affairs* 93, no. 6 (November 1, 2017): 1339–56.

Badawy, Alexander. *The Tomb of Nyhetep-Ptah at Giza and the Tomb of Ankhmahor at Saqqara*. Berkeley, CA: University of California Press, 1978.

Badiou, Alain. *Being and Event*. Translated by Oliver Feltham. London: Bloomsbury, 2013.

Badiou, Alain. *Saint Paul: The Foundation of Universalism*. Translated by Ray Brassier. Stanford, CA: Stanford University Press, 2003.

Barwell, Richard. "On Infantile Paralysis and Its Resulting Deformities." *The Lancet* 2, no. 2564 (October 19, 1872): 551–2.

Bearman, P., C. E. Bosworth, E. van Donzel, and W. P. Heinrichs, eds. "Khafd." In *Encyclopedia of Islam*, 2nd ed., 2012. http://referenceworks.brillonline.c om/entries/encyclopaedia-of-islam-2/khitan-SIM_4296.

Beaty, J. H. "Some Peripheral Irritations Common in Young Boys." *Journal of Orificial Surgery* 7 (July 1898): 33–6.

Belgian Advisory Committee on Bioethics. "On the Ethical Aspects of Nonmedical Circumcision." *American Academy of Pediatrics*, May 8, 2017. https://www.health.belgium.be/sites/default/files/uploads/fields/fpshealth_ theme_file/opinion_70_web.pd.

Benatar, Michael, and David Benatar. "Between Prophylaxis and Child Abuse: The Ethics of Neonatal Male Circumcision." *The American Journal of Bioethics* 3, no. 2 (May 1, 2003): 35–48.

Derrida, Jacques. "Circumfession." In *Jacques Derrida*, edited by Geoffrey Bennington and Jacques Derrida, translated by Geoffrey Bennington. Chicago, IL: University of Chicago Press, 1999.

Benvenuto, Bice. *Concerning the Rites of Psychoanalysis, Or, The Villa of the Mysteries*. London: Routledge, 1995.

Berg, Emmett. "Proposed Circumcision Ban Ordered off San Francisco Ballot." *Reuters*, July 28, 2011. https://www.reuters.com/article/us-circumcision-sa nfrancisco-idUSTRE76R83D20110728.

Berlin Jewish Museum. "Snip It! Stances on Ritual Circumcision." n.d. https:// www.jmberlin.de/en/exhibition-snip-it.

Bettelheim, Bruno. *Symbolic Wounds: Puberty Rites & the Envious Male*. New York: Collier Books, 1968.

Biddick, Kathleen. *The Typological Imaginary: Circumcision, Technology, History*. Philadelphia, PA: University of Pennsylvania Press, 2003.

Bird, Brian. "A Study of the Bisexual Meaning of the Foreskin." *Journal of the American Psychoanalytic Association* 6 (1958): 287–304.

Bloodstained Men. "Homepage." n.d. bloodstainedmen.com.

Bodenner, Chris. "How Similar Is FGM to Male Circumcision? Your Thoughts." *The Atlantic*, May 13, 2015. https://www.theatlantic.com/health/archive/2015/05/male-circumcision-vs-female-circumcision/392732/.

Bonner, Kate. "Male Circumcision as an HIV Control Strategy: Not a 'Natural Condom.'" *Reproductive Health Matters* 9, no. 18 (2001): 143–55.

Bonomi, Carlo. "Baginsky, Adolf." In *The Freud Encyclopedia: Theory, Therapy, and Culture*, edited by Edward Erwin, 41–2. New York: Routledge, 2002.

Bonomi, Carlo. *The Cut and the Building of Psychoanalysis*. London: Routledge, 2015.

Bonomi, Carlo. "The Relevance of Castration and Circumcision to the Origins of Psychoanalysis: 1. The Medical Context." *The International Journal of Psychoanalysis* 90, no. 3 (June 2009): 551–80.

Boon, James A. *Verging on Extra-Vagance: Anthropology, History, Religion, Literature, Arts . . . Showbiz*. Princeton, NJ: Princeton University Press, 1999.

Bowie, Malcolm. *Lacan*. Cambridge, MA: Harvard University Press, 1993.

Boyarin, Daniel. *A Radical Jew: Paul and the Politics of Identity*. Berkeley, CA: University of California Press, 1997.

Boyarin, Daniel. "Freud's Baby, Fliess's Maybe: Homophobia, Anti-Semitism, and the Invention of Oedipus." *GLQ: A Journal of Lesbian and Gay Studies* 2, no. 1 and 2 (January 4, 1995): 115–47.

Boyarin, Daniel. "'This We Know to Be the Carnal Israel': Circumcision and the Erotic Life of God and Israel." *Critical Inquiry* 18, no. 3 (1992): 474–505.

Boyarin, Daniel. *Unheroic Conduct: The Rise of Heterosexuality and the Invention of the Jewish Man*. Berkeley, CA: University of California Press, 1997.

Boyle, Gregory, Ronald Goldman, J. Steven Svoboda, and Ephrem Fernandez. "Male Circumcision: Pain, Trauma, and Psychosexual Sequelae." *Journal of Health Psychology* 7, no. 3 (May 1, 2002): 329–43.

Brennan, Teresa. *Between Feminism and Psychoanalysis*. Edited by Teresa Brennan. London: Routledge, 1989.

Brennan, Teresa. *The Interpretation of the Flesh: Freud and Femininity*. London: Routledge, 1992.

Breuer, Josef, and Sigmund Freud. *On The Psychical Mechanism of Hysterical Phenomena: Preliminary Communication from Studies on Hysteria*, Vol. 2. London: Hogarth Press, 1893.

Bromley, Scott (@Scott_Bromley). "Thank You, Fox News, for Showing Why the Protests Broke out Today." *Twitter*, January 6, 2021. https://twitter.com/Scott_Bromley/status/1346968318100467712.

Bronselaer, Guy A., Justine M. Schober, Heino F. L. Meyer-Bahlburg, Guy T'Sjoen, Robert Vlietinck, and Piet B. Hoebeke. "Male Circumcision Decreases Penile Sensitivity as Measured in a Large Cohort." *BJU International* 111, no. 5 (May 2013): 820–7.

Burke, Nan. "Reprise: Female Circumcision and the Control of Women." *Cambridge Quarterly of Healthcare* 3 (1994): 440.

Butler, Judith. *Bodies That Matter: On the Discursive Limits of "Sex."* London: Routledge, 1993.

Butler, Judith. *Gender Trouble: Feminism and the Subversion of Identity.* London: Routledge, 1990.

Butler, Judith. *Undoing Gender.* London: Routledge, 2004.

Campanile, Carl. "'Code of Silence' Blocking DOH from Finding Herpes-Infection Mohelim." *New York Post*, March 10, 2017.

Campbell, Douglas A. *The Deliverance of God: An Apocalyptic Rereading of Justification in Paul.* Grand Rapids, MI: William B. Eerdmans Publishing Company, 2013.

Cappell, Ezra, and Jessica Lang, eds. *Off the Derech: Leaving Orthodox Judaism.* Albany, NY: SUNY Press, 2020.

Caputo, John D., and Linda Martín Alcoff, eds. *St. Paul among the Philosophers.* Bloomington, IN: Indiana University Press, 2009.

Carlson, Shanna T. "Transgender Subjectivity and the Logic of Sexual Difference." *Differences* 21, no. 2 (August 18, 2010): 46–72.

Carpenter, Laura M. "On Remedicalisation: Male Circumcision in the United States and Great Britain." *Sociology of Health & Illness* 32, no. 4 (2010): 613–30.

Cavanagh, Sheila L. "Transpsychoanalytics." *Transgender Studies Quarterly* 4, no. 3–4 (2017): 326–57.

Chapman, Norman. "Some of the Nervous Affections Which Are Liable to Follow Neglected Congenital Phimosis in Children." *Medical News (Philadelphia)* 41 (1882): 314–17.

Chiesa, Lorenzo. *Subjectivity and Otherness: A Philosophical Reading of Lacan.* Cambridge, MA: MIT Press, 2007.

"Circumcision and Law." In *Wikipedia*, March 1, 2021. https://en.wikipedia.org/ w/index.php?title=Circumcision_and_law&oldid=1009546234.

Circumcision Choice. "How Intactivists Exploited the Coronavirus." *circumcisionchoice*, October 28, 2020. https://www.circumcisionchoice.com/ single-post/covid19.

Circumcision Reference Library. "American Academy of Pediatrics Circumcision Statements." Accessed March 22, 2021. http://www.cirp.org/ library/statements/aap/.

Circumcision Reference Library. "Conservative Treatment of Phimosis: Alternatives to Radical Circumcision." Accessed March 30, 2021. http://www .cirp.org/library/treatment/phimosis/.

Cixous, Hélène. "Sorties: Out and Out: Attacks/Ways Out/Forrays." In *The Newly Born Woman*, by Hélène Cixous and Catherine Clement, translated by Betsy Wing. Minneapolis, MN: University of Minnesota Press, 1986.

Cixous, Hélène, and Jacques Derrida. Jewish Book Week. The Language of Others: Hélène Cixous, Jacques Derrida. Interview by Jacqueline Rose, 2004. http://www.jewishbookweek.com/sites/default/files/Hélène%20Cixous,%20J acques%20Derrida%20Jacqueline%20Rose%2001.03.04.pdf.

Clopper, Eric. "Eric Clopper's Defense Fund." https://www.gofundme.com/f/eri
c-cloppers-defense-fund. Accessed March 29, 2021. https://www.gofundme
.com/f/eric-cloppers-defense-fund.

Cockshut, R. W. "Circumcision." *British Medical Journal* 2 (1935): 764.

Cohen, Shaye J. D. *Why Aren't Jewish Women Circumcised?: Gender and
Covenant in Judaism*. Berkeley, CA: University of California Press, 2005.

Coleman, Doriane Lambelet. "The Seattle Compromise: Multicultural
Sensitivity and Americanization." *Duke Law Journal* 47, no. 4 (February
1998): 717.

Conference of European Rabbis. *Circumcision - Pro and Contra*, 2015. https://
www.youtube.com/watch?v=yq0e6K0qpNA.

Conrad, Peter. "Medicalization and Social Control." *Annual Review of Sociology*
18, no. 1 (August 1992): 209–32.

Copjec, Joan. *Read My Desire: Lacan against the Historicists*. Cambridge, MA:
MIT Press, 1994.

Cox, Guy, and Brian J. Morris. "Why Circumcision: From Prehistory to the
Twenty-First Century." In *Surgical Guide to Circumcision*, edited by David A.
Bolnick, Martin Koyle, and Assaf Yosha, 243–59. London: Springer, 2012.

Critchley, Macdonald, and Eileen A. Critchley. *John Hughlings Jackson: Father of
English Neurology*. Oxford: Oxford University Press, 1998.

Cryle, P. M., and Alison Moore. *Frigidity: An Intellectual History. Genders and
Sexualities in History Series*. New York: Palgrave Macmillan, 2011.

Darby, Robert. *A Surgical Temptation: The Demonization of the Foreskin and
the Rise of Circumcision in Britain*. Chicago, IL: University of Chicago Press,
2005.

Darby, Robert. "Pathologizing Male Sexuality: Lallemand, Spermatorrhea,
and the Rise of Circumcision." *Journal of the History of Medicine and Allied
Sciences* 60, no. 3 (July 1, 2005): 283–319.

Darby, Robert. "The Child's Right to an Open Future: Is the Principle Applicable
to Non-Therapeutic Circumcision?" *Journal of Medical Ethics* 39, no. 7 (July
1, 2013): 463–8.

Darby, Robert, and John Cozijn. "The British Royal Family's Circumcision
Tradition: Genesis and Evolution of a Contemporary Legend." *SAGE Open* 3,
no. 4 (January 1, 2013).

Daskalakis, Demetre, and Julia Schillinger. "2020 Alert #2: Three New Cases of
Neonatal Herpes Infection Following Ritual Jewish Circumcision." *New York
City Department of Health*, n.d. https://www1.nyc.gov/assets/doh/downloads
/pdf/han/alert/2020/neonatal-herpes.pdf.

Dave, S., A. Johnson, K. Fenton, C. Mercer, B. Erens, and K. Wellings. "Male
Circumcision in Britain: Findings from a National Probability Sample
Survey." *Sexually Transmitted Infections* 79, no. 6 (December 2003): 499–500.

Davidson, Arnold. "Assault on Freud." *London Review of Books*, July 5, 1984.
https://www.lrb.co.uk/the-paper/v06/n12/arnold-davidson/assault-on-freud.

Davidson, Arnold. *The Emergence of Sexuality: Historical Epistemology and the
Formation of Concepts*. Cambridge, MA: Harvard University Press, 2004.

Dawkins, Richard (@richarddawkins). "If Circumcision Has Any Justification AT ALL, It Should Be Medical Only. Parents' Religion Is the Worst of All Reasons -- Pure Child Abuse." *Twitter.* @richarddawkins (blog), November 19, 2013. https://twitter.com/richarddawkins/status/402716873369726977.

Dawson, Benjamin E. "Circumcision in the Female: Its Necessity and How to Perform It." *American Journal of Clinical Medicine* 22, no. 6 (June 1915): 520–3.

Dean, Jodi. *Žižek's Politics.* New York: Routledge, 2006.

Dearden, Lizzie. "German Parliament Votes in Favour of Partial Burqa Ban." *The Independent*, April 28, 2017.

Derrida, Jacques. *Archive Fever: A Freudian Impression.* Translated by Eric Prenowitz. Chicago: University of Chicago Press, 1998.

Derrida, Jacques. *Dissemination.* Translated by Barbara Johnson. London: Continuum, 2004.

Dickens, Charles. *The Uncommercial Traveller.* Edited by Daniel Tyler. Oxford: Oxford University Press, 2015.

Didi-Huberman, Georges. *Invention of Hysteria: Charcot and the Photographic Iconography of the Salpêtrière.* Translated by Alisa Hartz. Cambridge, MA: MIT Press, 2003.

District Court of Cologne. Amtsgericht Cologne Judgement, no. 528 Ds 30/11 (September 21, 2011).

Doctors Opposing Circumcision. "Medical Organization Statements." Accessed March 30, 2021. https://www.doctorsopposingcircumcision.org/for-profess ionals/medical-organization-statements/.

Dolar, Mladen. "'I Shall Be with You on Your Wedding-Night': Lacan and the Uncanny." *October* 58 (October 1, 1991): 5–23.

Douglas, Mary. *Purity and Danger: An Analysis of Concepts of Pollution and Taboo.* London: Routledge, 2002.

Dysch, Marcus. "Jeremy Corbyn 'must Do More' to Address Concerns, Says Board of Deputies after Meeting." *The Jewish Chronicle*, February 9, 2016 edition. Accessed March 11, 2021. https://www.thejc.com/news/uk/jeremy -corbyn-must-do-more-to-address-concerns-says-board-of-deputies-after -meeting-1.59213.

Earp, Brian. "Between Moral Relativism and Moral Hypocrisy: Reframing the Debate." *Kennedy Institute of Ethics Journal* 26, no. 2 (June 2016): 105–44.

Earp, Brian. "Female Genital Mutilation and Male Circumcision: Should There Be a Separate Ethical Discourse?" *Practical Ethics*, February 18, 2014. http:// blog.practicalethics.ox.ac.uk/2014/02/female-genital-mutilation-and-male- circumcision-time-to-confront-the-double-standard/.

Earp, Brian. "The Ethics of Infant Male Circumcision." *Journal of Medical Ethics* 39, no. 7 (2013): 418–20.

Earp, Brian. "Infant Circumcision and Adult Penile Sensitivity: Implications for Sexual Experience." *Trends in Urology & Men's Health* 7, no. 4 (2016): 17–21.

Earp, Brian, and Robert Darby. "Does Science Support Infant Circumcision? A Skeptical Reply to Brian Morris." *The Skeptic* (blog), 2014. https://www.ske ptic.org.uk/magazine/onlinearticles/infant-circumcision/.

Earp, Brian, and Rebecca Steinfeld. "Gender and Genital Cutting; A New Paradigm." *Euromind*, April 6, 2017. http://euromind.global/en/brian-d-earp -and-rebecca-steinfeld/?lang=en.

Eilberg-Schwartz, Howard. *God's Phallus: And Other Problems for Men and Monotheism*. Boston: Beacon Press, 1995.

Eilberg-Schwartz, Howard. *The Savage in Judaism: An Anthropology of Israelite Religion and Ancient Judaism*. Bloomington, IN: Wiley, 1990.

Ellis-Petersen, Hannah. "Inside Delhi: Beaten, Lynched and Burnt Alive." *The Guardian*, March 1, 2020, sec. World News. http://www.theguardian.com/ world/2020/mar/01/india-delhi-after-hindu-mob-riot-religious-hatred-natio nalists.

Eric, Clopper. *Sex & Circumcision: An American Love Story by Eric Clopper*, 2018. https://www.youtube.com/watch?v=FCuy163srRc.

Ettinger, Bracha. *The Matrixial Borderspace*. Minneapolis, MN: University of Minnesota Press, 2006.

European Commission. "Denmark: Renewed Debate on Circumcision of Boys." *European Web Site on Integration*. Accessed March 30, 2021. https://ec.euro pa.eu/migrant-integration/news/denmark-renewed-debate-on-circumci sion-of-boys.

Evans, Mihail. "A History around Housman's Circumcision." *Historical Reflections/Reflexions Historiques* 40, no. 3 (December 1, 2014): 68–90.

Fanon, Frantz. *Black Skin, White Masks*. Translated by Charles Markmann. London: Pluto Books, 2008.

Feinberg, Joel. "The Child's Right to an Open Future." In *Whose Child? Children's Rights, Parental Authority, and State Power*, edited by William Aiken and Hugh LaFollette, 124–53. Totowa, NJ: Rowman and Littlefield, 1980.

Felman, Shoshana. "Turning the Screw of Interpretation." *Yale French Studies*, 55/56 (1977): 94–207.

Ferenczi, Sandor. *Thalassa: A Theory of Genitality*. London: Routledge, 2018.

Filipovic, Jill. "How Intactivists Are Ruining the Debate on Circumcision." *Feministe*, September 18, 2013. www.feministe.us/blog/.../how-intactivists-ar e-ruining-the-debate-on-circumcision/.

Fink, Bruce. *Lacan to the Letter: Reading Écrits Closely*. Minneapolis, MN: University of Minnesota Press, 2004.

Fishman, Sterling. "The History of Childhood Sexuality." *Journal of Contemporary History* 17, no. 2 (1982): 269–83.

Fogg, Ally. "Male Circumcision: Let There Be No More Tragedies Like Baby Goodluck." *The Guardian*, December 17, 2012.

Fonagy, Peter. *Attachment Theory and Psychoanalysis*. London: Routledge, 2018.

Forster, J. Cooper. *The Surgical Diseases of Children*. London: John W. Parker and Son, 1860.

Foucault, Michel. *The History of Sexuality, Vol. 1: The Will to Knowledge*. Translated by Robert Hurley. London: Penguin, 1998.

Fox, Marie, and Michael Thomson. "Short Changed? The Law and Ethics of Male Circumcision." *The International Journal of Children's Rights* 13, no. 1–2 (January 1, 2005): 161–82.

Freud, Anna. "The Role of Bodily Illness in the Mental Life of Children." *Psychoanalytic Study of the Child* 7 (1952): 69–81.

Freud, Sigmund. "An Autobiographical Study." In *The Standard Edition of the Complete Psychological Works of Sigmund Freud*, edited and translated by James Strachey 20:1–74. London: Hogarth Press, 1925.

Freud, Sigmund. "Analysis of a Phobia in a Five-Year-Old Boy." In *The Standard Edition of the Complete Psychological Works of Sigmund Freud*, edited and translated by James Strachey 10:1–150. London: Hogarth Press, 1909.

Freud, Sigmund. "Charcot." In *The Standard Edition of the Complete Psychological Works of Sigmund Freud*, edited and translated by James Strachey 3:7–23. London: Hogarth Press, 1893.

Freud, Sigmund. "Civilization and Its Discontents." In *The Standard Edition of the Complete Psychological Works of Sigmund Freud*, edited and translated by James Strachey 21:57–146. London: Hogarth Press, 1930.

Freud, Sigmund. "Contributions to a Discussion on Masturbation." In *The Standard Edition of the Complete Psychological Works of Sigmund Freud*, edited and translated by James Strachey 12:239–54. London: Hogarth Press, 1912.

Freud, Sigmund. "Moses and Monotheism." In *The Standard Edition of the Complete Psychological Works of Sigmund Freud*, edited and translated by James Strachey 23:1–138. London: Hogarth Press, 1939.

Freud, Sigmund. "New Introductory Lectures on Psycho-Analysis." In *The Standard Edition of the Complete Psychological Works of Sigmund Freud*, edited and translated by James Strachey 22:1–182. London: Hogarth Press, 1933.

Freud, Sigmund. "On The Grounds for Detaching a Particular Syndrome From Neurasthenia Under The Description 'Anxiety Neurosis.'" In *The Standard Edition of the Complete Psychological Works of Sigmund Freud*, edited and translated by James Strachey 3:85–115. London: Hogarth Press, 1894.

Freud, Sigmund. "On the History of the Psycho-Analytic Movement." In *The Standard Edition of the Complete Psychological Works of Sigmund Freud*, edited and translated by James Strachey 14:1–66. London: Hogarth Press, 1914.

Freud, Sigmund. "Project for a Scientific Psychology." In *The Standard Edition of the Complete Psychological Works of Sigmund Freud*, edited and translated by James Strachey 1:283–392. London: Hogarth Press, 1950.

Freud, Sigmund. "Psycho-Analytic Notes on an Autobiographical Account of a Case of Paranoia (Dementia Paranoides)." In *The Standard Edition of the Complete Psychological Works of Sigmund Freud*, edited and translated by James Strachey 12:1–82. London: Hogarth Press, 1911.

Freud, Sigmund. "Report on My Studies in Paris and Berlin." In *The Standard Edition of the Complete Psychological Works of Sigmund Freud*, edited and translated by James Strachey 1:3–18. London: Hogarth Press, 1956.

Freud, Sigmund. "Sexuality in the Aetiology of the Neuroses." In *The Standard Edition of the Complete Psychological Works of Sigmund Freud*, edited and translated by James Strachey 3:259–85. London: Hogarth Press, 1898.

Freud, Sigmund. "The Aetiology of Hysteria." In *The Standard Edition of the Complete Psychological Works of Sigmund Freud*, edited and translated by James Strachey 3:187–221. London: Hogarth Press, 1896.

Freud, Sigmund. "The Interpretation of Dreams." In *The Standard Edition of the Complete Psychological Works of Sigmund Freud*, edited and translated by James Strachey 4:9–627. London: Hogarth Press, 1900.

Freud, Sigmund. "The Neuro-Psychoses of Defence." In *The Standard Edition of the Complete Psychological Works of Sigmund Freud*, edited and translated by James Strachey 3:41–61. London: Hogarth Press, 1894.

Freud, Sigmund. *The Origins of Psycho-Analysis: Letters to Wilhelm Fliess, Drafts and Notes, 1887–1902*. Edited by Marie Bonaparte, Anna Freud, and Ernest Kris. Translated by James Strachey and Eric Mosbacher. New York: Basic Books, 1954.

Freud, Sigmund. "Three Essays on the Theory of Sexuality." In *The Standard Edition of the Complete Psychological Works of Sigmund Freud*, edited and translated by James Strachey 7:123–246. London: Hogarth Press, 1905.

Freud, Sigmund. "Three Essays on the Theory of Sexuality." In *The Standard Edition of the Complete Psychological Works of Sigmund Freud*, edited and translated by James Strachey, Vol. 7. London: Hogarth Press, 1909.

Freud, Sigmund. "Totem and Taboo: Some Points of Agreement between the Mental Lives of Savages and Neurotics." In *The Standard Edition of the Complete Psychological Works of Sigmund Freud*, translated by James Strachey 13:7–162. London: Hogarth Press, 1913.

Freud, Sigmund, and Josef Breuer. "Studies on Hysteria." In *The Standard Edition of the Complete Psychological Works of Sigmund Freud*, edited and translated by James Strachey, Vol. 2. London: Hogarth Press, 1895.

Frisch, Morten, Yves Aigrain, Vidmantas Barauskas, Ragnar Bjarnason, Su-Anna Boddy, Piotr Czauderna, Robert P. E. de Gier, et al. "Cultural Bias in the AAP's 2012 Technical Report and Policy Statement on Male Circumcision." *Pediatrics*, March 18, 2013. http://pediatrics.aappublications .org/content/early/2013/03/12/peds.2012-2896.abstract.

Frisch, Morten, and Jacob Simonsen. "Ritual Circumcision and Risk of Autism Spectrum Disorder in 0- to 9-Year-Old Boys: National Cohort Study in Denmark." *Journal of the Royal Society of Medicine* 108, no. 7 (July 2015): 266–79.

Frosh, Stephen. *Hate and the "Jewish Science": Anti-Semitism, Nazism and Psychoanalysis*. London: Palgrave Macmillan, 2005.

Gairdner, Douglas. "The Fate of the Foreskin: A Study of Circumcision." *British Medical Journal* 2 (December 24, 1949): 1433–8.

Gartland, Michael, and Carl Campanile. "De Blasio Orders Mohels Linked to Infant Herpes to Stop 'Unsafe' Circumcisions." *New York Post*, March 29, 2017.

Gaskell, Katherine M., Marina Johnson, Victoria Gould, Adam Hunt, Neil RH
    Stone, William Waites, Ben Kasstan, et al. "Extremely High SARS-CoV-2
    Seroprevalence in a Strictly-Orthodox Jewish Community in the UK."
    London School of Hygiene & Tropical Medicine, 2021. https://datacompass.
    lshtm.ac.uk/id/eprint/2084/.
Gauchet, Marcel. *L'inconscient Cérébral*. Paris: Seuil, 1992.
Geller, Jay. *On Freud's Jewish Body: Mitigating Circumcisions*. New York:
    Fordham University Press, 2007.
George, Sheldon. *Trauma and Race: A Lacanian Study of African American
    Racial Identity*. Waco, TX: Baylor University Press, 2016. https://muse.jhu
    .edu/book/44556/.
Gherovici, Patricia. *Please Select Your Gender: From the Invention of Hysteria to
    the Democratizing of Transgenderism*. New York: Routledge, 2010.
Gherovici, Patricia. *Transgender Psychoanalysis*. New York: Routledge, 2017.
Gilman, Sander L. *Freud, Race, and Gender*. Princeton, NJ: Princeton University
    Press, 1995.
Gilman, Sander L. *The Jew's Body*. New York: Routledge, 1992.
Gilman, Sander L. "The Struggle of Psychiatry with Psychoanalysis: Who Won?"
    Critical Inquiry 13, no. 2 (1987): 293–313.
Glick, Leonard. *Marked in Your Flesh: Circumcision from Ancient Judea to
    Modern America*. New York: Oxford University Press, 2005.
Gollaher, David. *Circumcision: A History Of The World's Most Controversial
    Surgery*. New York: Basic Books, 2001.
Gozlan, Oren, ed. *Current Critical Debates in the Field of Transsexual Studies*.
    London: Routledge, 2018.
Gozlan, Oren. *Transsexuality and the Art of Transitioning: A Lacanian Approach*.
    New York: Routledge, 2014.
Granshaw, Lindsay, and Roy Porter. *The Hospital in History*. London: Routledge,
    1989.
Gray, L. C. "The Question of Reflex Disturbances from Genital Irritation." *The
    Medical Record* 20 (November 19, 1881): 575–81.
Gray, Landon. *The Effect of Genital Irritation in the Production of Nervous
    Disorders*. New York: Union-Argus Steam Printing Establishment, 1882.
Greenberg, Zoe. "When Jewish Parents Decide Not to Circumcise." *The New
    York Times*, July 25, 2017, sec. Well. https://www.nytimes.com/2017/07/25/
    well/family/cutting-out-the-bris.html.
Greenblatt, Samuel. *John Hughlings Jackson and the Conceptual Foundations of
    the Neurosciences: Outline and Hypothesis*. Firenze: Leo S. Olschki Editore,
    1999.
Gross, Abraham. "The Blood Libel and the Blood of Circumcision: An
    Ashkenazic Custom That Disappeared in the Middle Ages." *The Jewish
    Quarterly Review* 86, no. 1/2 (1995): 171–4.
Gualtieri, Tom. "Our Bodies, Our Choices." *The Weeklings* (blog), August 31,
    2012. http://www.theweeklings.com/tgualtieri/2012/08/31/our-bodies-our-c
    hoices-part-i/.

Gunning, Isabelle. "Arrogant Perception, World-Travelling and Multi-Cultural Feminism: The Case of Female Genital Surgeries." *Columbia Human Rights Law Review*, no. 23 (1991): 189–248.

Hall, Catherine. *White, Male and Middle-Class: Explorations in Feminism and History*. Cambridge: Polity Press, 1992.

Hallman, J. C. "J. Marion Sims and the Civil War — a Rollicking Tale of Deceit and Spycraft." *Montgomery Advertiser*, September 28, 2018. https://eu.mont gomeryadvertiser.com/story/opinion/2018/09/28/dr-j-marion-sims-and-civ il-war-rollicking-tale-deceit-and-spycraft-slaves-experiments/1443452002/.

Hallman, J. C. "Monumental Error." *Harper's Magazine*, November 1, 2017. https ://harpers.org/archive/2017/11/monumental-error/.

Hallward, Peter. *Badiou: A Subject to Truth*. Minneapolis, MN: University of Minnesota Press, 2003.

Hammond, William. *On a Hitherto Undescribed Form of Muscular Incoordination*. New York: Putnam's Sons, 1887.

Harris, Oliver. *Lacan's Return to Antiquity: Between Nature and the Gods*. London: Routledge, 2016.

Heath, Stephen. "Joan Riviere and the Masquerade." In *Formations of Fantasy*, edited by Victor Burgin, James Donald, and Cora Kaplan, 45–61. London: Routledge, 1986.

Heckford, Nathaniel. "Circumcision as a Remedial Measure in Certain Cases of Epilepsy, Chorea, &c." In *Clinical Lectures and Reports at the Medical and Surgical Staff of the London Hospital*, Vol. 2. London: John Churchill & Sons, 1865.

High Court of Justice in England, Her Majesty's. R (on the application of) Quincy Bell and A -v- Tavistock and Portman NHS Trust and others, No. CO/60/2020 (December 1, 2020).

Hochhauser, Simon. "Don't Compare Male Circumcision with FGM." *The Telegraph*, July 30, 2014.

Hodges, Frederick. "The Ideal Prepuce in Ancient Greece and Rome: Male Genital Aesthetics and Their Relation to Lipodermos, Circumcision, Foreskin Restoration, and the Kynodesme." *The Bulletin of the History of Medicine* 75 (Fall 2001): 375–405.

Hoffman, Lawrence A. *Covenant of Blood: Circumcision and Gender in Rabbinic Judaism*. Chicago, IL: University of Chicago Press, 1996.

Hook, Derek. "Lacan, the Meaning of the Phallus and the 'Sexed' Subject." In *The Gender of Psychology*, edited by Tamara Shefer, Floretta Boonzaier, and Peace Kiguwa, 60–84. Lansdowne: Juta Academic Publishing, 2006.

Hutchinson, John. "A Plea for Circumcision." *Archives of Surgery* II (1890): 15.

Ignatiev, Noel. *How the Irish Became White*. New York: Routledge, 2008.

Intaction. "Female Genital Cutting," n.d. http://intaction.org/american-female -genital-cutting/.

Introcaso, Camille E., Fujie Xu, Peter H. Kilmarx, Akbar Zaidi, and Lauri E. Markowitz. "Prevalence of Circumcision among Men and Boys Aged 14 to 59 Years in the United States, National Health and Nutrition Examination

Surveys 2005–2010." *Sexually Transmitted Diseases* 40, no. 7 (July 2013): 521–5.

Irigaray, Luce. *Marine Lover of Friedrich Nietzsche*. Translated by Gillian Gill. New York: Columbia University Press, 1991.

Irigaray, Luce. *The Irigaray Reader*. Edited by Margaret Whitford. Translated by David Macey. Cambridge, MA: Blackwell, 1991.

James, Henry. *The Turn of the Screw and Other Stories*. Edited by T. J. Lustig. Oxford: Oxford University Press, 2008.

Jameson, Fredric. "Cognitive Mapping." In *The Jameson Reader*, edited by Michael Hardt and Kathi Weeks, 227–87. Oxford: Blackwell, 2000.

Johnsdotter, Sara. "Discourses on Sexual Pleasure after Genital Modifications: The Fallacy of Genital Determinism (a Response to J. Steven Svoboda)." *Global Discourse* 3, no. 2 (June 1, 2013): 256–65.

Johnson, Athol. "On an Injurious Habit Occasionally Met with in Infancy and Early Childhood." *The Lancet* 1, no. 1910 (April 7, 1860): 344–5.

Jonathan, Seidel, Judith R. Baskin, and Leonard V. Snowman. "Circumcision." In *Encyclopedia Judaica*, edited by Michael Berenbaum and Fred Skolnik, 2nd ed. Vol. 4, 730–5. Detroit: Macmillan Reference USA, 2007.

Jones, Ernest. *The Life and Work of Sigmund Freud, The Last Phase, 1919–1939*. Vol. 3. New York: Basic Books, 1957.

Jones, Ernest. *The Life and Work of Sigmund Freud, Years of Maturity, 1901–1919*. Vol. 2. London: Hogarth Press, 1967.

Jones, Gareth. "Circumcision Ban Makes Germany 'Laughing Stock' - Merkel." *Reuters*, July 17, 2012.

Judd, Robin. *Contested Rituals: Circumcision, Kosher Butchering, and Jewish Political Life in Germany, 1843–1933*. Ithaca, NY: Cornell University Press, 2007.

Kellogg, John Harvey. *Plain Facts for Old and Young: Embracing the Natural History and Hygiene of Organic Life*. Burlington, IA: I.F. Segner, 1887.

Kennedy, Amanda. "Circumcision Is a Feminist Issue . . . and so Is How We Talk about It." *Feministing* (blog), July 15, 2015. http://feministing.com/2015/07/15/circumcision-is-a-feminist-issueand-so-is-how-we-talk-about-it/.

Kennedy, Amanda. "Masculinity and Embodiment in the Practice of Foreskin Restoration." *International Journal of Men's Health* 14, no. 1 (2015): 38–54.

Kennedy, Amanda, and Lauren M. Sardi. "The Male Anti-Circumcision Movement: Ideology, Privilege, and Equity in Social Media." *Societies without Borders* 11, no. 1 (2016): 1–30.

Khan, Masud. "Foreskin Fetishism and Its Relation to Ego Pathology in a Male Homosexual." *The International Journal of Psycho-Analysis* 46 (1965): 64–80.

Kim, DaiSik, Sung-Ae Koo, and Myung-Geol Pang. "Decline in Male Circumcision in South Korea." *BMC Public Health* 12 (December 11, 2012): 1067.

Kitahara, M. "A Cross-Cultural Test of the Freudian Theory of Circumcision." *International Journal of Psychoanalytic Psychotherapy* 5 (1976): 535–46.

Kittay, Eva Feder. "Mastering Envy: From Freud's Narcissistic Wounds to Bettelheim's Symbolic Wounds to a Vision of Healing." *The Psychoanalytic Review* 82, no. 1 (1995): 125–58.

Klausner, Alexandra. "I Left the Hasidic Community to Become a Nude Model." *New York Post*, September 20, 2016.

Klein, Melanie. "Early Stages of the Oedipus Conflict." *The International Journal of Psycho-Analysis* 9 (January 1, 1928): 167–80.

Kol, Ish. *Mohels*, 2013. https://www.youtube.com/watch?v=IbHREE7qT8U.

Kolano, Uta, and Das Erste Schroder. *Gott Und Die Welt: Familie 2.0 - Taufe Oder Beschneidung? (Baptism or Circumcision)*. ARD, 2014. https://pr ogramm.ard.de/TV/Programm/Alle-Sender/?sendung=2872112094444 685.

Kotsko, Adam. "Politics and Perversion: Situating Žižek's Paul." *Journal for Cultural and Religious Theory* 9, no. 2 (2008): 43–52.

Krafft-Ebing, Richard von. *Psychopathia Sexualis*. 12th ed. London: William Heinemann, 1939.

Kristeva, Julia. *Revolution in Poetic Language*. Translated by Margaret Waller. New York: Columbia University Press, 1984.

Krohn, Paysach J. *Bris Milah: Circumcision*. New York: Mesorah, 1985.

Lacan, Jacques. *Le séminaire livre IV. La relation d'objet, 1956–1957*. Paris: Seuil, 1998.

Lacan, Jacques. "The Direction of the Treatment and the Principles of Its Power." In *Écrits*, translated by Bruce Fink, 489–542. New York: Norton, 2006.

Lacan, Jacques. "The Function and Field of Speech and Language in Psychoanalysis." In *Écrits*, translated by Bruce Fink, 197–268. New York: Norton, 2006.

Lacan, Jacques. "The Mirror Stage as Formative of the I Function as Revealed in Psychoanalytic Experience." In *Écrits*, translated by Bruce Fink, 75–81. New York: Norton, 2006.

Lacan, Jacques. *The Seminar of Jacques Lacan. Book III, The Psychoses, 1955– 1956*. Edited by Jacques-Alain Miller. Translated by Russell Grigg. New York: Norton, 1997.

Lacan, Jacques. *The Seminar of Jacques Lacan. Book V, Formations of the Unconscious, 1957–1958*. Edited by Jacques-Alain Miller. Translated by Russell Grigg. Cambridge: Polity, 2017.

Lacan, Jacques. *The Seminar of Jacques Lacan. Book VII, The Ethics of Psychoanalysis, 1959–1960*. Edited by Jacques Alain-Miller. Translated by Dennis Porter. New York: Norton, 1997.

Lacan, Jacques. *The Seminar of Jacques Lacan. Book VIII, Transference, 1960– 1961*. Edited by Jacques-Alain Miller. Translated by Bruce Fink. Cambridge: Polity, 2015.

Lacan, Jacques. *The Seminar of Jacques Lacan. Book X, Anxiety, 1962–1963*. Edited by Jacques-Alain Miller. Translated by A.R. Price. Cambridge: Polity, 2014.

Lacan, Jacques. *The Seminar of Jacques Lacan. Book XI, The Four Fundamental Concepts of Psychoanalysis, 1964*. Edited by Jacques-Alain Miller. Translated by Alan Sheridan. London: Norton, 1998.

Lacan, Jacques. *The Seminar of Jacques Lacan. Book XVII, The Other Side of Psychoanalysis, 1969-1970*. Edited by Russell Grigg. New York: Norton, 2008.

Lacan, Jacques. *The Seminar of Jacques Lacan. Book XX, On Feminine Sexuality, the Limits of Love and Knowledge (Encore), 1972-1973*. Edited by Jacques Alain Miller. Translated by Bruce Fink. London: Norton, 1999.

Lacan, Jacques. "The Signification of the Phallus." In *Écrits*, translated by Bruce Fink, 575-84. New York: Norton, 2006.

Lacan, Jacques. "The Subversion of the Subject and the Dialectic of Desire in the Freudian Unconscious." In *Écrits*, translated by Bruce Fink, 671-702. New York: Norton, 2006.

Laplanche, Jean. *Essays on Otherness*. Edited by John Fletcher. London: Routledge, 1998.

Laplanche, Jean. "Gender, Sex, and the Sexual." *Studies in Gender and Sexuality* 8, no. 2 (March 22, 2007): 201-19.

Laplanche, Jean. *Life and Death in Psychoanalysis*. Translated by Jeffrey Mehlman. Baltimore, MD: Johns Hopkins University Press, 1985.

Laplanche, Jean. *New Foundations for Psychoanalysis*. Translated by David Macey. Oxford: Basil Blackwell, 1989.

Laplanche, Jean. "The Theory of Seduction and the Problem of the Other." *The International Journal of Psycho-Analysis* 78 (August 1997): 653-66.

Laplanche, Jean, and Serge Leclaire. "The Unconscious: A Psychoanalytical Study." *Yale French Studies*, no. 48 (January 1, 1972): 118-75.

Laplanche, Jean, and J. B. Pontalis. "Auto-Erotism." In *The Language of Psychoanalysis*, translated by Donald Nicholson-Smith. London: Hogarth Press, 1973.

Laqueur, Thomas Walter. *Solitary Sex: A Cultural History of Masturbation*. New York: Zone Books, 2003.

Laycock, Thomas. *A Treatise on the Nervous Diseases of Women: Comprising an Inquiry into the Nature, Causes, and Treatment of Spinal and Hysterical Disorders*. London: Longman, Orme, Brown, Green, and Longmans, 1840.

Leader, Darian. *Why Do Women Write More Letters Than They Post?* London: Faber and Faber, 1996.

Lederer, Susan E. *Flesh and Blood: Organ Transplantation and Blood Transfusion in 20th Century America*. New York: Oxford University Press, 2008.

Leicht, Justus. "German Left Party Opposes Religious Circumcision." *World Socialist Website*, October 9, 2012. https://www.wsws.org/en/articles/2012/10/circ-o09.html%EF%BB%BF.

Lemaire, Anika. *Jacques Lacan*. Translated by David Macey. London: Routledge, 1977.

Levenson, Jon. "The New Enemies of Circumcision." *Commentary* 109, no. 3 (March 2000): 29-36.

Levine, Jon. "Andrew Yang's Anti-Circumcision Stance Cuts Deep: Jewish Leaders." *New York Post* (blog), January 10, 2021. https://nypost.com/2021/0 1/09/andrew-yangs-anti-circumcision-stance-cuts-deep-jewish-leaders/.

Lévi-Strauss, Claude. "Social Problems: Ritual Female Excision and Medically Assisted Reproduction." In *We Are All Cannibals, and Other Essays*, translated by Jane Marie Todd, 37–48. New York: Columbia University Press, 2016.

lord_autist. "R/Foregen - Foregen Brings Me Hope and Relief." *reddit*. Accessed March 29, 2021. https://www.reddit.com/r/Foregen/comments/8s806l/forege n_brings_me_hope_and_relief/.

Louden, Kathleen. "AAP Retracts Controversial Policy on Female Genital Cutting." *Medscape*, June 2, 2010.

Loudon, Irvine. "Why Are (Male) Surgeons Still Addressed as Mr?" *British Medical Journal* 321, no. 7276 (December 23, 2000): 1589–91.

Lupton, Julia Reinhard. "Ethnos and Circumcision in the Pauline Tradition: A Psychoanalytic Exegesis." In *The Psychoanalysis of Race*, edited by Christopher Lane, 192–210. New York: Columbia University Press, 1998.

Lydson, Frank G. *The Surgical Diseases of the Genito-Urinary Tract, Venereal and Sexual Diseases*. New York: The F. A. Davis Company, 1899.

Lyons, Barry. "Male Infant Circumcision as a 'HIV Vaccine.'" *Public Health Ethics* 6, no. 1 (April 1, 2013): 90–103.

MacDowell, Mississippi. "The Chasam Sofer's Ruling on Metzitzah Be-Peh." *On the Main Line* (blog), April 16, 2012. http://onthemainline.blogspot.co.uk /2012/04/chasam-sofers-ruling-on-metzitzah-be.html.

Maimonides, Moses. *The Guide of the Perplexed*. Edited and translated by Shlomo Pines. Chicago, IL: University of Chicago Press, 1963.

Malev, Milton. "The Jewish Orthodox Circumcision Ceremony -- Its Meaning from Direct Study of the Rite." *Journal of the American Psychoanalytic Association* 14, no. 3 (1966): 510–17.

Marcus, Steven. *The Other Victorians: A Study of Sexuality and Pornography in Mid-Nineteenth-Century England*. London: Transaction Publishers, 2009.

Marotta, Brendon. *American Circumcision*, 2017. https://www.imdb.com/title/ tt7628146/.

Martin, Dale. "The Promise of Teleology, the Constrains of Epistemology, and Universal Vision in Paul." In *St. Paul among the Philosophers*, edited by John D. Caputo and Linda Martín Alcoff, 91–108. Bloomington, IN: Indiana University Press, 2009.

Masson, Jeffrey Moussaieff. *A Dark Science: Women, Sexuality and Psychiatry in the Nineteenth Century*. New York: Farrar, Straus and Giroux, 1986.

Masson, Jeffrey Moussaieff. *The Assault on Truth: Freud's Suppression of the Seduction Theory*. New York: Ballantine Books, 2003.

Mazor, Joseph. "The Child's Interests and the Case for the Permissibility of Male Infant Circumcision." *Journal of Medical Ethics* 39, no. 7 (2013): 421–8.

McCarthy, Mary, and Philip Roth. "An Exchange." *New Yorker*, December 28, 1998.

McGowan, Todd. *Enjoying What We Don't Have: The Political Project of Psychoanalysis*. Lincoln, NE: University of Nebraska Press, 2013.

McGowan, Todd. *Universality and Identity Politics*. New York: Columbia University Press, 2020.

McGregor, Deborah Kuhn. *From Midwives to Medicine: Birth of American Gynecology*. New Brunswick, NJ: Rutgers University Press, 1998.

McLaren, Carrie. "Porn Flakes: Kellogg, Graham, and the Crusade for Moral Fiber," n.d. https://www.turboraketti.org/ifa/Porn%20Flakes.pdf.

Melkorka, Licea. "This Hasidic Couple's Kinky Open Marriage Could Get Them 'Shunned Forever.'" *New York Post*, March 12, 2017.

Millot, Catherine. *Horsexe: Essay on Transsexuality*. Translated by Kenneth Hylton. New York: Autonomedia, 1990.

Mitchell, Juliet. "Sexual Difference in the New Millennium." *Birkbeck College*, June 24, 2017. http://backdoorbroadcasting.net/2017/06/sexual-difference-in-the-new-millennium/.

Mitchell, Juliet. *Siblings: Sex and Violence*. Cambridge: Polity, 2003.

Morgan, William. "The Rape of the Phallus." *Journal of the American Medical Association* 193, no. 3 (July 19, 1965): 123–4.

Morris, Brian J., Stefan A. Bailis, and Thomas E. Wiswell. "Circumcision Rates in the United States: Rising or Falling? What Effect Might the New Affirmative Pediatric Policy Statement Have?" *Mayo Clinic Proceedings* 89, no. 5 (May 2014): 677–86.

Morris, Brian J., and John N. Krieger. "The Contrasting Evidence Concerning the Effect of Male Circumcision on Sexual Function, Sensation, and Pleasure: A Systematic Review." *Sexual Medicine* 8, no. 4 (December 2020): 577–98.

Morris, Brian J., and Thomas E Wiswell. "'Circumcision Pain' Unlikely to Cause Autism." *Journal of the Royal Society of Medicine* 108, no. 8 (August 2015): 297.

Moscucci, Ornella. "Clitoridectomy, Circumcision, and the Politics of Sexual Pleasure in Mid-Victorian Britain." In *Sexualities in Victorian Britain*, edited by Andrew H. Miller. Bloomington, IN: Indiana University Press, 1996.

Moscucci, Ornella. *The Science of Woman: Gynaecology and Gender in England, 1800–1929*. Cambridge: Cambridge University Press, 1993.

Munzer, Stephen R. "Secularization, Anti-Minority Sentiment, and Cultural Norms in the German Circumcision Controversy." *University of Pennsylvania Journal of International Law* 37, no. 2 (2016): 503–82.

Nagle, Angela. *Kill All Normies: The Online Culture Wars from Tumblr and 4chan to the Alt-Right and Trump*. Winchester: Zero Books, 2017.

Nanos, Mark. "The Myth of the 'Law-Free' Paul Standing between Christians and Jews." *Studies in Christian-Jewish Relations* 4, no. 1 (April 21, 2011): 1–21.

Neuman, William. "City Orders Sims Statue Removed From Central Park." *The New York Times*, April 16, 2018, sec. New York. https://www.nytimes.com/2018/04/16/nyregion/nyc-sims-statue-central-park-monument.html.

Nobus, Dany. "That Obscure Object of Psychoanalysis." *Continental Philosophy Review* 46, no. 2 (August 2013): 163–87.

Nunberg, Herman. "Circumcision and Problems of Bisexuality." *The International Journal of Psycho-Analysis* 28 (1947): 145–79.

Ohr, C. H. "Genito-Reflex Neurosis in the Female." *The American Journal of Obstetrics and Diseases of Women and Children* 26 (1883): 168–80.

Osserman, Jordan. "Is the Phallus Uncut? On the Role of Anatomy in Lacanian Subjectivization." *Transgender Studies Quarterly* 4, no. 3–4 (December 2017): 497–517.

Osserman, Jordan, and Foivos Dousos. "Psychoanalysis and 'Post-Truth' Conference." Accessed March 23, 2021. https://youtube.com/playlist?list=P LxXvI8Dj8ue0XiFVTFDP3eawaJ2kH6UyW.

Otterman, Sharon. "Regulation of Circumcision Method Divides Some Jews." *The New York Times*, September 12, 2012.

Owings, Maria, Sayeedha Uddin, and Sonja Williams. "Trends in Circumcision for Male Newborns in U.S. Hospitals: 1979–2010." *Center for Disease Control*, August 2013. https://www.cdc.gov/nchs/data/hestat/circumcision_2013/ circumcision_2013.htm.

Palfreyman, Harriet. "Visualising Venereal Disease in London c.1780–1860." PhD Dissertation, University of Warwick, 2012. http://wrap.warwick.ac.uk /55107/.

Philo. "The Special Laws." In *Philo*, translated by F. H. Colson, Vol. 7, 98–473. Cambridge, MA: Harvard University Press, 1937.

Plato. *Symposium*. Translated by Robin Waterfield. Oxford: Oxford University Press, 2008.

Public Policy Advisory Network on Female Genital Surgeries in Africa. "Seven Things to Know about Female Genital Surgeries in Africa." *Hastings Center Report* 42, no. 6 (November 1, 2012): 19–27.

Punzi, Elisabeth H. "Freud's Jewish Identity, Circumcision, and the Theory of Castration Anxiety: Problem or Pride?" *Mental Health, Religion & Culture* 17, no. 10 (November 26, 2014): 967–76.

Reik, Theodor. *Ritual: Four Psychoanalytic Studies*. New York: Grove Press, 1962.

Reinhard, Kenneth. "Toward a Political Theology of the Neighbor." In *The Neighbor: Three Inquiries in Political Theology*, edited by Slavoj Žižek, Kenneth Reinhard, and Eric Santner, 11–75. Chicago: University of Chicago Press, 2013.

Reinhard, Kenneth. "Universalism and the Jewish Exception: Lacan, Badiou, Rosenzweig." *Umbr(a)* 1 (2005): 43–71.

Remondino, Peter Charles. "Circumcision and Its Opponents." *American Journal of Dermatology and Genito-Urinary Diseases* 6 (1902): 65–73.

Remondino, Peter Charles. *History of Circumcision from the Earliest Times to the Present*. Philadelphia: F.A. Davis, 1891.

Richardson, Everard. "Congenital Phimosis and Adherent Prepuce Producing Anomalous Nervous Phenomenon." *Transactions of the Medical Association of Georgia* 31 (1880): 143–9.

Riminton, Hugh (@hughriminton). "America Has Issues. So Many Issues." *Twitter*, October 26, 2020. https://twitter.com/hughriminton/status/13208 40031905312768.

Riviere, Joan. "Womanliness as a Masquerade." *International Journal of Psycho-Analysis* 10 (1929): 303–13.

Robinson, William J. "Circumcision and Masturbation." *Medical World* 33 (1915): 390.

Rodriguez, Sarah B. *Female Circumcision and Clitoridectomy in the United States: A History of a Medical Treatment*. Rochester, NY: University of Rochester Press, 2014.

Rogin, Michael. *Blackface, White Noise: Jewish Immigrants in the Hollywood Melting Pot*. Berkeley, CA: University of California Press, 1998.

Romberg, Moritz Heinrich. *A Manual of the Nervous Diseases of Man*. Edited and translated by Edward Sieveking. London: Sydenham Society, 1853.

Rose, Jacqueline. *Sexuality in the Field of Vision*. London: Verso, 2005.

Rose, Jacqueline. *The Case of Peter Pan or The Impossibility of Children's Fiction*. London: Macmillan, 1992.

Rose, Jacqueline. "Who Do You Think You Are? Trans Narratives." *London Review of Books*, May 5, 2016.

Rosenberg, Schmarya. "Why Do Haredim Do Metzitzah B'Peh?" *Failed Messiah* (blog), July 29, 2014. http://failedmessiah.typepad.com/failed_messiahcom /2014/07/why-do-haredim-do-metzitzah-bpeh-the-dangerous-circumcision -related-practice-that-has-killed-and-mai-345.html.

Rosenberg, Shmarya. "Hundreds Of Haredi Rabbis Order Jews To Violate Proposed Circumcision Law." *Failed Messiah* (blog), September 2, 2012. http: //failedmessiah.typepad.com/failed_messiahcom/2012/09/hundreds-of-hare di-rabbis-order-jews-to-violate-proposed-circumcision-law-123.html.

Rosenberg, Shmarya. "The History of Metzizah B'Peh." *Failed Messiah* (blog), n.d. http://failedmessiah.typepad.com/.a/6a00d83451b71f69e2017d3bf9fa3 7970c-pi.

Roth, Philip. *The Counterlife*. London: Jonathan Cape, 1987.

Roudinesco, Elisabeth. *Jacques Lacan & Co: A History of Psychoanalysis in France, 1925–1985*. Translated by Jeffrey Mehlman. Chicago, IL: University Of Chicago Press, 1990.

Salecl, Renata. *A Passion for Ignorance: What We Choose Not to Know and Why*. Princeton, NJ: Princeton University Press, 2020.

Salecl, Renata. *(Per)Versions of Love and Hate*. London: Verso, 2000.

Salisbury, Laura, and Andrew Shail, eds. *Neurology and Modernity: A Cultural History of Nervous Systems, 1800–1950*. New York: Palgrave Macmillan, 2010.

Santner, Eric. *My Own Private Germany: Daniel Paul Schreber's Secret History of Modernity*. Princeton, NJ: Princeton University Press, 1998.

Sartin, Jeffrey. "J. Marion Sims, the Father of Gynecology: Hero or Villain?" *Southern Medical Journal* 95, no. 5. Accessed March 26, 2021. http://www .medscape.com/viewarticle/479892.

Sayre, Lewis. *Lectures on Orthopedic Surgery and the Diseases of the Joints: Delivered at Bellevue Hospital Medical College, during the Winter Session of 1874–1875.* New York: D. Appleton and Company, 1876.

Sayre, Lewis. *On the Deleterious Results of a Narrow Prepuce and Preputial Adhesions.* Philadephia: WM. F. Fell & Co, 1887.

Sayre, Lewis. "Paralysis from Peripheral Irritation, so-Called 'Spinal Anaemia.'" *The Medical and Surgical Reporter (Philadelphia)* 35 (1876): 305–8.

Sayre, Lewis. "Partial Paralysis from Reflex Irritation, Caused by Congenital Phimosis and Adherent Prepuce." *Transactions of the American Medical Association* 21 (1870).

Sayre, Lewis. "Spinal Anaemia with Partial Paralysis and Want of Co-Ordiantion, from Irritation of the Genital Organs." *Transactions of the American Medical Association* 26 (1875): 255–74.

Scarfone, Dominique. "A Brief Introduction to the Work of Jean Laplanche." *The International Journal of Psychoanalysis* 94, no. 3 (June 2013): 545–66.

Schlich, Thomas. "Medicalization and Secularization: The Jewish Ritual Bath as a Problem of Hygiene (Germany 1820s–1840s)." *Social History of Medicine* 8, no. 3 (1995): 423–42.

Schmitt, Carl. *Political Theology: Four Chapters on the Concept of Sovereignty.* Edited and translated by George Schwab. Chicago, IL: University of Chicago Press, 2005.

Schmitt, Carl. *The Concept of the Political.* Translated by George Schwab. Chicago: University of Chicago Press, 1996.

Schofield, Daisy. "How Intactivist's Anti-Circumcision Movement Was Co-Opted by the Alt-Right." *Dazed*, April 9, 2020. https://www.dazeddigital.com/body/article/48684/1/how-intactivists-anti-circumcision-movement-was-co-opted-by-the-alt-right.

Schur, Max. "Some 'additional Day Residues' of the 'Specimen Dream of Psychoanalysis.'" In *Psychoanalysis -- a General Psychology: Essays in Honor of Heinz Hartmann*, edited by Rudolph M. Lowenstein, Lottie M. Newman, Max Schur, and Albert Solnit, 45–85. New York: International Universities Press, 1966.

Scott, Joan Wallach. *The Fantasy of Feminist History.* Durham, NC: Duke University Press, 2011.

Scull, Andrew. *Hysteria: The Disturbing History.* Oxford: Oxford University Press, 2011.

Sengoopta, Chandak. *The Most Secret Quintessence of Life: Sex, Glands, and Hormones, 1850–1950.* Chicago, IL: University of Chicago Press, 2006.

Shell-Duncan, Bettina, and Ylva Hernlund, eds. *Female "Circumcision" In Africa: Culture, Controversy, and Change.* Boulder, CO: Lynne Rienner Publishers, 2000.

Shepherdson, Charles. *Vital Signs: Nature, Culture, Psychoanalysis.* New York: Routledge, 2000.

Shire, Emily. "Why Ultra-Orthodox Jewish Babies Keep Getting Herpes." *The Daily Beast*, July 29, 2014. http://www.thedailybeast.com/articles/2014/07/29/why-ultra-orthodox-jewish-babies-keep-getting-herpes.

Shorter, Edward. *From Paralysis to Fatigue: A History of Psychosomatic Illness in the Modern Era*. New York: Free Press, 1992.

Shweder, Richard. "What about 'Female Genital Mutilation'? And Why Understanding Culture Matters in the First Place." In *Engaging Cultural Differences*, edited by Richard Shweder, Martha Minow, and Hazel Rose Markus, 216–51. New York: Sage, 2002.

Silverman, Eric. "Anthropology and Circumcision." *Annual Review of Anthropology* 33, no. 1 (October 2004): 419–45.

Silverman, Eric. *From Abraham to America: A History of Jewish Circumcision*. Lanham, MD: Rowman & Littlefield Publishers, 2006.

Sims, J. Marion. "Remarks on Battey's Operation." *British Medical Journal* 2, no. 885 (December 15, 1877): 840–2.

Sims, J. Marion. *The Story of My Life*. New York: Appleton, 1884.

Slavet, Eliza. *Racial Fever: Freud and the Jewish Question*. New York: Fordham University Press, 2009.

Sommer, Will. "Andrew Yang, Upstart Democratic Presidential Candidate, Comes Out Against Circumcision." *The Daily Beast*, March 19, 2019, sec. Politics. https://www.thedailybeast.com/andrew-yang-the-upstart-democratic-presidential-candidate-comes-out-against-circumcision.

Sorensen, Martin Selsoe. "Denmark Talks (Reluctantly) About a Ban on Circumcising Boys." *The New York Times*, June 2, 2018, sec. World. https://www.nytimes.com/2018/06/02/world/europe/denmark-circumcision.html.

Spitz, René. "Authority and Masturbation: Some Remarks on a Bibliographical Investigation." *Psychoanalysis Quarterly* 21 (1952): 490–527.

Stanley, Leo L. *Men at Their Worst*. New York: D. Appleton, 1943.

Stepansky, Paul E. *Freud, Surgery, and the Surgeons*. Hillsdale, NJ: The Analytic Press, 1999.

Stern, Mark Joseph. "How Intactivists Broke the Internet." *Slate*, September 18, 2013. http://www.slate.com/articles/health_and_science/medical_examiner/2013/09/intactivists_online_a_fringe_group_turned_the_internet_against_circumcision.html.

Stoppard, Lou. "Will Mandatory Face Masks End the Burqa Bans?" *The New York Times*, May 19, 2020, sec. Style. https://www.nytimes.com/2020/05/19/style/face-mask-burqa-ban.html.

Sulloway, Frank J. *Freud, Biologist of the Mind: Beyond the Psychoanalytic Legend*. Cambridge, MA: Harvard University Press, 1992.

Svoboda, J. Steven, Peter W. Adler, and Robert S. Van Howe. "Circumcision Is Unethical and Unlawful." *The Journal of Law, Medicine & Ethics: A Journal of the American Society of Law, Medicine & Ethics* 44, no. 2 (June 2016): 263–82.

talierch. "R/Foregen - Foregen Brings Me Hope and Relief." *reddit*. Accessed March 30, 2021. https://www.reddit.com/r/Foregen/comments/8s806l/foregen_brings_me_hope_and_relief/.

The Circumcision Complex. "Circumcision to Terrorism." n.d. http://www.circ umcisioncomplex.com/circumcision-to-terrorism/.

Tian, Ye, Wei Liu, Jian-Zhong Wang, Romel Wazir, Xuan Yue, and Kun-Jie Wang. "Effects of Circumcision on Male Sexual Functions: A Systematic Review and Meta-Analysis." *Asian Journal of Andrology* 15, no. 5 (September 2013): 662–6.

Tilney, Nicholas L. *Transplant: From Myth to Reality.* New Haven, CT: Yale University Press, 2003.

Valeii, Kathi. "How Men's Rights Activists Hijacked The Circumcision Debate." *The Establishment*, February 17, 2016. https://theestablishment.co/how-mens -rights-activists-hijacked-the-circumcision-debate-7b0389c3b9e.

Van Buren, Abigail. "Dear Abby: College Man Still Mad about Botched Circumcision." *Chicago Sun-Times*, March 21, 2016.

Van Haute, Philippe. *Against Adaptation: Lacan's Subversion of the Subject.* New York: Other Press, 2001.

Van Haute, Phillippe, and Thomas Geyskens. *Confusion of Tongues: The Primacy of Sexuality in Freud, Ferenczi and Laplanche.* New York: Other Press, 2004.

Verhaeghe, Paul. "Lacan on the Body." In *The New Klein-Lacan Dialogues*, edited by Julia Borossa, Catalina Bronstein, and Claire Pajaczkowska, 119–34. London: Karnac, 2015.

Verhaeghe, Paul, Stijn Vanheule, and Ann De Rick. "Actual Neurosis as the Underlying Psychic Structure of Panic Disorder, Somatization, and Somatoform Disorder: An Integration of Freudian and Attachment Perspectives." *The Psychoanalytic Quarterly* 76, no. 4 (October 2007): 1317–50.

Wade, Lisa. "Learning from 'Female Genital Mutilation': Lessons from 30 Years of Academic Discourse." *Ethnicities* 12, no. 1 (2012): 26–49.

Wald, Rebecca, and Lisa Braver Moss. *Celebrating Brit Shalom.* Notim Press, 2014.

Walker, Kenneth. "Surgical Procedures in General Practice: Circumcision." *The British Medical Journal* 2, no. 4069 (December 31, 1938): 1377–8.

Wall, L. Lewis. "Obstetric Vesicovaginal Fistula as an International Public-Health Problem." *Lancet (London, England)* 368, no. 9542 (September 30, 2006): 1201–9.

Wall, L. Lewis. "The Medical Ethics of Dr J Marion Sims: A Fresh Look at the Historical Record." *Journal of Medical Ethics* 32, no. 6 (June 2006): 346–50.

Wang, Andrew. "Federal Judge Dismisses Former Harvard Employee Eric Clopper's Lawsuit." *The Crimson*, December 1, 2020. https://www.thecrimson .com/article/2020/12/1/federal-judge-dismisses-clopper-lawsuit-against-the -crimson/.

waraukaeru. "R/Intactivists - Got Banned from r/Sex for Calling Circ What It Is!" *reddit.* Accessed March 29, 2021. https://www.reddit.com/r/Intactivists/ comments/8kipyx/got_banned_from_rsex_for_calling_circ_what_it_is/.

Washington, Harriet A. *Medical Apartheid: The Dark History of Medical Experimentation on Black Americans from Colonial Times to the Present.* New York: Knopf Doubleday Publishing Group, 2008.

Weininger, Otto. *Sex and Character: An Investigation of Fundamental Principles.* Edited by Daniel Steuer. Translated by Ladislaus Lob. Bloomington, IN: Indiana University Press, 2005.

Wensinck, A. J. "Khitan." In *Encyclopedia of Islam,* edited by P. Bearman, Th. Bianquis, C. E. Bosworth, E. van Donzel, and W. P. Heinrichs, 2nd ed., 2012. http://referenceworks.brillonline.com/entries/encyclopaedia-of-islam-2/khit an-SIM_4296.

Westerholm, Stephen. *Perspectives Old and New on Paul.* Grand Rapids, MI: William B Eerdmans Publishing Co, 2004.

WHO. "Clearing House on Male Circumcision for HIV Prevention." Accessed March 22, 2021. www.malecircumcision.org.

WHO. "Neonatal and Child Male Circumcision: A Global Review." Joint United Nations Programme on HIV/AIDS, April 2010. http://www.who.int/hiv/pub /malecircumcision/neonatal_child_MC_UNAIDS.pdf?ua=1.

Wim, Dekkers. "Routine (Non-Religious) Neonatal Circumcision and Bodily Integrity: A Transatlantic Dialogue." *Kennedy Institute of Ethics Journal* 19, no. 2 (2009): 125–46.

Wine, Sherwin. "Circumcision." *Humanistic Judaism* 6, no. 2 (1988): 4–8.

Winger, Anna. *Unorthodox.* Drama. Studio Airlift, Real Film Berlin, 2020.

Winnicott, D. W. "Circumcision." *The British Medical Journal* 1, no. 4071 (January 14, 1939): 86–7.

Wolfson, Elliot. "Circumcision and the Divine Name: A Study in the Transmission of Esoteric Doctrine." *The Jewish Quarterly Review* 78, no. 1/2 (1987): 77–112.

Worboys, Michael. *Spreading Germs: Disease Theories and Medical Practice in Britain, 1865–1900.* Cambridge: Cambridge University Press, 200AD.

Zampini, Jay M., and Henry H. Sherk. "Lewis A. Sayre: The First Professor of Orthopaedic Surgery in America." *Clinical Orthopaedics and Related Research* 466, no. 9 (September 2008): 2263–7.

Žižek, Slavoj. "Against Human Rights." *New Left Review* 34 (August 2005): 115–31.

Žižek, Slavoj. "Multiculturalism, or, the Cultural Logic of Multinational Capitalism." *New Left Review* 225 (1997): 28–51.

Žižek, Slavoj. *The Ticklish Subject: The Absent Centre of Political Ontology.* London: Verso Books, 2009.

Žižek, Slavoj, Eric Santner, and Kenneth Reinhard. *The Neighbor: Three Inquiries in Political Theology, with a New Preface.* Chicago, IL: University of Chicago Press, 2005.

Zupančič, Alenka. "The Case of the Perforated Sheet." In *Sexuation,* edited by Renata Salecl, 282–96. Durham, NC: Duke University Press, 2000.

Zupančič, Alenka. *The Odd One In: On Comedy.* Cambridge, MA: MIT Press, 2008.

Zupančič, Alenka. *Why Psychoanalysis?: Three Interventions.* Uppsala: Aarhus University Press, 2008.

Index